MW00332813

# INSATIABLE APPETITES

# INSATIABLE APPETITES

Imperial Encounters with Cannibals in the
North Atlantic World

KELLY L. WATSON

New York University Press

NEW YORK AND LONDON

NEW YORK UNIVERSITY PRESS
New York and London
www.nyupress.org

© 2015 by New York University
All rights reserved

For Library of Congress Cataloging-in-Publication data,
please contact the Library of Congress.

ISBN 978-0-8147-6347-6 (hardback)

Manufactured in the United States of America
10 9 8 7 6 5 4 3 2 1

Also available as an ebook

# Contents

# Figures

## Acknowledgments

I have been asked countless times to explain what possessed me to study cannibalism. My response always feels a bit unsatisfactory, both to me and to the questioner, because the truth is I'm not sure. I can pinpoint when the idea for this project came into being, but I can't quite figure out what interested me in the first place. Ultimately I think what drew me to this project and to a fascination with such a macabre subject is a less interesting question than it might seem. If there is one thing that this project has helped me to realize it is that I am not alone in being interested in tales of humans eating one another. Such a fascination has existed for millennia, and if I knew why I would have solved an eternal question of the human condition.

This book represents nearly a decade of thought and work. There are so many people, organizations, and institutions that have assisted me with this project that I am sure I will forget some of them, and for that I preemptively apologize. I have had the privilege of working alongside many wonderful scholars over the years, all of whom have earned my gratitude, including Bill Albertini, Ellen Berry, Rob Buffington, Kim Coates, Ed Danziger, Jeannie Ludlow, Don MacQuarie, Scott Martin, Jeff Myers, and Peter Way. Erin Labbie deserves particular thanks for her mentorship and friendship over the years. Her faith in me and her willingness to go above and beyond the call of duty will inspire and guide me for years to come. I am also thankful for the thoughtful, kind, and generous support of Ruth Herndon, who read my work, answered my questions, and graciously offered assistance whenever I needed it. Without the calm guidance of Susana Peña, you would not be reading these words before you. Her ability to remind me of the questions that really matter is of immeasurable importance. Amilcar Challu is not only a wonderful source of knowledge, suggestions, and assistance, but he has shown me unwavering support and helped to give me the confidence to become a scholar. Thank you to Andy Schocket, who never hesitates to tell me when I need to push myself and my ideas further; a compliment from him means more than the praise of many others combined.

Many of my colleagues and friends helped keep me on track by reading various versions of this text over the years, offering me support, and assisting me with translations, and to them I am eternally grateful. Thank you to Melodee Baines; Karin Barbee; Phil Bird; Jim Buss; Michael Carlson; Leslie Dorrough-Smith; Christine Eisel; Shirley Green; Cassandra Jones; Jennifer Kavetsky; Teresa Lorenz; Jeff Myers; Tracey Osborne; Ken Parsons; Kris Proctor; Charlotte Quinney; Jamie Stuart; Marcia Watson; the participants and organizers of the 2007 Four Corners of the Atlantic, 1500–2000 Interdisciplinary Atlantic Studies Workshop at the University of Michigan and Michigan State University; and the participants and organizers of the 2012 Race, Gender, and Sexualities in the Atlantic World Symposium through the Carolina Lowcountry in the Atlantic World Program at the College of Charleston.

I owe a debt of thanks to all of my friends and colleagues at Avila University, Bowling Green State University, and Saint Mary's College. I am forever thankful for their friendship, support, love, and trust. I am also indebted to Avila University for the generous course releases that allowed me to put the finishing touches on this book.

I would like to thank the staff at the Bowling Green State University Library, the John Carter Brown Library, the New York Public Library, and the countless other libraries whose holdings I consulted. Libraries are a vital part of our world that we should never take for granted.

This project would not have been possible without the generous grant from the Andrew W. Mellon Foundation to establish the Early American Places series. I would also like to thank the editorial staff at New York University Press, Clara Platter and Constance Grady as well as Debbie Gershenowitz for her guidance in the early stages.

Additionally I owe a great debt to the anonymous reviewers of this manuscript for their helpful and challenging feedback.

Finally, thank you to my family, who deserve the biggest thanks of all for putting up with me over the years: my parents, Wanda and Bill Watson, who have always shown me incomparable support, love, and honesty; my brother and sister, who not only are wonderful specimens of humanity but always keep me honest; my parents-in-law, Lois and Terry Zeh, who opened their house and their hearts to me so generously. They all deserve great thanks. I would also like to thank the DeGranges, who have always been like a second family to me. And I cannot express my gratitude adequately to my partner in life, Jason Zeh, for making me a better person and for always reminding me that I can do it.

# Introduction

*I think there is nothing barbarous and savage in that nation, from what
I have been told, except that each man calls barbarism whatever is not
his own practices; for indeed it seems that we have no other test of truth
and reason than the example and pattern of opinions and customs of
the country we live in. There is always the perfect religion, the perfect
government, the perfect and accomplished manners in all things.*
MICHEL DE MONTAIGNE, *"Of Cannibals,"* 1580

In his famous essay "Of Cannibals," Michel de Montaigne argues that
Western societies rarely judge other cultures on their own terms.[1]
Rather, in his estimation Europeans tend to project negative qualities onto others, so that the cultural practices they observe actually
mirror their own faults. Montaigne uses the practice of cannibalism
in Brazil to reflect on European civilization, arguing for a nuanced
understanding of difference and a careful examination of cultural
practices before declaring them barbarous.[2]

Despite the seriousness of his argument for cultural relativism,
Montaigne was not without a sense of humor. He ends the essay
with this clever line: "All this is not too bad—but what's the use?
They don't wear breeches."[3] He jokingly suggests that any reason or
intelligence possessed by Indians is negated by their lack of clothing. This phrase highlights the difficulties of the work that he asks
of his reader: no matter how hard one tries, cultural assumptions
are difficult to overcome.[4] A lack of proper clothing was a common
descriptor of savagery in medieval and early modern Europe, but
Montaigne underscores the absurdity of this assumption. Simply
because they did not don clothing, should Indians be assigned a
lower place in the hierarchy of humanity? "Of Cannibals," written in
1580, was an important essay and shaped intellectual thought about
imperialism and cannibalism in Europe, but beyond that it also
demonstrates the inevitable tensions that resulted when Europeans
encountered cannibals.

In this same essay Montaigne argues that "our eyes are bigger than our bellies, and that we have more curiosity than capacity; for we grasp at all, but catch nothing but wind."[5] This phrase plays with the idea of cannibalism, as it defines the limitations of an incorporative epistemology of imperialism. Montaigne hints at the limits of European knowledge about the New World and its peoples as he denigrates the rapid processes of imperialism and colonialism. Europeans rushed forth into the New World, conquered its peoples, destroyed its cities, and exploited its landscape without a thorough understanding of what they were doing and why they were doing it. Montaigne's passage depicts the European conquest of the Americas as greedy and impetuous. European powers claimed lands and divvied up resources successfully, yet as they grasped at everything, they ignored the wider implications of their desires.

Montaigne's metaphor for European imperialism provides a useful way of thinking about the discourse of cannibalism and the ways this discourse aided in the establishment and maintenance of imperial power in North America. Early modern writers rarely connected the supposed acts of cannibalism that they described with the larger issues of imperialism, yet hierarchy, dominance, and power were implicit in every account. The desire of the writers to record the supposed atrocities of Indigenous Americans for an eager readership back in Europe masked the true power of anthropophagic accusations. Through their accusations of cannibalism European writers implicitly and explicitly argued that Indians were inferior. As these conquerors, soldiers, priests, and settlers documented their perception of Indian barbarity, they underscored their preexisting belief in their own superiority. However, following Montaigne's warning that curiosity exceeded capacity, this book examines sources of cannibalism from a new perspective. Rather than taking descriptions of cannibalism in European accounts as either true representations of savage Indian acts or dismissing these descriptions as merely propaganda, I uncover the ways the imperial context affected the discourse of cannibalism represented in European texts as well as the ways the discourse of cannibalism changed the dynamics of imperial power in North America.[6] More specifically I also investigate the subtle and often hidden ways imperial power was gendered and was instrumental in redefining gendered and sexual norms.

*Insatiable Appetites* reveals new insights into historical documents, arguing for a recentering of gender in the analysis of the discourse of cannibalism. Recent discussions of cannibalism have tended to focus on the connection between cannibalism, savagery, and race. However, in the early modern period European understandings of cannibalism and savagery were more closely linked with gender and sexuality. Imperial power depended on the assertion of European superiority and the assumption of Indian inferiority, and the discourse of cannibalism played a key role in these determinations. As conquest always involved the domination of bodies in addition to land and resources, it is imperative to acknowledge and scrutinize the way that conquered bodies were gendered. Cannibalism is an embodied act, and an investigation of the discourse of man-eating illuminates the development of early modern ideas about race, gender, and sexuality. There is a great deal of scholarship that examines the racialized and gendered discourses of empire and colonialism, but there is a dearth of scholarly work that develops these ideas in the early modern North Atlantic.

My focus is on the discourse of cannibalism in European records from approximately 1492 until 1763. The objects of inquiry are primarily written texts, although some discussion of the role of images in the establishment and maintenance of imperial power is advanced as well. Through an analysis of these sources, I interrogate the construction of the idea of the cannibal in European empires rather than the actual practice of cannibalism among the Native people of the Americas. Not only is it virtually impossible to uncover concrete evidence of Indigenous practices solely through European records, but the idea of cannibalism and its associations with savagery were significantly more important in imperial discourse than were the actual rituals of human consumption.

Historically the consumption of certain body parts and some methods of corpse ingestion were treated as different from cannibalism. Human bodies were widely used for medicinal purposes in early modern western European nations and their colonies. Mummified remains of ancient and sometimes more recent origins were commonly prescribed as a treatment for a wide range of ailments. Human blood was used to treat epilepsy in England into the middle of the eighteenth century, for example.[7] While corpse medicine was ubiquitous, it was not without critics, including Montaigne himself.[8] Yet the producers and consumers of corpse medicine were not viewed as savage, bloodthirsty man-eaters, indicating that not all acts of the consumption of human bodies were viewed in the same way. Rather it was the cannibal practices of exogenous others that were linked with savagery, barbarism, and heathenism.

Acts of man-eating are generally placed into two broad categories, endo- and exocannibalism, referring to the consumption of insiders and outsiders, respectively. These categories loosely parallel the distinction between funerary and warfare cannibalism.[9] While the definition of cannibalism may seem quite clear at first glance, establishing the limits of what constitutes an act of cannibalism is actually quite complex. On the simplest level, a cannibal is a person who consumes the body of another human being. But how much of another person does one have to consume to be a cannibal? Does the accidental ingestion of bodily fluids, for example, make one a cannibal? Does it have to be an intentional act to constitute anthropophagy? Or, put another way, does the consumer have to willfully and knowingly consume human body parts to be a cannibal? Does the doctrine of transubstantiation make Roman Catholics cannibals? Is there a difference between consuming the bodies of those who have died and killing people in order to consume them? We could keep asking these kinds of questions ad nauseam, but ultimately what matters for my purposes is that all of the acts of man-eating discussed herein are linked with savagery.

Determining whether or not groups of people actually practiced anthropophagy is difficult and comes laden with thousands of years of inherited prejudices and inequities. To label a population cannibalistic has always been a strategy of defamation. Indeed even asking the question presupposes that one human consuming another has significance well beyond the fulfillment of nutritional needs, for one does not ask a question whose answer is meaningless. Thus the determination of anthropophagy reveals something about both the questioner and the object of inquiry. Modern-day descendants of purported cannibals in history often take umbrage at the characterization of their ancestors. This is quite understandable given the faulty and prejudicial historical records that scholars have relied on to make such determinations. In the particular case of historic accounts of Amerindian cannibalism, almost all records, with very few exceptions, were written by peoples bent on conquest, conversion, elimination, and/or control over those that they regarded as man-eaters. Yet denying the existence of the practice of cannibalism is itself a reinscription of European and Western-centric values. Furthermore both modern scholarship on cannibalism and the sources on which it relies have certain features in common, including "a schema of analyzing culture that does not easily admit the existence of a phenomenon that is Other without explaining that phenomenon as a totalized alterity or without totally explaining it away."[10] In other words, it is quite difficult to acknowledge the existence of cannibalism without passing judgment on the people who might have practiced it. How can we objectively acknowledge and interrogate a practice that is so wrought with preconceptions and obfuscation? There are no easy answers to this question, and we must tread carefully, paying close attention to our own prejudices and those of our sources. As this book focuses on discourse, most of the time it does not matter if an accusation of cannibalism is *true*; it matters more that the accusation had consequences and that it reflected the *mentalité* of the writer and his or her culture. This can feel rather unsatisfying as most people have an innate desire to *know*.

The act of man-eating (excluding corpse medicine) in medieval and early modern western European society was always associated with savagery and Otherness. Culturally sanctioned cannibalism threatened to destroy the basic foundations of Christian society, for if humans ate other humans, then they could not be easily separated from animals. The taboo against man-eating was in fact one of the key markers of civilization. For European writers, the failure to recognize the boundaries between human and animal, and the refusal to value the lives of humans above all other creatures, was an indicator of savagery and primitiveness. Civilization created order out of chaos, and the presence of cannibalism served as a reminder of the barbarity from which all humans supposedly emerged. Even more than other subjects dealt with in European sources, descriptions of cannibalism were particularly prone to exaggeration and projection.[11]

## Whither Cannibalism?

European writings about cannibalism can help us to understand the development of racism, patriarchy, and heterosexism in colonial and postcolonial contexts. An analysis of cannibalism is certainly not the only way the connections between gender and empire can be examined, yet the prominence of descriptions of cannibalism in European discourse demonstrates its importance. European men— and almost all of the pertinent writers were male—were captivated by the acts of cannibalism that they claimed to have discovered among the peoples of the Americas, and because of this they wrote about them often. Their descriptions reveal both a fascination with and revulsion for anthropophagous acts. The specific relationship between the discourse of cannibalism and the gendered nature of imperial power changed depending on the geographic, temporal, and imperial context. Due to the sheer volume of Western writings about cannibalism, savagery, and empire during the past five hundred years, this book cannot hope to cover every discussion in every moment. Instead I have chosen to focus on four distinct times and places in order to open up a conversation about the relationship between cannibalism, gender, sexuality, and race within the confines of empire and to establish a model through which we can better understand the nature of imperial expansion in North America.

Most scholarship that has discussed cannibalism, whether as an actual occurrence or as a discursive construction, has tended to focus exclusively on Latin America, and Brazil in particular. To date only modest consideration has been given to the study of cannibalism in North America. The extant sources dealing with cannibalism in North America are primarily concentrated in the following regions: the eastern seaboard of what is now the United States, southeastern Canada, the Great Lakes region, the American Southwest, Florida, the Caribbean, the Yucatán peninsula, and the Valley of Mexico.

In *Dangerous Liaisons: Gender, Nation, and Postcolonial Perspectives*, Anne McClintock writes, "The representation of male *national* power depends on the prior construction of *gender* difference."[12] In this way the nationalist masculine power of the nineteenth century and beyond depended on an earlier articulation of gender and power. Thus an examination of gender in the early modern world is essential for understanding the foundations of modernity. Following this assertion, *Insatiable Appetites* develops a theory of gender and empire through an exploration of the origins of masculine imperial power. In order to understand the institutions of patriarchy and racism in colonial or postcolonial situations, it is necessary to first interrogate the origins of such ideas. From where did the notion of gender difference that McClintock insists is a necessary precedent for masculine national power come? By examining the discourse of cannibalism in the conquest period of Atlantic North American history, the role that cannibalism played in the formation of European ideas about gender difference, sexual mores, and racial hierarchies is made clearer. As Ann Laura Stoler argues, we must place "questions of homo- and heterosexual arrangements and identities not as the seedy underbelly of imperial history . . . but as charged sites of its tensions."[13] Thus the fundamental anxieties on which imperial power rests are illuminated through an interrogation of the ways gender and sexual norms came to be within the confines of empire in North America. Implicit within ideas about barbarism in the early modern world was the inability of barbarians to conform to the established norms of gendered power and sexual practices. Cannibalism, then, existed alongside the perception of other inappropriate cultural practices in the writings of European men. The formation of masculine and, later, racist imperial power insisted on the perceived presence of cannibalism. In the early centuries of conquest, cannibalism above all else determined savagery, and savagery established one's place within the hierarchy on which civilization and imperialism rested.

An important aspect of the colonial project was the insistence of the colonizers on control of the bodies of the colonized. The body itself was a fundamental site on which imperial power was negotiated and enforced. Sexuality was one essential realm through which control was maintained; the threat of pollution through miscegenation was a common fear expressed by colonizers. The body became a permeable border through which an early form of biopower was enacted.[14] But while bodies were sites for the enforcement of imperial control, they were also sites for subversion. In the history of the Americas, the body was a contested space. Imperial power was enacted on the body, even while the body remained a space for resisting this power. The functions of the body had to be controlled and regulated in order for civilization to prosper. Thus the threat of uncontrollable bodies loomed large in the minds of early writers. The act of cannibalism signified an inability to control the body, where its victims were violated through penetration, ingestion, and incorporation. Cannibalism represented bodies out of control—bodies that functioned outside of the regulatory norms of Western Christendom. Because of this the fear of cannibalism was also a fear of alternative notions of embodiment.

Implicit within colonialist discourse is the assumption that the binary construction of civilization versus savagery and barbarism defines and constrains the world. While the definitions of civilization, savagery, and barbarism are variable, the European perception of cultural superiority was constant in the early modern Atlantic world. This was especially evident in commentary about norms of gender and sexuality. Europeans, most especially in the earliest years of contact, recorded Americans violating these norms with practices such as polygamy, serial monogamy, and promiscuity. Native communities often maintained political, social, and kinship networks that seemed at odds with European ways. Women's participation in warfare and government, the ease of divorce, the prohibition of interclan marriage, and looser restrictions on women's sexuality, among others, served as evidence of barbarism and thus inferiority.

Together the early European texts about the Americas, and the images they inspired, demonstrate the depth and complexity of discourses about cannibalism and encounter. What has been left out of much of the scholarly discourse on cannibalism to date is the role that gender played in labeling a group cannibalistic and in the consequences of this label. The cannibal was, and continues to be, simultaneously a racialized and gendered figure. In the period I discuss, ideas about both race and gender were not static. However, this did not preclude the existence of understandings of racialized and gendered difference. The distinction between what is *race* and what is *racialized* difference is slightly muddy; however, the key distinction in terms of this book is that, in general, European writers in the late fifteenth through the mid-eighteenth century did not directly equate skin color and other physical characteristics, which would later become descriptors of "race," with inferiority.[15] Rather Europeans understood the differences between themselves and the Indians they encountered in the Americas in ways that also took into account geographic, religious, cultural, and gendered elements. In other words, Europeans did not consider the variances in physical appearance between themselves and Indians to be the primary indicator of Indian inferiority. Rather European men justified their perception of their own superiority over Native peoples through a range of complex indicators, including but not limited to geography, religion, culture, and norms of gender and sexuality.[16] Skin color did not serve as a straightforward heuristic that indicated savagery in this period; rather the determination of the savagery of a group of people relied on assumptions about proper human behavior and beliefs coupled with physiognomy.

The binary construct of civilization/savagery provides a clearer framework for understanding the ways Europeans articulated difference and otherness. The term *savage* encompassed a range of behaviors, beliefs, and assumptions about Others and was used by European writers to describe those behaviors, beliefs, and actions. However, both *civilization* and *savagery* were variable terms, and writers indicated that there existed degrees of each. For example, the seventeenth-century French writer Pierre D'Avity listed what he believed were the five indicators of brutishness: the inability (or refusal) to use reason, a savage diet, nakedness, poor quality of shelter, and a lack of government.[17] Possessing these characteristics indicated that a particular group of people was suitable for conquest.

Race, as expressed through an understanding of physical and phenotypical characteristics that represented moral worth, social standing, and intellectual potential, would play a much more important role in the discourse of cannibalism in later centuries. By the nineteenth century the connection between emerging ideas of scientific racism and cannibalism was firmly established. In the period I discuss, gender was of greater importance to the discourse of cannibalism and was central in determining the effect that such discourse had on imperial power dynamics. Within the complex set of indicators of savagery and civilization, understandings of gender and gendered practices were fundamentally important for Europeans in establishing the place of a particular group within the hierarchy of human beings. Civilization itself was viewed primarily as a gradual process of cultural, social, religious, and intellectual developments. Therefore the so-called savage peoples of the Americas were seen as inferior and primordial and their understandings of sexuality and gender were viewed as equally atavistic and dangerous. For Europeans the figure of the cannibal hearkened back to an earlier era, a savage time that had been all but eliminated by the march of civilization. When these conquerors encountered "real live" cannibals, it was easy to see them as holdovers from the past.[18] Furthermore not only were the conquerors truly men, but they had complex understandings of Native peoples as feminized and as failed men.

My decision to focus on the "discovery" of America in 1492 should not be taken as an acceptance of this date as the first European interaction in the "New World."[19] Nor should it be taken as an acceptance of the great historical division between premodern and early modern, as such divisions are always messy and fraught with assumptions. The shift from medieval to modern did not occur in a moment, and medieval ideas and traditions played an important role in the early modern world. The discovery of the Americas by Columbus did not, as is often repeated, spur an immediate rethinking of historical processes.[20] Rather the "discoveries" made by Columbus set events in motion that would eventually radically reshape the histories of both Europe and the Americas. There is no specific year that clearly distinguishes the colonial from the nationalist period of North American history, as different parts of this vast landscape were colonized at different times and European imperialism did not end in one fell swoop; however, the end of the Seven Years War in 1763 provides a satisfying conclusion to this book.

The Treaty of Paris, which ended the Seven Years War, did not signal a complete end to European imperial expansion in the Americas. However, it did radically reshape the balance of power between France, Spain, and England in North America, greatly reducing the power of France and increasing that of England. Furthermore as the English became the dominant power on the eastern seaboard, groups of Indians, such as the Iroquois, were less able to play European groups against one another and carve out an influential space as middlemen, gatekeepers, and trading partners. Additionally, after the American Revolution, tales of cannibalism decreased rapidly in the eastern United States and were common only on the western frontiers. Thus the "triumph of civilization" in eastern North America meant that cannibalism ceased to be an important trope through which alterity was negotiated in that specific context. The firm establishment of imperial power in the Caribbean, Mexico, New France, and New England also led to the decline of writing about cannibalism. It seems that once the tangible threat of contact with savagery was eliminated, cannibalism was no longer an important topic of discussion in a particular region. Rather accusations of cannibalism lodged against Native peoples traveled along a moving imperial frontier. For example, in the nineteenth century accusations of cannibalism were much more often lodged against Africans as Europeans raced to carve up that continent for themselves.

The texts examined in this book come primarily from the late fifteenth to the eighteenth century as I compare and provide general findings about cannibalism and empire. In this vast swath of time, from "discovery" to the Seven Years War, Europeans writing of the New World witnessed and reported on the presence of cannibalism, enabling us to document the changes in these discourses over time.

Most academic scholarship on cannibalism has been written by anthropologists and literary theorists, although historians have not been completely silent. The works of such literary theorists as Tzvetan Todorov and Frank Lestringant have proven quite useful for their rich interpretations of the literature of conquest. Todorov's *The Conquest of America: The Question of the Other* is a linguistic and semiotic analysis of the ways Europeans constructed Indigenous Americans as

Other and an investigation of the effects of this imbalance of power. Although Todorov focuses primarily on the Spanish conquest of the New World, his ideas about Otherness resonate in other contexts as well. Frank Lestringant's *Cannibals: The Discovery and Representation of the Cannibal from Columbus to Jules Verne* is notable for its focus on how the idea of the cannibal impacted European thought. Lestringant documents the changes in European understandings of the figure of the cannibal over time in order to demonstrate its continued importance. Like Todorov, Lestringant primarily restricts his investigation to Central and South America. Furthermore he engages with the idea of the cannibal in the works of important French literature and philosophy.

Scholars of psychoanalysis have also taken an interest in cannibalism as a cultural phenomenon. In *Cannibalism: Human Aggression and Cultural Form*, Eli Sagan argues that cannibalism, as both a fantasy and an actual practice, stems from sublimated aggression. The psychoanalyst Melanie Klein provocatively argues that cannibalism is one of humanity's basest desires and that during infancy children must learn to effectively sublimate their desire for the consumption of the Other or risk developing psychological problems in later life.[21]

The use of psychoanalytic insights by literary scholars is quite common. The work of Maggie Kilgour, for example, examines cannibalism as a trope through which writers negotiate opposition between forms, such as inside and outside, consumer and consumed. The act of incorporation, which is at the center of all acts of cannibalism, is something to be both feared and desired, according to Kilgour. In this way cannibalism in literature reveals the primary tension between Self and Other.[22] Kilgour's work is featured in an interdisciplinary collection entitled *Cannibalism and the Colonial World*, which includes the work of other key researchers of cannibalism.[23] Together these essays trace the idea of cannibalism from the colonial to the postcolonial world, from literal acts to metaphor, and demonstrate a wide array of approaches to the study of cannibalism, although with a limited discussion of North America. Peter Hulme, who coedited *Cannibalism in the Colonial World*, and the anthropologist Neil Whitehead are among the most important scholars of Carib cannibalism, and anthropophagy in general.[24] Whitehead's careful reporting on the evidence of Carib cannibalism in European records is especially useful.

Anthropological studies of cannibalism can be grouped into several categories, all of which assert that cannibalism is reflective of larger cultural factors. Psychoanthropology, a branch of the field that examines culture through the lens of psychoanalysis, typically articulates cannibalism as a manifestation of internal psychological processes. Cultural materialist anthropologists, such as Marvin Harris, believe that cannibalism can be best understood as a response to environmental factors: an inadequate protein supply for example.[25] The well-known structural anthropologist Claude Lévi-Strauss asserted that one of the fundamental binaries on which all human cultures rest is the division between the raw and the cooked. This division plays out in a number of ways, including nature versus culture and civilized versus savage. He further argued that within the act of cannibalism, the way a body is cooked reveals important insights into the social status of the deceased person as well as about the society as a whole.[26] He argued that the boiling of bodies is the typical form of endocannibalism, and roasting is typical of exocannibalism; that is, outsiders are most like to be roasted, and in-group members are more likely to be boiled.[27] In his framework cannibalism is a feature of "primitive" societies, a kind of disordered consumption that is opposed to civilization and culture. Another fundamental human distinction for Lévi-Strauss and other structural anthropologists is the divide between men and women. Thus humanity is in a constant tug of war between two opposing forces, with cannibalism residing squarely within the primitive, savage, and feminine side of the binary.

The anthropologist William Arens continues to be a polemical figure in the study of cannibalism. In his controversial book, *The Man-Eating Myth: Anthropology and Anthropophagy*, he argues that there has never been a society that has positively sanctioned cannibalism. He operates under the assumption that all of the evidence for cannibalism was merely propaganda to support European imperialism and served only to emphasize the "primitiveness" of conquered peoples. However, the majority of modern anthropological scholarship agrees that many groups did in fact practice cannibalism.[28] What is often misunderstood about Arens is that he does not categorically deny the existence of cannibalism; rather he argues that whether or not cannibalism was a real social practice, it existed as a discursive trope. He asserts that the real or imagined existence of cannibalism does not diminish its importance in historical discourse.[29]

The ethnohistorian Thomas Abler confronts Arens in his article "Iroquois Cannibalism: Fact not Fiction" and debunks several of Arens's assertions.[30] Arens states that there is no definitive evidence of cannibalism in the *Jesuit Relations*, the compilations of reports from missionaries, which I discuss in greater detail in chapter 4. However, as Abler adroitly points out, thirty-one volumes contain references to cannibalism.[31] Certainly the mere preponderance of references in the *Jesuit Relations* does not prove that the practice actually occurred, but when viewed in concert with the evidence for Iroquois cannibalism in speeches and captivity narratives, it is quite clear that anthropophagy did occur.

This project lends itself naturally to a comparative analysis; in order to draw conclusions about discourses of cannibalism in early postencounter North America, it is necessary to evaluate a range of sources from several imperial contexts, in addition to the social and cultural traditions of the Native group in question. D. W. Meinig's characterization of the Spanish conquest as "stratification," the French conquest as "articulation," and the English conquest as "expulsion" serves as a useful model.[32] The means and goals of empire had consequences not only for the frequency of reports of cannibalism but also in regard to the power of such reports in propelling conquest and colonization.

In *American Pentimento: The Invention of Indians and the Pursuit of Riches*, Patricia Seed argues that the way the empires of England, Portugal, Spain, and France conceived of ownership of land, resources, and people shaped the development of imperial power in the Americas. For example, the Moorish influence on Iberian political thought after the Reconquista created the understanding that deposits of natural resources were put there by God for use by his people. The successful elimination of Muslim power in Spain was seen as proof by the monarchs and other elites that Spaniards were the true people of God, and therefore the resources were theirs for the taking. Spanish tradition also insisted on the payment of one fifth of all profit to the Crown. This complex understanding of public versus private ownership carried over into the issue of slavery. Seed argues that although the Spanish Crown expressed no concern about the coercion of Native labor in the pursuit of riches, Indian slavery was not condoned because it implied private ownership of labor and resources.[33] The development of the *repartimiento* system reflected this, as it apportioned Native labor into private hands in a trustee relationship, not full ownership.[34] Spaniards in general believed that the pursuit of riches was a common goal to benefit all of God's people. The control of natural resources obtained by the exploitation of Indian labor was of primary importance to the Spanish Empire in the Americas.

Drawing on Seed's insights, I argue that the ways a particular empire understood its relationship to land and Others was important in determining the place of cannibalism within discourse. For example, as Spaniards perceived the exploitation of natural resources as central to their imperial goals, they were more likely to carve out a subservient position for Indians in order to maintain a local labor force. In chapter 2 I examine how the slave trade and the mining of raw materials were directly related to accusations of cannibalism. In opposition to Spanish conceptions, Englishmen conceived of their efforts in the New World in more individualized ways and were far more interested in private landownership.[35] While success for the conquistadors may have been measured in gold and silver, success for the English was measured in landownership.[36] Based on these general priorities, the English colonists in North America tended to show less interest in affording Indians a space in their New World. Thus the prominence of cannibalism within English discourse, and the relationship between cannibalism and imperial power, differed from the Spanish and French versions and had consequences for the gendered nature of imperial power.

In order to understand the discourse of cannibalism (keeping in mind imperial context), it is necessary to understand the distinction between civilization and savagery and to acknowledge the power of this binary. The conquest of the New World rested on the assumption of a fundamental difference between the European and the Indian. No matter how profoundly different European ethnic groups believed in their own regional and cultural superiority within Europe itself, they nonetheless believed in the innate superiority of Christian Europeans over all others. Certainly the English believed, for example, that Catholicism was fundamentally flawed, but they nonetheless continued to operate under the assumption that a flawed belief in God was superior to no belief in God at all. In order to make the conquest of the Americas viable, Europeans had to see themselves, and their social and cultural traditions, as different from American ones.

Anthony Pagden discusses many of the heated Spanish arguments about Indian humanity in *The Fall of the Natural Man*. He demonstrates that mainstream Spanish thought came to recognize the shared humanity of Spaniards and Indians, even if Spaniards considered Indians to be inferior. They assumed that it was their job to provide Indians with the knowledge that was denied them by their fall from grace. Spanish thought presumed that one of the most fundamental tenets of humanity was that humans should not consume one another. God called humanity forth to prosper, populate, and control the world through his word and glory; consuming one another violates his divine will. A similar sentiment was echoed in other empires as well, and although the English and the French may have had different ideas about God and about their relationship with the land and peoples of the New World, they still believed that human consumption violated fundamental tenets of Christianity.

The modern concept of the Other is useful here. While it is difficult to provide a concrete definition of this term, in its simplest form Others are those who represent the opposite of the Self/Subject. The Other serves to provide a Subject with a point of reference for something it is not and must strive not to be. Although the Other represents what a society should not be, there is also often a fetishistic reverence for the Other. It stands in opposition to the Self, the Subject, the Signifier. In order to define itself, a being must determine what it is not. The Subject is not merely constructed in opposition to its Object, however, as the reverse is also true. The "civilized" being exists because of the cannibal, just as the cannibal takes form because of the existence of the civilized world.

In *The Location of Culture*, Homi Bhabha puts forth a methodology for the analysis of the Other in discourse: "My reading of colonial discourse suggests that the point of intervention should shift from the ready recognition of images as positive or negative, to an understanding of the *process of subjectification* made possible (and plausible) through stereotypical discourse."[37] The cannibal was a key site for mapping subjectification for European writers, as the opposition between presumed American cannibal savages and civilized Europeans became a fundamental trope through which early modern ideas about identity, and especially masculinity, were formed. While there are texts that are more "sympathetic" to the cannibal, for most the cannibal is the supreme representative of savagery. To oversimplify the matter slightly, it was not because Native peoples were cannibals that Europeans felt they needed civilizing, but that because they needed civilizing they must be cannibals.

## Cannibalism versus Anthropophagy

It is important to separate the very real physical act of anthropophagy from the idea of the cannibal. The cannibal is a construct produced by imperialism and maintained through discourse. The image of the cannibal was the product of a complex set of interactions and assumptions. As Hulme argues, "To concentrate on the notion of a dialogue is to insist on two emphases, not always present in discussions of cannibalism; on the agency of those described as cannibals—difficult to access but necessary to posit; and on the relationship between describer and described, between Europe and its others. The figure of the cannibal is a classic example of the way in which that otherness is dependent on a prior sense of kinship denied, rather than on mere difference."[38] Thus in order to understand the idea of the cannibal, one must first understand the complex power dynamics inherent in interactions between Europeans and American Indians, as well as prevalent beliefs about alterity. Many sources reveal instances when Native peoples called Europeans cannibals and feared them for their cannibalistic reputation.[39] What differentiates this kind of relationship is the imbalance of power between colonizer and colonized. This difference most clearly manifests in European dominance of the written record. The image of the savage cannibal Native has lingered and prospered over time; the figure of the bloodthirsty cannibal European, however, has not. Cannibalism still remains perhaps the most powerful and enduring image of savagery.[40]

Before moving forward into a description of the chapters to follow, I must present an idea that is fundamental to this work and any study of cannibalism. As some readers may know, the modern English words *cannibal* and *cannibalism* are the etymological descendants of word *Carib*. The Carib tribe, as I argue in chapter 2, in addition to having inspired the name of the Caribbean and the term that we now use to describe man-eating, was one of the main targets of European accusations of savagery. In discourse Caribs were placed in opposition to their supposedly more docile neighbors, the Arawaks. Despite the etymological relationship between *Carib* and *cannibalism*, the language employed in early works on the Caribbean to describe the act of man-eating and the people now known as the Caribs was quite complex, and it is not always clear if a writer is referring to the Caribs, to man-eaters, or to both. Columbus and others sometimes wrote about the Caniba, or people of the great Khan.[41] Much important linguistic work has been done on the use of the words *Caniba*, *Caribes*, *Carib*, and others in early writings, but suffice it to say that while the meanings that Columbus and others attached to these words cannot be fully recovered, these early writings established a precedent

FIGURE I.1  "Allegorical image of America." Engraving.
Frontispiece in Ferdinando Gorges, *America Painted to the Life
the True history of the Spaniards proceeding in the conquests of the
Indians, and of their civil wars among themselves* (London, 1659). It
was quite common for the American continents to be represented
in allegorical form as a cannibal woman. (Courtesy of the John
Carter Brown Library at Brown University.)

in which *Carib* became equivalent to *cannibal*. However the modern word came to be, it is important to note that *cannibalism* and *cannibal* differ from the more formal descriptive terms *anthropophagy* and *anthropophagite*. Cannibals and cannibalism came to be associated with a whole host of other savage traits and bear a heavy discursive legacy.[42] *Anthropophagy*, on the other hand, derives from the Greek and simply means human-eating. This book primarily examines cannibalism, not anthropophagy. I am not strictly concerned with acts of human-eating but rather with the development of the discourse of cannibalism and all of the historical and etymological baggage that this term carries with it. In fact there is a debate within anthropology as to whether or not the term *cannibalism* should be reserved for use "for the ideology that constitutes itself around an obsession with anthropophagy."[43] However, despite the important conceptual differences between these two terms, I use them interchangeably to prevent excessive repetition.

The primary sources discussed herein were chosen based on a number of criteria. While there are some accounts in the historical record about Europeans consuming one another, especially in times of starvation or extreme stress, these are rare and remarkable.[44] There are also numerous accounts of shipwreck cannibalism among Europeans, most famously in the wrecks of the French frigate *Méduse* and the English ship *Mignonette*.[45] These occurrences were always dealt with differently in European texts than those perpetrated by Natives, as there was never the assumption of a cultural pattern of cannibalism. While starvation cannibalism was considered singularly abhorrent by some, as evidenced by Jean de Léry's writings about the siege of the Sancerre in France in 1572–73, for example, it was nonetheless treated as a momentary aberration.[46] The most prevalent type of cannibalism presented in European chronicles was performed by Native people on Native people. Less common, but still notable, were accounts of Natives consuming Europeans.

This book draws primarily from published works in part because of the popularity of accounts of cannibalism and exploration, but primarily because of its focus on discourse. *Insatiable Appetites* cannot claim to encompass every possible source that includes anthropophagous references; instead I focus on those that contain substantive references. The evidence discussed in the following chapters is limited to explicit references to cannibalism. I do not assume that the use of a term like *bloodthirsty* to describe Native peoples is an indicator of the practice of cannibalism, yet there was clearly a connection between the European conceptions of warrior bloodlust and the desire to consume human flesh. Finally, whenever possible, the sources discussed in this book are limited to observational accounts rather than strictly philosophical works, such as the writings of Montaigne.

The vast majority of sources examined in this book are available in English translation, and I have typically cited these versions for the ease of the reader and because of their widespread availability. The texts were originally composed in a range of languages, including French, German, Latin, Spanish, Italian, Greek, Old English, and Portuguese. I consulted original sources whenever possible, but for those texts in Greek, Portuguese, Old English, Italian, and German I was forced to rely exclusively on available translations. The translations were selected based on both publication date and widespread acceptance. For most of the sources that I read in translation only, I consulted several different versions. For example, Michele Cuneo's essay discussed in chapter 2 was originally written in Italian, and the available English translations vary slightly. This was particularly noticeable in the translation of the phrase "una Camballa belissima," which is variously translated as a gorgeous or beautiful, cannibal or Carib, woman or girl. Such choices obviously impact the interpretation of this key passage. Most translations use "gorgeous cannibal woman," and as such I have chosen to do the same. While the use of translations undoubtedly impacts my interpretation of the sources, care was taken to ensure that the impact was as limited as possible.

Sources on cannibalism are not evenly distributed across empires. The Spanish records are by far the most extensive and are particularly strong on cannibalism in sixteenth-century Mexico. French sources yield a reasonable amount of information, and the records of Jesuit missionaries in the Great Lakes region are especially robust. English sources, however, are far more difficult to come by. These disparities in the historical record speak not only to the differences among the Native peoples encountered but also to the priorities of empire and the period in which considerable intervention occurred. Large-scale English efforts, for instance, occurred much later on the Atlantic seaboard and overall were far less interested in incorporating Native peoples into the Anglo-American world.

The chapters that follow are organized in chronological order, but each also explores the discourse of cannibalism from a specific subject position within an imperial and geographic context. For example, in the case of the French Empire in the Americas, I focus on the writings of Jesuit missionaries in Canada. The limited perspective of the Jesuits cannot be easily extrapolated to make conclusions about the French Empire writ large, but the uniqueness of the encounters between Catholic priests and the Iroquois can provide insight into the relationship between religion, the discourse of cannibalism, and imperial power. In this way no one chapter fully represents the discourse of cannibalism from the position of empire; rather together they speak to the ways in which the discourse of cannibalism was fundamental to the establishment and maintenance of European imperial power, in all of its manifestations, in North America.

The first chapter, "Inventing Cannibals," provides an overview of the classical and medieval discourses of man-eating. Drawing from authors such as Herodotus, Pliny, Isidore of Seville, and Marco Polo, I demonstrate the place of anthropophagy within the literature of monstrosity and travel writing, as well as the role of cannibalism in the construction of Otherness. Ultimately I elucidate the intellectual heritage of European travelers to the Americas in order to shed light on the biases, heuristics, and preconceptions that they brought with them to the New World.

Chapter 2, "Discovering Cannibals," investigates the emergence of the idea of the cannibal in the writings of European explorers of the Caribbean. Beginning with Christopher Columbus and continuing through to Amerigo Vespucci, I establish the development of the idea of cannibalism, as opposed to anthropophagy. The encounter between European men, who hailed from a variety of homelands, and the Caribs and the Arawaks was fundamental in creating the discourse of cannibalism. These encounters did not happen in a vacuum, and these writers drew explicitly from medieval and classical ideas. However, they also radically reshaped the power of the discourse of cannibalism. Furthermore in these writings the discourse of cannibalism was gendered based on preexisting understandings of gender, sexuality, and monstrosity. In these accounts European men expressed great fear about the cannibalistic appetites of Carib women, which reflected their fear of the unknown and its feminine nature.

In the context of the conquest of Mexico explored in chapter 3, the conquistadors expressed much less fear of the anthropophagous appetites of the women they encountered. They used accusations of cannibalism to justify their conquest of the Aztecs and to further the establishment of the superiority of Spanish masculinity. The descriptions of horrific sacrifices and cannibalism practiced by the Aztecs enabled Hernán Cortés and his men to argue for the superiority of Spanish civilization. Additionally, continuing a practice established in the Caribbean, these men connected cannibalism with savagery and assumed that people who practiced man-eating were also prone to sexual indiscretions. By calling them cannibals, they made the bodies of the Aztecs ripe for conquest. This conquest took place on the battlefield, but also in the bedroom. Cortés was the prototypical masculine imperial hero who exploited the bodies and labor of the Native women he encountered. His successes not only portended the erasure of the "abominable" customs of cannibalism and sacrifice among the Aztecs but helped to establish a stratified society in which power was masculine and women's participation in political matters was voided.

Chapter 4 focuses on the discourse of cannibalism in New France, specifically through the documents of the *Jesuit Relations*. Unlike Cortés, Columbus, or Vespucci, the Jesuit missionaries did not arrive in North America desirous of the bodies of its inhabitants; they sought souls instead. As an avowedly celibate order, the Jesuits sought to prove their masculinity by enduring the trials of the wilderness and the cruelties perpetrated by the Indians, particularly the Iroquois. Their accounts of martyrdom and cannibalization at the hands of their potential converts not only drew more dedicated missionaries to Canada but also reiterated the seriousness and importance of their cause. The goals of the French Empire were less clearly articulated than their English and Spanish neighbors, and their settlements in the Americas were typically smaller and more distant from one another. The French sought to first establish economic relations with the Indians in order to profit rather than fully conquering and dominating the land and peoples. Thus the accusations of cannibalism in the *Jesuit Relations* spurred religious interest in the peoples of Canada rather than inspiring full-scale conquest.

Chapter 5 examines the discourse of cannibalism in the English Empire, focusing particularly on New England. Captivity narratives provide the richest source of references to cannibalism; however, English writers were far less preoccupied than the French and Spanish with man-eating in general. I argue that this is due to the legacies of Spanish and French efforts, the practices of the Native groups they encountered, and the particular goals of English colonization. The English were much less interested than the French or the Spanish in making space for Indians in their new empire. Captivity narratives demonstrate that discussions of cannibalism reinforced the development of a new understanding of Anglo-American masculinity that defined itself against the wilderness and its inhabitants. The ability to endure the threat of cannibalism and other trials at the hand of the Indians allowed the English to justify their presence in the Americas and assert their power over the lands and its people.

# 1 / Inventing Cannibals: Classical and Medieval Traditions

In a famous and gruesome tale from ancient Mediterranean mythology, the god Kronos (Saturn in the Roman incarnation) swallowed his children out of fear that he would lose his power at the hands of his son, as had been prophesied by his parents. Prior to eating his off-spring, he had also castrated his father, Uranus, in a fit of jealous rage. After watching Kronos consume all but one of their children, Kronos's sister-wife, Rhea, tricked him into eating a stone instead of their son Zeus. Later, as predicted, Zeus took revenge on his father and freed his brothers and sisters from Kronos's body.[1] Thus from acts of castration and cannibalism the leader of the Olympic Pantheon rose to power. Centuries later, in the 1820s, the Spanish artist Francisco Goya would memorialize this fateful event in the painting *Saturn Devouring His Son*. This story is only one of many mythological tales of cannibalism that have lasted the ages.

While humans consuming other humans has likely occurred since time immemorial, the Western idea that there are certain peoples who are prone to consuming other humans and that man-eating is directly related to other "savage" characteristics finds its origin in the ancient Mediterranean world. From these ancient traditions medieval genres like travelogues and bestiaries emerged. Thus by the time that Columbus arrived in the Caribbean, he carried nearly two thousand years of discursive cannibal history with him. Before jumping into an analysis of cannibalism in the late fifteenth- and early sixteenth-century Caribbean, we must first understand the intellectual tradition inherited by early modern Europeans. Explorers, soldiers, settlers, and priests brought with them evolving traditions about how to interact and engage with difference. They inherited the belief that peoples who inhabit the far reaches of the world and people unlike themselves were often man-eaters. This chapter traces ideas about cannibalism from Ancient Greece to medieval western Europe through a survey of some of the most influential texts.

## The Origins of Anthropophagy in the Ancient Mediterranean

In Herodotus's *Histories*, he describes several types of man-eating practiced by both Greek and non-Greek peoples, including acts of vengeance cannibalism, starvation cannibalism, and ritualized man-eating. The first of these tales of cannibalism, in book I, is an act of vengeance by a group of Scythian hunters angered by the harsh treatment they received at the hands of Cyaxares, the king of Media, when they returned empty-handed from a hunt. Herodotus writes, "They [the Scythians] felt that this treatment from Cyaxares was unwarranted, and they decided after consideration to chop up one of their young pupils, prepare him for the table in the way they had usually prepared wild animals, and serve him up to Cyaxares."[2]

The second story of cannibalism in *The Histories* also involves vengeance. Astyages, the son of Cyaxeres, had a dream that his daughter Mandane would bring great danger to his kingdom. So, in order to preserve his power, Astyages married her to an inferior nobleman, a Persian named Cambyses. Soon Mandane became pregnant, and Astyages had another dream, which foretold that her offspring would rule in his place. Once the child was born, Astyages called upon a trusted relative named Harpagus and asked him to kill his grandson. Harpagus had no choice but to agree, but he was unable to complete the task himself, so he passed it on to a herdsman named Mitradates. Rather than kill the boy, Mitradates and his wife, who had just given birth to a stillborn child, passed him off as their own and put their deceased child in his place as evidence of the deed. Years later Astyages discovered that his grandson, called Cyrus, was still alive and brought Harpagus before him to answer for his crime. After pretending to be happy with this turn of events, Astyages told Harpagus to invite his own son to greet Cyrus. "However, when Harpagus' son arrived, Astyages murdered him and dismembered him. He baked some of his flesh, stewed the rest and prepared it all for the table."

After Harpagus had eaten, Astyages asked him if he enjoyed the feast and called the servants to bring in a platter containing the boy's head, hands, and feet. Rather than recoil in terror or grief, Harpagus told the king that he could do no wrong and returned home with his son's remains. Years later, at the urging of Harpagus, Cyrus rebelled against his grandfather and ruled in his place, thus fulfilling Astyages' dream premonition. In another story of cannibalism in the sordid, sad tale of the kingdom of Media, troops under Cyrus's father, Cambyses, resorted to cannibalism in the face of starvation on an ill-fated attempt to conquer Ethiopia. Cambyses had been warned that this mission was foolhardy, but it took the desperate cannibalistic acts of his soldiers to finally convince him of this.[3]

While the Scythians are implicated in the revenge cannibalism of book I of *The Histories*, it is in book IV that they receive greater scrutiny and become the paradigmatic cannibals. Herodotus begins by describing the conquests of the Scythians and Darius's plan to seek vengeance on them for their acts of aggression against the Medes. He then relates several different versions of the origins of the Scythian people, one of which traces their descent to the offspring of Heracles and Echidna, a snake-human hybrid. Much of book IV is taken up with a detailed description of the people and places in the region of Scythia. But despite the anthropophagous reputation of the Scythians, it is in fact their neighbors that Herodotus accuses of institutionalized cannibalism: "North of this agricultural region there is a vast uninhabited area, and then there are the Cannibals, who have their own distinct way of life and are not Scythian at all."[4]

There are other people Herodotus accuses of occasionally committing acts of cannibalism, but the Cannibals are the only group to be defined by these acts. For example, he describes the funerary practices of the Issedones, who prepare a special feast on the occasion of a father's death made of sacrificial animals and the dead man's body.[5] Herodotus is actually quite careful to distinguish among types of man-eating. He passes only minimal judgment on ritualized cannibalism, like that practiced by the Issedones. Acts of revenge cannibalism similarly are not judged as significantly worse than other acts of revenge, all of which bear severe consequences for those involved and their descendants. In other words, in tales of revenge cannibalism, it is not that a human being is killed and consumed that causes repercussions; more often it is the rashness and pride of the perpetrators that come back to haunt them. Thus Herodotus distinguishes between cannibalism (ritual, starvation, revenge) and Cannibals (people who actively seek to consume human flesh).

Throughout *the Histories*, Herodotus makes sure to give his reader all available information on a topic even if he does not find his sources very credible. For example, of the different versions of the origins of the Scythians that he relates, he indicates which he finds most reasonable. He is unconvinced by the version preferred by the Scythians themselves, which ties their origins to Heracles and Echidna. That does not mean, however, that Herodotus's conclusions are always plausible. In his lengthy narrative on the regions surrounding Scythia, he describes a group of people living on the edges of the kingdom: "Far past this rugged region, in the foothills of the mountain range, live people who are said—men and women alike—to be bald from birth; they are also supposed to have snub noses and large chins, to have a distinct language, to dress like Scythians and to live off trees." Beyond the lands of the bald people, Herodotus reports, he has only the sparest of evidence. He claims that the bald people tell of "goat-footed men living in the mountains, and that on the other side of the mountains there are other people who spend six months of the year asleep," but he does not trust these reports. In fact in book III he offers a statement similar to that of Montaigne more than a thousand years later: "If one were to order all mankind to choose the best set of rules in the world, each group would, after due consideration, choose its own customs; each group regards its own as being by far the best."[6] Thus much more than most writers who followed him, Herodotus treats the act of cannibalism carefully and with a crude nod to cultural relativism.

Much has been written about the plausibility or implausibility of the existence of Herodotus's Cannibals, but whether or not he is to be trusted on the topic, other classical writers followed his example and believed that Scythia and other regions on the edges of the "civilized world" were populated by man-eaters.[7] Strabo describes the cannibalistic practices of the Celtic inhabitants of the British Isles, who are "more savage" than others in the region, practice incest, and are "man-eaters as well as heavy-eaters." To shore up this claim, which he admits comes from less than trustworthy sources, he looks to the reputation of the Scythians for support: "And yet, as for the matter of man-eating, that is said to be a custom of the Scythians also and in cases of necessity forced by sieges, the Celti, the Iberians and several other peoples are said to have practiced it." Thus, it is because the anthropophagy of the Scythians is so notorious that he finds the tales of Irish cannibalism to be somewhat credible. Furthermore, like Herodotus, Strabo maintains that there is a difference between resorting to cannibalism out of necessity and being a Cannibal, although he does seem to criticize acts of starvation cannibalism, as he asserts that only those on the fringes of "civilization" have resorted to it.[8]

Pliny the Elder echoes these sentiments in book VII of his *Natural History*. In the opening pages of this section, he discusses the authoritativeness of his work, pointing to men like Herodotus as his trustworthy sources: "We have pointed out that some of the Scythian tribes and in fact a good many, feed on human bodies—a statement that perhaps may seem incredible if we do not reflect that races of this portentous character have existed in the central region of the world, named Cyclopes and Laestrygones, and that quite recently the tribes of the parts beyond the Alps habitually practised human sacrifice, which is not far removed from eating human flesh."[9] Furthermore, Pliny argues, even if some of the things he describes may seem fantastic or dubious, given that humans tend to regard the unfamiliar with suspicion, they are all supported by the best sources that he could find. He presents himself as a skeptic who is naturally inclined to view evidence with measured suspicion. When describing parts of Africa for which his information is dubious, he refers to them as "imaginary."[10] And when he describes a litany of monstrous humans, he presents such specimens as real to the best of his knowledge, including people born with horse hooves; humans with ears large enough to cover their whole body; a race known as the Blemmyes who have no heads, only a mouth and eyes on their chest; and people with strap-like feet who must crawl instead of walk.[11] In this way he assures readers that even if one or more of the claims he makes turn out to be false, the rest of the work should not be discredited as he was merely working from the knowledge of others.

In addition to physically monstrous humans, Pliny discusses humans whose cultural practices and traditions are the cause of their monstrosity. For example, the Gamphasantes "do not practice marriage but live with their women promiscuously" and "go naked, do not engage in battle, and hold no intercourse with any foreigner," while the people of the Atlas tribe do not dream like other humans nor assign proper names to individuals, which have caused them to fall "below the level of human civilization." The aptly named Cave-dwellers live in caves, eat snakes, and are unable to speak.[12] Monstrous humans, then, are those whose bodies are well outside the normal range for humanity or whose cultures fail to meet the minimum standard for rationality and civilization as Pliny defines them.

In his descriptions of the various kinds of humans that exist in the world, Pliny specifies three places where monstrous humans are most likely to live: sub-Saharan Africa, the central Asian steppes, and Southeast Asia. In other words, monstrous humans reside in the places farthest from the influence of Mediterranean civilization. Out of all of these regions, it is the area around Scythia in the central Asian steppes that receives the most attention. Pliny lists the various tribes that fall under the general umbrella term Scythian. Some of these tribes he designates as civilized and others as savage. Those groups that inhabit the edges of the Scythian world are the recipients of most of Pliny's condemnation. Some of the lands just beyond the "Scythian promontory" are too snowy to be inhabited, while others are "uncultivated because of the savagery of the tribes that inhabit it. This is the country of the Cannibal Scythians who eat human bodies; consequently the adjacent districts are waste deserts thronging with wild beasts lying in wait for human beings as savage as themselves."[13] The lands inhabited by the Cannibal Scythians appear to mirror the savagery of its supposed inhabitants. Savage people inhabit savage lands.

Book VII of *Natural History* is devoted to describing humanity's various forms and capacities. A number of monstrous groups live in the lands just beyond the Scythians, including "people dwelling in forests who have their feet turned backward behind their legs"; people who "drink out of human skulls and use the scalps with the hair on as napkins hung round their necks"; and Albanians, who "are born with keen grey eyes and are bald from childhood."[14] These descriptions underscore an important element of the intellectual tradition that early modern Europeans would inherit: the conflation of physical and cultural "deformities" into a single category described variously as savage, barbarous, or monstrous. In this way an individual who looks like a "normal" human but turns out to be a cannibal is as far from "civilized" as physically divergent creatures like Cynocephali or Cyclopes.

Pliny spends the rest of book VII discussing human physiology, devoting considerable space to sex and reproduction. He links the earlier section on monstrosity with the section on physiology through the example of the "Hermaphrodites formerly called androgynes" and individuals who had transformed from female to male or vice versa. Thus individuals (and in some cases whole tribes) who are born with ambiguous genitalia provide the necessary link between variations of the human form and the "science" of sex and reproduction. Pliny reports that humans are the only species who indulge in procreative copulation all year round rather than during a fixed season. Human gestation, in his estimation, ranges from six to ten months. Pregnant women first feel the movement of the fetus on the fortieth day if it is male and on the ninetieth day if it is female. The birth of male children was reportedly easier for the mother. Together these beliefs about reproduction reinforce the notion of maleness as humanity's default (and more "natural") state.[15]

Like other classical writers, Pliny found the female sex both degraded and frighteningly powerful. Women's bodies were believed to do mysterious things that could have a profound impact on the environment. Contact with menstrual blood, for example, "turns new wine sour, crops touched by it become barren, grafts die, seeds in gardens are dried up, the fruit of trees falls off, the bright surface of mirrors [in] which it is merely reflected is dimmed, the edge of steel and the gleam of ivory are dulled, hives of bees die, even bronze and iron are at once seized by rust, and a horrible smell fills the air; to taste it drives dogs mad and infects their bites with an incurable poison." Thus women were in some way always monstrous. Even in death, the corpses of men float on their back, while women float on their face "as if nature spared their modesty after death," preserving the idea that women and men are fundamentally different in both form and capacity.[16] Such sentiments were echoed often by early modern Europeans in their encounters with Indigenous Americans.

## Early Christianity

At roughly the same time that Pliny was composing the *Natural History,* the religious teachings of Jesus and his disciples began spreading around the Mediterranean. The early years of Christianity were difficult for its adherents; they faced suppression and vilification for their beliefs, including accusations of anthropophagy. As evidenced by writers like Herodotus, Strabo, and Pliny, such claims about those who resided outside of civilization were not uncommon. The allegations against the Christians, however, remind us that one did not need to be geographically removed from the polis to be considered uncivilized or Other. Individuals whose cultural or religious practices differed from the masses, whose traditions remained mysterious, or who posed a threat to society as a whole could easily find themselves suspected of anthropophagy. Traditionally scholars have understood the accusations against the early Christians as a misinterpretation of the ritual of the Eucharist by the pagan majority. While this symbolic correlation seems obvious (and in fact will be deployed by English settlers against their French neighbors in America nearly a millennium and a half later), the Anglican theologian Andrew McGowan argues that this simplistic explanation fails to account for the fact that other groups were accused of cannibalism who possessed no such ritual.[17]

In the first century ce, Christians were accused of both cannibalism and incest. Much of the discussion about Christian practices among the pagan Romans centered on what transpired at their ritual meals. Pliny the Elder's nephew, referred to as Pliny the Younger, wrote a letter to Emperor Trajan while serving as the governor of Bithynia-Pontus (in modern-day Turkey) regarding his interactions with Christians. In addition to providing a useful window into the prevailing Roman policy toward Christians at the time, Pliny the Younger's letter also hints at the mystery surrounding Christian meals. In his account of his initial investigations into the crimes of Christians, he argues that their "pertinacity and inflexible obstinacy" alone "should certainly be punished," and he also hints at other questionable practices. He reports on the confessions of several Christians who described their religious practices: after pledging themselves to Christ, "it was their custom to depart and meet again to take food; but it was ordinary and harmless food, and they had ceased this practice after my edict in which, in accordance with your orders, I had forbidden secret societies."[18] According to Pliny the Younger, the accused Christians steadfastly maintained that their ritual meals were harmless. The need to defend their ritual meals reinforces the fact that speculation ran rampant in the Roman world.

Other sources from the first few centuries of the Common Era also mention the slanderous accusation of cannibalism against Christians. The second-century Christian apologist Athenagoras writes, "Three things were alleged against us: atheism, Thyestean feasts, Oedipodean intercourse," and asserts that if any evidence of such crimes could be found among the Christian population, then they deserved to be punished.[19] The charge of Thyestean feasts refers to the legendary conflict between Thyestes and his brother Atreus over the Mycenaean throne. Thyestes' children were served to him as an act of vengeance over his seduction of Atreus's wife, Aerope. Later Thyestes raped his own daughter, thus committing a reversal of Oedipal incest.[20] Athenagoras dismisses the charges against Christians as absurd but nonetheless devotes a great deal of time to refuting them. He argues that the charges of incest and sexual impropriety are illogical given that Christians focus their corporeal lives on preparation for the eternal spiritual one and as such are not "enslaved to flesh and blood, or overmastered by carnal desire," following the Pauline belief in the spiritual superiority of celibacy. He argues that the Romans are accusing the Christians of the very things that they themselves are guilty of: sodomy, prostitution, and more. In a curious passage Athenagoras accuses non-Christian Romans of being pederasts, adulterers, and sodomites, indicating that he believes such acts of promiscuity are innately cannibalistic as they do violence to the body: "These adulterers and pæderasts defame the eunuchs and the once-married (while they themselves live like fishes; for these gulp down whatever falls in their way, and the stronger chases the weaker: and, in fact, this is to feed upon human flesh, to do violence in contravention of the very laws which you and your ancestors, with due care for all that is fair and right have enacted)."[21] Christians were accused not only of sexual impropriety and man-eating but also of incestuous orgies and the consumption of babies. Their supposed crimes went well beyond the violation of social norms; they were believed to be in violation of natural law itself.

The accusations of incest and anthropophagy were widely reported by men like Theophilus of Antioch, Justin Martyr, Origen, Lucian, Clement of Alexandria, Tertullian, and in great detail by Minucius Felix.[22] These were not mere rumors, as they had real and tragic consequences for Christians in the Roman Empire, as is evidenced by the case of the Christians of Lyon and Vienne in 177. After a particularly tumultuous year, in which the Christian population came under increasing suspicion, Christians were forced to stand before the governor to face charges of incest and cannibalism. For these crimes the defendants were executed and became martyrs. An imperial edict stated that Roman citizens should be decapitated, not tortured, but although one of the defendants was a Roman citizen, he was tortured before being thrown to the beasts with his fellow believers in Christ.[23] The denial of the appropriate sentence in this case indicates that perhaps accusations of such a horrific crime as cannibalism rendered the privileges of Roman citizenship null and void.

Ultimately fear of unknown religious practices led to rumor and conjecture, resulting in the accusation of cannibalism, for why would a group want to keep their meal practices secret if not for some nefarious purpose? Toward the end of his letter to Trajan, Pliny the Younger refers to the growth of Christianity as a contagion that is spreading quickly.[24] The danger inherent in not knowing becomes even more frightening if the mystery appears to be growing. As Christian adherents spread throughout the Roman world, their hidden and mysterious rites took on a new and terrifying face. Centuries later, men like Columbus and Vespucci would write of their fears of the contagious nature of practices like cannibalism and sodomy.

## Classical Cannibal Discourse

Taken together all of these accusations of cannibalism in the classical world help us to better understand a number of important precedents that would profoundly shape the minds of early modern explorers, conquerors, evangelists, and settlers as well as those back in Europe reading of the American experience. While ancient Western writers accused a variety of peoples of cannibalism, the Scythians stand out as the most notorious group.[25] Their alleged anthropophagy was prevalent in the literature, as was their supposed uncouthness and stupidity. Herodotus was careful to distinguish between the Scythians and the Androphagi, for example, underscoring the fact that although some Scythian practices might be savage and cannibalistic, they were not solely defined by their supposed anthropophagus ways. In spite of Herodotus's contradictory and complicated depiction of Scythian peoples, it is the negative aspects of their culture that proliferated in popular discourse.[26] The first-century Jewish chronicler Josephus, for example, described the Scythians as "reveling in the murder of humans, and only slightly better than wild beasts."[27]

The proliferation of the myth of Scythian cannibals across time and space demonstrates the staying power of such accusations. But even more important, these accusations of anthropophagy against the groups collectively called the Scythians not only created the trope of cannibalism in the Central Asian steppes but helped to establish precedents regarding who cannibals were, what they were like, and where they lived. These accusations also constrained ways of thinking about cannibalism in the ancient Mediterranean world, for if Scythians were cannibals, then one knew what a cannibal was: a Scythian. This kind of circular logic will be repeated throughout the Middle Ages and the early modern period. Those who were believed to be cannibals because of their geographic location (or other defining characteristics, such as cultural practices or appearance) become themselves the very definition of "cannibals." Thus the definition of cannibal is more complicated than merely one human who consumes another, encompassing a web of assumptions about Otherness as well.

The endurance of the Scythian reputation for cannibalism also reveals how whole groups of people were conflated into artificial categories and how the differences between them were minimized. The category of Scythian encompassed a rather poorly defined group of people inhabiting a region whose boundary was equally vague. Discursively, however, these differences and vagaries mattered little. The Scythians *were* cannibals, whoever they were and wherever they lived. Again this pattern will be repeated often in the following millennia.

The anthropophagus accusations lodged at other groups, like Celts and Christians and even starving soldiers, reveal another important discursive legacy of the ancient world. If one were reading Herodotus, Pliny, or Strabo in a Mediterranean metropole like Athens or Rome, it might seem that the vast majority of cannibals live on the edges of civilization, places whose landscapes mirrored the savagery of their people. In other words, the overall impression from these works is that the cannibal always lives *elsewhere*. Yet these authors also described acts of human consumption that supposedly occurred a lot closer to home. In each of these examples, however, the act of cannibalism was an act of desperation or revenge, not a defining cultural practice. While the unfortunate Harpagus might have unknowingly consumed his own son, this act is presented as an isolated incident that arose from the intertwining of prophecy, vengeance, and overzealous passion. In this case cannibalism occurred under extreme circumstances rather than as a habitual act. The driving force of bloodlust is undeniable in such tales, but the object of rage and hatred is pointed in a specific direction rather than indiscriminately at all human beings; the paradigmatic cannibal society was presumably one in which the bonds of shared humanity were weak and all human beings were potential food sources. Even when Cambyses' troops were driven to cannibalism in the desert, it was out of desperation, not desire.

In the case of the Christians in the Roman Empire, however, a complicated situation developed in which a group a people who inhabited "civilization" were accused of ritualized, institutionalized cannibalism. The Christians were not an undifferentiated Other living somewhere on the fringes of civilization; they were not people who had been raised as savages, yet they chose to abandon their traditions and follow a path leading to inhumanity. Living among civilized people did not automatically make them part of civilization. In contrast to Pliny's lurid descriptions of cannibalistic monsters in the far reaches of the world, the Christians who were accused of cannibalism in the second century seemed to have chosen rather than inherited the practice of anthropophagy. This presents a challenge to the simplistic assertion that cannibals are always fundamentally Other. If there are people living in Rome or Antioch who are secretly cannibals, then the threat of savagery and consumption is much closer at hand. One need not travel to distant lands to be exposed to threats to one's body and spirit. These accusations highlight the distinction between the internal and external Other. Not only is this important in furthering our understanding of the concept of the Other, but it will be important in tracing the discourse of cannibalism through medieval Europe and the early modern Americas, for the strategies necessary to combat the threat of savage man-eaters need to change if the cannibals are literally among us.

Underscoring many of the descriptions of man-eaters in the classical world was the symbolic linkage of people who consumed other human beings with monsters and the monstrous. In the case of Pliny the Elder, the two were often conflated; he describes cannibals as both humans and monsters in the *Natural History*. Some of his richest descriptions of monsters appear in the chapter devoted to man, whom he considers the highest of all animals. Given this, it seems clear that for Pliny, the human race came in many forms with a large number of variations. Alongside Scythian cannibals he includes a description of Cyclopes, people whose feet are turned backward, Androgyni, individuals whose saliva can cure snakebites, and others who possess body parts with a variety of magical abilities.[28] What, then, are the parameters for defining humanity? It is not size, skin color or texture, sexual dimorphism, number of extremities, possession of certain sensory organs, nor sociality, language, or culture. Rather the reader is left with a confused understanding of humanity. What is clear, however, is that not all humans were equal in Pliny's mind.

The line between human and inhuman, or perhaps more precisely human and monster, was (and continues to be) a site of negotiation. Can one become a monster? When does a human become a monster? Is it achieved through acts or physical appearance? For modern-day readers, the designation *monster* when used in reference to human beings tends to be awarded based on actions. For example, one might come across the following sentence: "Adolf Hitler was a monster." This usage of the term feels familiar as it is not referring to Hitler as physically monstrous but rather that his horrific actions were the root of his monstrousness. At least in polite conversation, we tend not to use *monster* as a descriptor for people whose bodies deviate from the norm. Furthermore modern readers tend not to believe that the Cyclopes, mermaids, or Blemmyes are or ever were real. Since the Enlightenment there has been a clear shift away from the belief that humanity is widely diverse in form and an increased skepticism about the existence of seemingly monstrous or magical beings. But for much of the first two millennia of the Common Era, belief in such creatures was widespread. Yet while the other monstrous creatures described by Pliny have been rejected as mere fantasy, the man-eater who dwells on the fringes of civilization has not been rejected so readily. The figure of the cannibal is a central site through which the very definition of human is negotiated. As we move forward in time, it is important to take note of whether or not cannibals were perceived as monstrous humans or humanoid monsters.

Finally, before moving on to a discussion of the discourse of the can-nibal in the European Middle Ages, we must pause one more time to interrogate the place of gender, sex, and sexuality. For most classical writers, the default form of humanity was male, and thus any refer-ence to so-called Cannibals primarily signified men. The connection between reported acts of cannibalism and sexual deviance is also important. Taboo sex and cannibalism both represented the corruption of the body; each was seen an embodied act whose existence challenged the hegemonic power of the given society. Thus, regardless of what gov-ernment or religion held sway, the control of bodies and bodily acts was reserved for the state. It was common in ancient Greece for enemies to be denied proper burial, as is detailed in Sophocles' play *Antigone*. The rituals associated with death often center on control of the body. For early Christians the issue of body disposal was fraught with tension as debates over the nature of resurrection, whether it would be bodily or spiritual, raged. The denial of a proper burial or bodily disposal might mean that an individual would never achieve eternal life. In a similar fashion, for early Christians, even while one was still alive defilement of the body risked one's eternal salvation.

Within the early Christian Church itself there were accusations that certain hidden and mysterious sects did actually perform the kinds of rights that the Romans accused them of. In the fourth century Bishop Epiphanius of Salamis believed that a Gnostic Christian sect known as the Phibionites or Borborites took part in all kinds of illicit and damning acts, including cannibalism:

> They [the Phibionites] set the table with lavish provisions for eating meat and drinking wine. But then, after a drinking bout and practically filling the boy's veins, they next go crazy for each other. And the husband will withdraw from his wife and tell her—speaking to his own wife!—"Get up, perform the Agape with the brother." . . . For besides, to extend their blasphemy to heaven after making love in a state of fornication, the woman and man receive the male emission on their own hands. And they stand with their eyes raised heavenward but the filth on their hands, and pray, if you please—the one called Stratiotics and Gnostics—and offer that stuff on their hands to the actual Father of all, and say, "We offer thee this gift, the body of Christ." And then they eat it and partake of their own dirt, and they say, "This is the body of Christ; and this is the Pascha, because of which our bodies suffer and are made to acknowledge the passion of Christ."[29]

This lurid description highlights the way acts of cannibalism and sexuality were linked. Not only were they believed to have happened during a single ritual, but their pairing suggests that sexual impropriety set one on a path toward rejection of all that "civilization" held dear. In the vast majority of classical tales of cannibalism, it is the body of an infant or a young man who is consumed, linking the act of human consumption with homosexual acts. In the previous example, semen is both an offering for God and the body of Christ itself. If we understand that accusations of cannibalism in some way represent the fear of the most horrific elements of human nature, and the fear that such horrors existed hidden in plain sight even in the "civilized world," then the connection between cannibalism and sexuality (in particular nonprocreative sex) takes on greater importance. The fear of cannibalism carries with it the fear of female desire and "inappropriate" male desire. When the norms of gender and sexuality are subverted, when women commit adultery or become promiscuous or when men copulate with other men, the social body itself is threatened. The presence of unbridled indulgence of the flesh (whether through sex or consumption) indicated a society and a social order that was out of control.

## Medieval Western Europe

As Christianity spread and the early Church was still developing its canon, a large number of texts about Jesus and his disciples were written, most of which have since been deemed apocryphal. Among these was the *Acts of Andrew*, written around the middle of the third century. The most common version of the *Acts* traces the proselytizing efforts and miracles of Saint Andrew after the death and resurrection of Jesus. In addition to the more well-known and accepted version, another account of Andrew's exploits was written in Greek at the end of the fourth century. This version, called the *Acts of Andrew and Matthias*, the *Acts of Matthew and Andrew in the City of Cannibals*, or the *Acts of Andrew and Matthias among the Anthropophagi*, is a much more fanciful rendition of the tale. The edition that remains is an Old English translation of a no longer extant Latin translation of the original Greek.[30] The traditional *Acts of Andrew* mentions nothing about cannibalism, which is a prominent feature of the more dubious *Acts of Andrew and Matthias*.

The *Acts of Andrew and Matthias* begins with Saint Matthew's journey to spread the gospel of Jesus in the city of Marmadonia (Mermodonia in some versions), which was supposed to be in Scythia. The Marmadonians are described in less than flattering terms: "The men who were in this city ate no bread and drank no water, but ate men's flesh and drank their blood. And whatever foreign man who came into the city, it says that they immediately seized him and put out his eyes, and they gave him a potion to drink that was blended with much witchcraft, and when he drank this drink, immediately his heart was undone and his mind overturned." Unsurprisingly Matthew is captured and imprisoned upon his arrival in the city. While in prison, he prays to God for his deliverance. God answers, telling him that after twenty-seven days Andrew will come to his rescue. The Lord convinces Andrew to go to Marmadonia and rescue Matthew. Andrew then boards a ship, which turns out to be helmed by God himself in disguise, who warns him of the great torments that he will suffer on this mission. However, God also assures Andrew that it will be worth it as there are many among the cannibals who will make great converts. When he arrives in Marmadonia, Andrew swiftly rescues Matthew from prison and begins to spread the word of God throughout the city. Soon afterward the jailors "came so that they could lead the men out and make them into food, and they found the doors of the prison open and the seven guards lying dead," causing them great consternation. A fight between the Devil, on the side of the Marmadonians, and Andrew ensues, during which Andrew is imprisoned and tortured. While captive Andrew sends forth a flood through the city from his mouth, drowning the children and animals, while God surrounds the city with fire so that no one can escape. After this the cannibal Marmadonians repent and become devout followers of Christ.[31]

This rather absurd tale provides a nice bridge between the accusations of cannibalism lodged at Christians in the late Roman Empire and the discourses of cannibalism in medieval Europe. The story makes Christians' denial of their man-eating rituals explicit as it presents them as warriors against the scourge of cannibalism. While this reversal turns one aspect of prevalent cannibal discourses on its head, it preserves much of the spirit of cannibalism as an Othering device. It also reinforces the idea that cannibalism is common on the fringes of civilization, especially in Scythia. By the fourth century, when Christians dominate in Rome, they are presented as heroes over pagan cannibals. No longer were the Christians the enemy within.

From the fall of the Roman Empire to Columbus's landing in the Caribbean, tales of cannibalism were prevalent throughout western Europe. Such tales took a number of different forms, from travel literature to romances, church histories, and folk tales. The tendency for stories of cannibalism to locate man-eaters on the fringes of civilization continued, and so the Scythians remained a common recipient of these accusations. Instead of pointing fingers at Christians in the late Roman Empire, the accusations shifted toward other groups whose beliefs, rituals, and practices seemed mysterious, savage, or heretical. Common among these accused man-eaters were Jews, Muslims, pagans, witches, Africans, and Asians. As with the classical examples above, I will proceed chronologically, focusing on a number of key texts that appear to have had the greatest impact on Europeans in the Americas.[32]

Following the example set by Pliny in the *Natural History* (among others), the seventh-century Spanish bishop Isidore of Seville compiled an encyclopedia, called *Etymologiae*, which had a profound impact on medieval culture and knowledge. Over the next millennium, Isidore's work was published and republished so often that nearly a thousand copies survive to this day, a staggering number in comparison to other extant medieval manuscripts. Isidore drew heavily from classical writers, including Pliny the Elder, Tertullian, and

Martial; much of the *Etymologiae* is merely a rehashing, and often a direct borrowing, of earlier sources. It should come as no surprise that cannibalism is among the vast number of topics that Isidore discusses. In his exhaustive list of the peoples of the world, he describes the Scythians and their various neighbors and subdivisions. He indicates that the Scythians are descended from Magog, the second son of Japheth (the supposed forebear of all Europeans), who was the son of Moses. Isidore describes the Thracians as the most ferocious of all peoples living around Scythia. Echoing Pliny the Elder, he writes, "Indeed, they were the most savage of all nations, and many legends are recorded about them: that they would sacrifice captives to their gods, and would drink human blood from skulls." He says that the Albanians are born with white hair ("because of the incessant snow"), differing slightly from Pliny, who argued that they were bald from childhood. Despite these descriptions of the Scythians and their neighbors, Isidore specifically locates the homeland of the Cannibals as somewhere beyond India. "The Anthropophagians . . . feed on human flesh and are therefore named 'man-eaters.'"[33]

He also describes many different kinds of monstrous humans, the Plinian races, as they have come to be called, but adds a new dimension to the subject. Since Isidore is writing from a Christian perspective, unlike many of the sources he draws from, he cannot discuss monsters without clarifying their place in God's creation. As he tells us, there are no beings that are contrary to nature, and nothing can be contrary to God's will. He is concerned with developing a more rational approach to understanding monsters and human monstrosities and is careful to distinguish between beings that are portents and those that are unnatural. Nonetheless he reports on the existence of Cynocephali, Cyclopes, Blemmyes, Sciopodes, Giants, Pygmies, the Hippopodes, and the Panotians (people with ears so large that they cover their whole body). While not all of these monstrous beings lived in Scythia, several did, and Isidore reports that among the tribes that reside in this region "some cultivate the land, whereas others are monstrous and savage and live on human flesh and blood."[34] Thus the *Etymologies* maintain the earlier traditions of representing cannibals as both actual monsters, residing near monsters, or being like monsters. Anthropophagi do not appear to fit neatly into any category, but it seems that Isidore views man-eaters as human—perhaps monstrous but human nevertheless.

Isidore presents a common premodern understanding of human temperament as directly related to the climate and geography of the region that a group inhabits: "People's faces and coloring, the size of their bodies, and their various temperaments correspond to the various climates. Hence we find Romans are serious, the Greeks easy-going, the Africans changeable, and the Gauls fierce in nature and rather sharp in wit, because the character of their climate makes them so."[35] This climatic theory of human development will be echoed repeatedly by European travelers to the Americas well into the modern era.

A few centuries after Isidore of Seville composed his encyclopedic work, European Christians embarked on series of conquests of the Holy Land. The accounts of the First Crusade, which lasted from 1096 until 1099, add another important, and perplexing, layer to the medieval discourse on cannibalism. While one might expect that the Catholic Crusaders would follow earlier precedents and accuse their Muslim enemies of cannibalism, this is not the case. Rather the first-hand reports describe Catholic soldiers consuming Muslims. In 1098, during the Siege of Ma'arra, in modern-day Syria, there were a surprising number of reports that the Crusaders ate the bodies of their enemies. While the reports agree that bodies were consumed, the how, why, and who are not quite as clear. Some chroniclers blame the acts on a perhaps fictitious group of impoverished soldiers known as the Tarfur, reinforcing that even if acts of cannibalism did happen, they were committed by an outsider group. Equally important, however, is the fact that these reports stressed that the only bodies the Crusaders consumed belonged to Muslims; even when driven to desperate acts, the soldiers maintained a distinction between the bodies of their compatriots and those of their enemies. Symbolically, of course, treating the bodies of one's enemies as food dehumanizes them. But it also, in some ways, dehumanizes the consumer. As the historian Jay Rubenstein notes, however, "behind each narrative direction lies a common impulse: the recognition of cannibalism not as an aberration from the ethos of holy war but as an aspect of it."[36] In a holy war, which is by its nature understood as justified, the means must always support the ends. This same logic will be repeated by English settlers in North America who resorted to cannibalism to survive in a world that they believed was hell-bent against them.

## Medieval Travel Narratives

Typically in the Middle Ages cannibals were portrayed as either distant foreigners from the East, witches, Jews, or savage forest-dwelling

wild men. The cannibal was always an individual who resided outside of mainstream Christian culture. European traditions about the
Other reinforced a civilizing agenda, in which strangers were meant
to be converted to the proper Christian way of life or eliminated.
Because these processes were set in motion long before the first European set foot in the "new world," the writings of early explorers tended
to focus on the differences between themselves and the inhabitants of
the Americas. As it was common in medieval Europe for individuals
to label peoples and cultures that were quite different from their own
as cannibalistic, this led to an abundance of references to cannibalism
in the Americas. Additionally medieval European writings were rife
with references to the threatening powers of women, as evidenced by
the numerous accounts of witches, for example. The medieval tendency to portray women's sexual freedom as threatening was continued in the Americas.[37]

Writings about travel to exotic lands were enormously popular in
the Middle Ages, and it was not uncommon for these accounts to feature descriptions of cannibalism. Two of the most important travel
narratives for our concerns are those of Marco Polo and John Mandeville. Columbus read both of their works and to varying degrees
used them as guides for his own explorations. Polo's writings helped
Columbus to determine what he believed to be the circumference of
the Earth (he turned out to be quite wrong).[38] More important, however, it was Polo's writings that kept Columbus searching for Cathay
(China), Cipangu (Japan), and the Great Khan. Just as Columbus's
quest was shaped by Polo's own journey, so too did Polo impact discourses of cannibalism.

The travelogue of Marco Polo remains one of the most enduring narratives of the later Middle Ages. The *Travels* were actually written down
by Rustichello of Pisa, who shared a prison cell with Polo in Genoa in
the late thirteenth century. The work itself is a blend of travel narrative,
fantastic history, and romance. Polo traveled much of the known world,
from Acre to Beijing around the Indian peninsula and back to Constan-
tinople. He traveled to the seat of Mongol power and met with Kublai
Khan, who asked Polo, along with his father and uncle, who traveled
with him, to carry a letter to Pope Clement IV requesting an official
delegation of Christians. Polo's opinions on the peoples he encountered
range from outright disgust to measured admiration.

Alongside marvels of ingenuity, wealth, and engineering, Polo's
narrative discusses marvels of custom, behaviors that were decidedly

outside the norms of Roman Catholic societies. He was fascinated in particular by women's sexual licentiousness. In the majority of cultures he discusses, women are depicted as either chaste and modest or overly passionate and without shame. He describes the women of Cathay as "excel[ling] in modesty," which profoundly shapes their lives. These women go to great lengths to preserve their hymens (and thus the assumption of their virginity): "The maidens always walk so daintily that they never advance one foot more than a finger's breadth beyond the other, since physical integrity is often destroyed by a wanton gait." He was fascinated and appalled by the range of sexual practices that he heard about on his journey. In central Asia he met a group of people whose notions of hospitality went well beyond acceptability in Polo's mind. When a stranger arrived, the host was warm and welcoming, offering his house, and his wife, to the guest. The host then departed for several days, leaving the guest to do "what he will with her, lying with her in one bed just as if she were his own wife; and they lead a gay life together. All of the men of this city and province are thus cuckolded by their wives; but they are not the least ashamed of it. And the women are beautiful and vivacious and always ready to oblige." A lack of "proper" attitudes regarding gender and sexual norms was enough for Polo to describe a group of people as "liv[ing] like beasts."[39]

The first reference to anthropophagic practices in the *Travels* comes from a description of religious leaders in Tibet and Kashmir. According to Polo, holy men in these regions are filthy and have "no regard for their own decency or for the persons who behold them." They are so physically and spiritually abhorrent that they eat the corpses of convicted criminals (but never those who die a natural death). In a region of China subject to the Great Khan, Polo tells of a group of bloodthirsty people who "relish human flesh," whose armies are devoted to killing men for their feasts of flesh and blood. However, it was not until Polo and his companions arrived in the South Pacific that he reported extensively on the presence of monstrous humans and cannibals. Residing on islands between India and Japan is a group of people who kidnap all strangers to ransom them for money. If their ransom demands are not met, however, they kill and consume the captive in a great feast, for "human flesh they consider the choicest of all foods." One might question why these people bother with ransom demands if human flesh is their favorite delicacy, but perhaps Polo is implying that their greed supersedes their unnatural

uff die zeit des heilige bischoffs S. Kilians/ welcher den hertzogen vnd das volck diser stat zů Christlichem glauben bekert/ Welches hertzogen sun uff dē berg zů Würtzburg die erste kirchen in dͤ Er Marie der gebenedeiten iunckfrawen gebuwē hat Der bischoff zů Würtzburg wirt ei hertzog des frāckenlands geheissen. Von Heliopoli das.59.cap.

Eliopolis ein nāhaffte statt in Egypten gelegen/ zů teutsch dͤ Sonnen stat genāt/ wañ die hitz dͤ sonnen da so gar groß ist zů etlichen zeiten das kau zů glauben ist. Dise stat ist fast reich an gold vñ māch erley kauffmanschafft/ aber dͤ bodē ist

nit fast fruchtpar vō wege vberiger dörre/ vñ das dͤ Nilus da nit so ein gewaltigen vßgang hat als an andern orte in egyptē/ als hieuor in disem bůch angezögt ist/ das volck ist vast schwartz/ vñ get nackend/ on allein vmb die schā bedeckt es sich mit seiden od leinwat. Die menschē werden da gar selten alt. In diser statt sicht mā teglichs on zal vil Camel tierer vñ in gͤ waser zů notdürf tigen dingen tragen. Da sicht mā mancherlei fiß intreibē zů narung dͤ mēschen/ grosse hāmel wie die kuw bey vns sein/ das volck ist fast begerig milch zůtrincken/ wañ die selbig kület vnd settiget sie wol.

Von Caniballen das.60.ca.

Die Canibali seind eins grimes schützliches volck/ sesse huns köpfen glech das eine grauset dͤ sie an sicht/ vñ habend ein Insul innē/ welche Christofel dauber vō Ianua bei kurtzen iarē erfunden hat. Dise Insul ist vast groß vnd hat vil ander insulen vmb sich zůring vmb/ Die Canibali gond ale nakend on allein das sie sich zierē mit Papagallen federn mancherley farb/ seltzam durch

---

FIGURE 1.1 "Dog-headed cannibals on a Caribbean island." Hand-colored woodcut. In Lorenz Fries, *Uslegung der Mercarthen oder Cartha Marina* (Strasbourg, 1525). This image of the Americas closely resembles Marco Polo's description of cynocephali in Southeast Asia. (Courtesy of the John Carter Brown Library at Brown University.)

anthropophagous appetites. He refers to this group as idolaters (which in this case implies that they are pagans of some sort), but near Java, Polo describes an island on which people living in the cities are Muslim and those in the country are pagan. The people who reside in the mountains "live like beasts," eating human flesh and other unclean animals, and they worship "whatever they see first in the morning."[40] While Polo certainly has no great love for Islam, he does believe that Muslims are less "savage" than believers in animistic religions.

There are fewer references to monsters, monstrous humans, and other supernatural marvels in the *Travels* than one might expect. Polo is skeptical about some accounts, reporting that the Pygmies supposedly brought back from India are in fact elaborate frauds created from monkeys. However, he readily accepts more dubious creatures, such as unicorns. He describes people who have tails "as thick as [a] dog['s]" but are not covered in hair, as he expected.[41] The most well known of the creatures that Polo encountered are the dog-headed men who supposedly inhabit the Andaman Islands.[42] He describes them as idolaters who live like beasts, but more remarkably "all the men of this island have heads like dogs, and teeth and eyes like dogs; for I assure you that the whole aspect of their faces is that of big mastiffs. They are a very cruel race: whenever they can get hold of a man who is not one of their kind, they devour him."[43] Not only are the residents of the Andaman Islands cynocephalic, but they are also man-eaters. The question of whether or not they are fully human is important, for cannibalism implies the consumption of the same species; a dog that eats a human being is not a cannibal but simply a man-eater. If we are to accept that humans come in a variety of physical forms, including with the heads of other animals, then the Andaman Islanders are guilty of consuming their own species. However, if we discount the possibility of diverse humans forms, then the Cynocephali are a different species altogether and so cannot be the recipient of moral condemnation for their act.

The dubious fourteenth-century travel narrative of Sir John Mandeville also describes the "evil customs" of lands to the east. It is likely that Mandeville never actually existed but was a character created by an unknown individual. Yet his travelogue was enormously popular and appealed to the desires of some literate Europeans who wished to retake Jerusalem and continue the Crusades. Far more copies of his narrative survive than Polo's; it remained a best seller well into the sixteenth century and was especially popular in England. The work itself drew from the writings of other travelers, Crusader histories, general chronicles, and encyclopedic works. Mandeville describes women who transform into dragons, give birth to snakes, or reside in women-only lands. He also writes about people in Africa with feet so large that they can be used like parasols, and giants, Cyclopes, and centaurs in Asia who are the offspring of human women and demons.[44] Following the patterns of the sources he drew from, the author of Mandeville's travels indicates that the farther one travels from Europe, the more marvels one will encounter but also the more riches and natural resources the lands will possess. It seems that the lands occupied by the most monstrous beings were often the richest.

Similar to Polo's work, much of Mandeville's *Travels* is devoted to reporting the gendered and sexual customs of the people he encounters. He describes widespread polygyny but also women who dress indecently or like men, and even one island where a class of men are charged with deflowering all brides on the night of their wedding to other men. In the land of the legendary Christian prince of India, Prester John, Mandeville finds uncommon virtue among vice, noting that Prester John has multiple wives but has sex with them only four times a year for procreative purposes.[45]

Unlike the true tales of Crusader cannibalism, Mandeville reserves his accusations of anthropophagy for non-Europeans only. His portrayal of the practices of the people of the Isle of Lamary presage many of the descriptors that European writers would later employ to depict American cannibals. The people of Lamary are described as unabashedly naked, promiscuous, and communalist. However, it was their practice of cannibalism that most astonished Mandeville: "In that country there is a cursed custom, for they eat more gladly men's flesh than any other flesh. . . . Thither go merchants and bring with them children to sell to them of the country, and they buy them. And if they be fat they eat them anon. And if they be lean they feed them till they be fat and then they eat them. And they say, that it is the best and sweetest of all the world." Not only are the people of Lamary cannibals, but they also trade in the flesh of children. Curiously, however, he explains that they do not wear clothes because Adam and Eve were naked, suggesting that the people of Lamary have some primitive understanding of Christianity. Beyond Lamary, and in fact beyond the entrance to Hell, another group of cannibals reportedly live ready to capture any unfortunate passersby. In addition to enjoying the flesh of men more "than any other flesh," these people were supposedly twenty-eight to thirty feet tall. Mandeville also tells a tale about a group of priests in the lands beyond Prester John's country who disarticulate the corpses of people and feed most of the remains to birds. The head is reserved for the son of the dead man, who takes it home and serves it to his friends and family during a great feast. He then uses his dead father's skull as a drinking vessel.[46] This story, along with many of Mandeville's other tales of cannibals, come almost word for word from the less well-known fourteenth-century travelogue of Friar Odoric of Pordenone.[47] The dog-headed cannibals are also mentioned in Odoric's writings.[48]

## Discursive Precedents for the New World

It may seem logical to dismiss cannibalism as an element of the past, something that we have moved beyond, but this ignores the contribution of cannibalism in constructing modern identity. Cannibalism is an inseparable feature of racism, colonialism, and sexism. The trope of cannibalism was employed by European writers as an important justification for the subjugation of peoples. It was the discursive presence of cannibalism, which was consistently linked to understandings of gender and sexuality, that indicated savagery long before race, as we understand it in the modern context, became fully developed.

When Portuguese caravels began exploring the African coast in the first half of the fifteenth century, they were in possession of technological advances that allowed them to travel farther and faster and to navigate more efficiently. These explorations and conquests, particularly in the Canary Islands, set the stage for the conquest of the Americas. The Spanish and the Portuguese first tested their imperial machines on Atlantic islands, subjugating people and establishing mercantilist ventures that would lead to unprecedented royal profits and a new thirst for expansion. Columbus did not decide in isolation to venture west to discover a new route to Asia; he was born into a rapidly changing world dominated by Italian merchants with a burgeoning desire to possess and consume the world's resources. He was not simply curious about what lay to the west; he wanted to find riches and respectability there. He was driven by competing desires for gold, for glory, and for God. As we all are, Columbus was a product of his time. Born into a world on the cusp of modernity, he inherited intellectual legacies about the wonders of the far reaches of the globe from the medieval world, just as he possessed the mercantilist, empirical desires of early modern empires.

Medieval tales of cannibalism reveal a fascination with the unknown and a profound wonder at the diversity of the world. Cannibals were almost always portrayed as outsiders; whether they lived within the boundaries of "civilization" or somewhere far from European influence, they were Other. Travel writings demonstrate that the connections evident in classical discourse between sexuality, gendered norms, and cannibalism persisted. Even when a group of people was not explicitly described as cannibalistic, "improper" consumptive patterns went hand in hand with other supposedly deviant practices. For example, Mandeville describes a group of people on a far-flung island who have a wide array of edible animals available to them yet limit themselves to certain animals and never consume the myriad fowl or rabbits among them. These people "eat flesh of other beasts and drink milk. In that country they take their daughters and sisters to their wives, and their other kinswomen. And if there be ten men or twelve men or more dwelling in an house, the wife of everych of them shall be common to them all that dwell in that house; so that every man may lie with whom he will of them on one night, and with another, another night. And if she have any child, she may give it to what man that she list, that hath companied with her, so that no man knoweth there whether the child be his or another's."[49] Mandeville places a description of their dietary habits right next to a report on their sexual and kinship practices. Taken together, this and other descriptions of exotic people in medieval travel narratives clearly demonstrate a pervasive belief in the connection between seemingly disordered sexuality and eating habits. Not only were other humans the most improper food to eat, but cannibalism was perceived as both gastronomic and sexual.

In addition to the concept of Otherness and the connection between sex and cannibalism, medieval narratives reinforce the link between anthropophagy and imperial expansion. From Herodotus to Marco Polo, the concerns of empires, city-states, and rulers were intimately tied to the accusations of cannibalism. As empires and cities grew and expanded, they came into contact with new groups of people, many of whom resisted foreign influence. The peoples inhabiting the areas to the north and east of the Black Sea proved to be formidable obstacles to both Hellenic and Roman expansion. For centuries these Scythians were also considered to be the consummate cannibals. In one way or another all of the accusations of cannibalism discussed herein are connected to the expansion of empires and cultures but not always outright conquest. Thus even though Columbus did not sail west with an army at his back, he did bear with him a millennium's worth of axioms about Otherness. Well before any documented interactions between Americans and Europeans, including Vikings in Newfoundland, new lands and strange new peoples were quite often already believed to be savage and cannibalistic. The categorization of the peoples of the Americas, setting aside any evidence of anthropophagous practices, was perfectly consistent with European expectations.

# 2 /   Discovering Cannibals: Europeans, Caribs, and Arawaks in the Caribbean

In the Pulitzer Prize–winning book *Admiral of the Ocean Sea: A Life of Christopher Columbus* from 1942, Samuel Eliot Morison attempts to capture the awe-inspiring wonder of the discovery of the Americas. He describes the experience as earth-shattering, ushering in a new era of human experience: "Every tree, every plant that the Spaniards saw was strange to them, and the natives were not only strange but completely unexpected, speaking an unknown tongue and resembling no race of which even the most educated of the explorers had read in the tales of travelers from Herodotus to Marco Polo. Never again may mortal men hope to recapture the amazement, the wonder, the delight of those October days in 1492 when the New World gracefully yielded her virginity to the conquering Castilians."[1] Morison's choice to describe the American continents as a virginal woman and Spanish exploration as sexual conquest follows a long-standing pattern. The notion of land as feminine and conquest as masculine appears often in the literature of imperialism.[2] But the Americas did not willingly yield their virginity to Europe, as he suggests; rather Europe claimed and constructed the continents as pure and unspoiled in order to create a narrative of consent. Describing the encounter as consensual denies the fact that the Americas had minimal agency in regard to the Columbian encounter. There was no real choice: Columbus showed up without their permission and laid claim to lands and people who could not object because they were not even aware that a claim was being made. If one were compelled to describe the first meeting of

Europeans and Americans in sexual terms, rape would be a much more appropriate metaphor.

Morison also highlights the novelty of the encounter between America and Europe while connecting it to the same historic context that I discussed in chapter 1. He argues that even with the knowledge of earlier traditions of contact with strange people and far-flung lands, something unique and unprecedented occurred when men from Europe met the men and women of the Americas for the first time. Accordingly this chapter uncovers the novelty and continuity of the discursive traditions of cannibalism in the context of the first encounters in the Caribbean. Furthermore I examine the connection that Morison makes between sexuality and conquest. The discussion will predominantly focus on the Caribs of the Lesser Antilles, for it is on these islands that the fearsome cannibals reportedly resided.[3] However, particularly in the section on Amerigo Vespucci, I discuss mainland Carib peoples as well.[4]

The figure of the cannibal remains one of the most enduring images of the European conquest of America, and while Columbus was most certainly not the first person to indicate the existence of savage cannibals in a faraway land, his momentous voyage ushered in a new era in which cannibals replaced anthropophagi.[5] This chapter explores the discourse of cannibalism in the context of the discovery and early exploration of the Caribbean, addressing the ways the discourse of cannibalism drew from earlier classical and medieval precedents and developed in new directions in a unique context, beginning with a discussion of the development of the discourse of cannibalism in writings about the four voyages of Columbus. Then I examine how descriptions of cannibalism differed in the writings of Amerigo Vespucci, especially regarding the gendered nature of cannibal discourse. Finally, I will briefly examine the visual rhetoric of man-eating.

The discourse of Carib cannibalism was gendered in a variety of complex and sometimes contradictory ways. Europeans writings about the New World demonstrated preconceived notions about proper displays of gender and sexuality, and these assumptions led them to construct Indians as inferior Others. In my examination the intersections of the discourses of cannibalism, sex, and gender in the Caribbean, the development of European ideas about alterity and difference, which were fundamental to the establishment and maintenance of European power in the New World, becomes clearer. Furthermore this exploration provides greater insight into how Europeans expanded their power in the Americas and the justifications that this power rested upon, both in the Caribbean and in other regions.

The Caribs took the symbolic place of the Scythians as the paradigmatic cannibals in the minds of European writers in the early sixteenth century.[6] Europe was first made aware of the Caribs/Kalinago by neighboring Arawak/Taíno Indians of the Greater Antilles, who informed Columbus and his crew about the fearsome tribe to the east who came over the sea to terrorize and consume them.[7] European writings implied that the Arawaks and Caribs were long-standing enemies.[8] This supposed enmity has come down to us as a reflection of the divide between "good Indians" and "bad Indians." The Caribs, from the first moment of European contact, were portrayed as villains who terrorized the innocent Arawaks and posed a significant impediment to European expansion. Their reputation for cannibalism became one of the most damning pieces of evidence of their savagery and accordingly their availability for conquest. On his first voyage Columbus did not venture into the Lesser Antilles, but he undertook the second journey across the Atlantic with the express purpose of finding the islands of the Caribs.[9] Thus the purported presence of cannibalism in the West Indies was an important catalyst for early exploration and conquest. By the mid-sixteenth century the practice of cannibalism would also determine the Europeans' ability to enslave a given population.

The men who participated in these voyages of exploration-turned-exploitation came from many different parts of Europe and did not possess a unified understanding of Otherness. Yet, as discussed in chapter 1, there were some generalized tropes with which they would have been familiar. Even though Columbus sailed for Spain, he was Italian by birth, as was Vespucci, who sailed for both Spain and Portugal. Italian mariners dominated the seas in the fifteenth century and led the way in the conquest of America. Despite the multiethnic nature of the crew on voyages to the Caribbean, the writings about these voyages all indicate that European men brought preexisting traditions about encounter with difference with them on their journey. The discovery of the Americas represented the first time that Europeans were exposed to such a large, unknown, and seemingly barbaric population.[10] There were innumerable accounts of savages, wild men, and witches living in Europe, as well as tales of cannibals at the edges of the civilized world, but what distinguished the encounter with the Americans was its scale, not necessarily its novelty.[11]

Based on intellectual traditions of monstrosity and cannibalism, Columbus fully expected to encounter amazing and monstrous creatures when he arrived in the New World.[12] The cannibals of Columbus's day were part of the same family of monsters as dog-headed men, though today we consider the existence of cannibals as less dubious.[13] While the cannibals of Europe's imagination may have been considered among the monstrous and magical, this was no longer the case less than a century after discovery. Through an examination of the writing of Columbus, Vespucci, and others, the way the figure of the cannibal became disassociated with the realm of the imaginary and instead came to represent real, living people with disastrous consequences becomes clearer as well.

The beginnings and ends of historical epochs are always fuzzy, and while there is no clear moment in which the medieval world ends, Columbus's discovery of the Americas was a harbinger of modernity. In many ways he was a man straddling the medieval and the modern; he challenged conventional wisdom about geography (although, contrary to the prevalent American cultural myth, people of his time knew that the world was round), traveled widely throughout Europe and Africa, and opened Europe's eyes to the vast lands to the west. At the same time, he was obstinate in his belief that he had discovered the western route to Asia and found evidence to confirm his belief without recognizing the glaring errors in his observations. Furthermore his way of understanding difference was shaped by medieval epistemologies.[14]

## First Impressions

In a journal entry from November 4, 1492, Columbus mentions cannibalism for the first time, more than three weeks after the first sighting of land on October 12.[15] This initial observation is often overlooked because it does not relate directly to "real" Indians, but it is nonetheless very important. The entry, as abstracted by Fray Bartolomé de las Casas, reads, "He [Columbus] understood also that, far from there, there were one-eyed men, and others, with snouts of dogs, who ate men, and that as soon as one was taken they cut his throat and drank his blood and cut off his genitals."[16] Columbus accepted the presence of wondrous creatures, like the fabled dog-headed men, albeit with a dollop of skepticism.[17] He and his crew never encountered these creatures, although he did find a couple of mermaids who turned out not to be as beautiful as he anticipated.[18] Despite that, he still insisted that they were in fact mermaids. Similarly he insisted that the islands of the Caribbean were actually India, in spite of the evidence to the contrary. He exhibited a curious combination of empirical observation coupled with confidence in his ability to interpret data based on a preconceived understanding of the outcome. Like most others of his time, he knew what he would find in the New World and simply looked for evidence to confirm his assumptions.[19] Rather than letting his observations speak for themselves, Columbus insisted on the existence of truth in medieval and classical texts that he simply needed to confirm. In this way he was no great innovator or discoverer, for he was discovering only what he believed had already been proven to exist. His real discovery from his perspective, then, was the route that he took to get to Asia, not learning of new lands and new peoples.

In his famous letter to Luis de Santángel, the finance minister who was instrumental in convincing the Crown to fund the voyage, Columbus remarked that because of God's divine will the lands that had been "talked or written" about by men but were known only through "conjecture, without much confirmation from eyesight, amounting only to this much that the hearers for the most part listened and judged that there was more fable in it than anything actual," had finally been observed and were now known to Christendom.[20] In the past several decades, much doubt has been cast on the novelty of Columbus's discovery, but that is not at issue here. It does not matter that he was not the first European to set foot in the Western Hemisphere, but rather that his actions started a chain of events that radically altered the course of history. Through his writings and their legacy he originated an idea of the cannibal that not only affected the way scholars and laypeople speak about indigeneity, savagery, and civilization but had real tangible effects on people's lives.

There are very few surviving records of Columbus's voyages in his own words; the vast majority of what remains are summaries and abstracts of his work written by his contemporaries. Bartolomé de Las Casas abstracted and edited Columbus's journal of his first voyage and published it as part of his larger work, *Historia de las Indias*. Las Casas's book contains some of the actual language from the no longer extant journal, as well as editorial summaries of other portions. Ferdinand Columbus also abstracted and summarized his father's journal in a biography about him that survives in a Latin translation from 1571.[21] The state of the historical records makes it difficult to know where Columbus ended and the editorial hand began. In the passage quoted earlier, from Las Casas's record of the journal of the first voyage, Columbus did not really doubt the veracity of the existence of dog-headed cannibals or men with one eye. However, in his widely published letter to Santángel, which was written in his own hand and published in Barcelona in April 1493, Columbus displayed a measured skepticism about the wonders of the New World.[22] He wrote, "Down to the present, I have not found in those islands any monstrous men, as many expected, but on the contrary all the people are very comely."[23] Considering precedent, one might reasonably expect that men with dog heads would be considered monstrous.

Columbus wrote that he had not obtained any information about the existence of monsters in the Indies except for an island that was inhabited by those who other Indians "regard as very ferocious, who eat human flesh." The people, he reported, plundered the other islands in their canoes. These cannibals were "no more ill-shaped than the others, but have the custom of wearing their hair long, like women." Their ferocity was starkly contrasted by the excessive cowardice that Columbus attributed to other Indians. Finally, he indicated that the cannibals consorted with the people of the Island of Matinino, which was populated only by women who "practice[d] no female urges," a tale that bears a striking resemblance to one told by Marco Polo and legends of Amazons in general.[24] In this description of the peoples of the Caribbean islands, he denies the existence of monsters in the West Indies but confirms the presence of cannibals and the Amazon-like women of Matinino, with whom the cannibals mated. According to his letter, Columbus did not doubt that the cannibals were indeed human; they may have behaved monstrously, but they were not actually monsters. While his journal contains the record of what occurred on his journey, including that the Natives told him of the existence of the fabled dog-headed people, his letter to Santángel was more careful and did not relate such tales as reflections of reality.

After departing from Palos de la Frontera in Andalusia on August 3, 1492, the *Niña*, *Pinta*, and *Santa María* headed first to the Canary Islands, finally heading for the unknown west on September 6.[25] Columbus and his crew explored the islands that we now call the Greater Antilles, including Hispaniola and Cuba. It was here that he encountered the Arawaks.[26] His first written impressions of this group of Indians stressed their docility, generosity, and of course their nudity.[27] During this initial contact he also learned that they were being terrorized by a fearsome neighboring tribe. Ferdinand Columbus reported, "Some Indians had scars left by wounds on their bodies; [we] asked by signs what had caused them, they replied, also by signs that the natives of other islands came on raids to capture them and they had received their wounds defending themselves."[28] Columbus's journal contains a similar account of this fateful meeting.[29]

Throughout these first travels in the Caribbean, Columbus claims to have heard often about the atrocities of the neighboring Caribs. He recorded on November 23, 1492, that the Indians expressed great fear of the island of Bohío, where well-armed one-eyed cannibals resided.[30] He doubted what the Arawaks told him; he wondered if perhaps their people were simply taken captive and, because they did not return, were assumed to have been eaten. He remarked that they expressed the same fear about him and his men when they first encountered them. The Arawaks' fear inspired him with the hope that based on their superior technology and organization, these Caribs might in fact be the same people of the Great Khan for whom he had been searching. Despite the number of times the Arawaks reportedly told him that the Caribs had one eye or the faces of dogs, he did not believe them, and his excitement to meet the Great Khan only increased. At one point he believed that he encountered some Carib individuals based solely on their hideous appearance. However, he did not record much of importance about this encounter, and based on the navigational records of his journey, it is unlikely that these individuals were actually Caribs.[31]

In addition to the stories of being terrorized at the hands of cannibalistic seafaring Caribs, the Arawaks also told the Europeans about the legendary women of the island of Matinino. Columbus recorded that only women lived on this island and that they did not practice the traditional employs of their sex, but rather were fierce warriors. These women were said to be the consorts of the Carib warriors, who at a certain time of the year traveled to Matinino to mate with them. Male children were returned to their Carib fathers, and female children were raised by the women.[32] Together the cannibals and the women of Matinino fascinated Columbus and filled him with the desire to encounter them on his second voyage. Herodotus indicated that the Amazons lived in a region bordering Scythia and the cannibals and tells a similar story about sex between Scythian men and Amazonian women.[33] Although Columbus never explicitly connects the Caribbean with Scythia, he nonetheless transposes the geographical and sexual relationship between cannibals and Amazons onto the New World.

On his first voyage of discovery, Columbus did not find great caches of gold or spices, but his encounters with Indians provided him with clues about their possible location and what he believed to be the location of the Great Khan. The writings from this voyage reveal a profound ambivalence about the presence of cannibalism in the Caribbean. At times the admiral seems quite skeptical about what is revealed to him; at other times, however, he appears eager to hear about the sophistication of the man-eaters and the possible presence of gold in their midst. His diary and the published letter to Santángel further emphasize this ambivalence; he recorded that the cannibals were supposedly one-eyed and dog-headed, yet he doubted the truth of this. He was less skeptical about their cannibalistic ways but still did not unquestioningly accept it.

Neither Columbus, his son Ferdinand, nor Las Casas provides much detail about the gendered or sexual practices of Caribbean Natives. However, Columbus was intrigued by their nudity and remarked upon it a number of times.[34] He fixated on the beauty of some of the Indians, but in the published versions of his accounts, he stops short of describing sexuality in any detail.[35] He wrote that the men on Hispaniola only possessed one wife each, "except for the king, who could have as many as twenty."[36] The sexual practices of the women of Matinino and their Carib lovers did appear of some interest to the admiral, perhaps because of their relative strangeness.

The connection between sexuality and cannibalism became more firmly established in accounts of the second voyage and subsequently in the writings of Michele da Cuneo and Amerigo Vespucci. Additionally the first reference to cannibalism described dog-headed beings who drank blood and removed the genitals of their victims. In the coming decades Caribs would be widely accused of castrating and consuming their victims. This particular threat to masculinity embodied the most deep-seated fear of European men: not only did the Caribs practice strange sexual behaviors, but they also enacted their rage and vengeance on virile men, first by removing their "manhood," then by ingesting and incorporating male bodies into their own.

There were a number of published secondhand accounts that deal with the admiral's first voyage to the Americas. For example, Allegretto Allegretti wrote in 1493, "On one island there are men who eat other men from a nearby island, and they are great enemies to each other and do not have any type of weapons."[37] Allegretti displays none of the ambivalence evidenced in Columbus's writings. He also incorrectly asserts that none of the islanders had any weapons, which was directly contradicted by the letter to Santángel, which was published in the same month in which Allegretti wrote his account.[38] Allegretti also claims that the Indians welcomed the Spaniards by presenting them with "many young virgins," an event that does not occur in the extant records of Columbus.

In his chronicle of the history of Venice from 1493, Domenico Malipiero repeats that the Indians of the New World were generous, timid, and good-natured. However, he also notes, "The island called Santa Maria has people like the others, except they have very long hair and eat human flesh, and they go about in the vessels referred to above [canoes] abducting men from other islands."[39] In this passage the Caribs and those that eat human flesh are clearly conflated. Interestingly Malipiero seems to suggest that the length of their hair is as important and interesting as their man-eating. He does not doubt that the cannibals are men and not monsters, nor does he express doubt about the veracity of the Arawak descriptions of them.

Another example of the circulation of tales from the first voyage comes from the account of an Augustinian monk named Giacomo Filippo Forest da Bergamo, written in 1493. He repeats a story that Columbus tells in his letter to Santángel, that there is an island in the Caribbean on which all of the people are born with tails. This is an example of the direct passing on and recirculating of knowledge about discovery. Bergamo also writes, "The admiral took those people [from Hispaniola, home of the short-lived first European settlement, La Navidad], who were living like wild animals and brought them to a more cultivated way of life." This statement nicely encapsulates the burgeoning civilizing agenda of Europe: through the beneficence of European men, the New World "savages" were taught to use the land properly (through cultivation) and thus were brought from bestiality to rationality. Bergamo also repeats the tale of the women of Matinino and notes that on the Island of Charis there is "a very fierce race of men who eat human flesh."[40]

In his popular book *De Orbe Novo*, the prominent theologian Peter Martyr d'Anghiera relates the tales of cannibals recorded by Columbus with some embellishment. He writes that the peaceful men of Hispaniola live in great fear of their formidable neighbors, whom they refer to as Cannibals and Caraibes. Martyr tells the oft-repeated story of the castrated captives taken by the cannibals, but he provides a level of detail not previously seen:

> The cannibals captured children, whom they castrated, just as we do chickens and pigs we wish to fatten, and when they were grown and became fat they ate them. Older persons, who fell into their power, were killed and cut into pieces for food; they also ate the intestines and the extremities, which they salted just as we do hams. They did not eat women, as this would be considered a crime and an infamy. If they captured any women they kept them and cared for them, in order that they might produce children; just as we do with hens, sheep, mares, and other animals.[41]

Martyr dehumanizes both the Caribs and their captives in this passage. He indicates that the Caribs treated other humans like animals, a practice that calls into question the superiority and uniqueness of the human species. Furthermore, by consistently referring to the captives as animals, Martyr emphasizes the presumption of the bestiality and barbarity of Indians.

Martyr, an Italian like the admiral, was an important humanist in Spain and served in the household of Ferdinand and Isabella. He collected information about the discovery and conquest of the Americas and over the course of his life published a detailed account of these events. He had access to Columbus's writings, many of which are no longer extant, and therefore his work is an invaluable resource for understanding the genesis of the idea of the cannibal. It is nearly impossible to determine what was embellished in his account and what was derived from sources that have disappeared. What is clear, however, is that New World cannibals were becoming infamous. Martyr believed that the actions of the Caribs toward the other Caribbean peoples were akin to the ways that Europeans treated their livestock. In this way he simultaneously connected the victims of the cannibals and the cannibals themselves with animal-like behavior.

## Traveling Tales

Records of Columbus's first voyage indicated the presence of cannibalism in the Americas but did not provide much in the way of detail or certainty. It was on the second voyage that the discourse of the cannibal really began to emerge. According to crewmember Diego

Álvarez Chanca, the second voyage was expressly intended to bring Europeans and Caribs into contact for the first time.[42] Writing several years after the voyage, Allesandro Zorzi, who was not an eyewitness, concurs that Columbus "had been commissioned . . . to persecute and destroy their enemies, those very wicked men, the Cannibals."[43]

Columbus and his crew set out from the Canary Islands on October 13, 1493. By November 3 they had their first view of the island of Dominica in the Lesser Antilles. After sailing around the western islands, they proceeded to Cuba, Puerto Rico, and Hispaniola. On this voyage Columbus had his first real encounter with men he believed were the fearsome cannibal Caribs. The eyewitness evidence from the second voyage comes from several letters written by members of the expedition. There is Nicolò Scillacio's translation of a letter he received from a crewmember named Guillelmo Coma, which was first published in 1504.[44] Another important source is a letter written by Dr. Diego Alvarez Chanca that was only uncovered and printed in the nineteenth century. There are also numerous secondhand assemblages of the events, the most important of which are the writings of Peter Martyr d'Anghiera from late 1494 and early 1495.

Early on in the second voyage Columbus and his men encountered a group of women who claimed to have escaped the voracious jaws of the Caribs. They fled to the Spaniards for salvation, but instead of freedom the women were given gifts to give to the Caribs. After this, according to Ferdinand Columbus, the women begged the Spaniards to take them along and indicated by gestures that their captors were man-eaters. The Spaniards eventually relented and allowed the women to remain with them. Ferdinand Columbus, who was not present on this voyage, reported that these women felt more comfortable in the hands of strangers than "among those wicked, cruel men who had eaten their children and husbands. It is said the Caribs do not eat or kill women, but keep them as slaves."[45] This assertion reoccurs throughout the early accounts of Caribbean exploration. The agents of the Spanish Crown indicated that the appetites of Caribs were so disordered and antithetical to civilization that they ate men and used women as beasts of burden. Unfortunately for these and other women the Spaniards encountered, life with the admiral and his men was not likely to have been much better. If they did not die from disease, they were likely sold into slavery and probably died soon afterward.

In his biography of his father, Ferdinand Columbus does not dwell on the practices of Native Americans and thus does not devote much time to the cannibalistic appetites of the Caribs. His biography was written after his father's death in 1506, and as fourteen years had passed since the initial encounter, the supposed atrocities of the Indians were less important to Ferdinand than redeeming his father's character, which was paramount. However, Ferdinand does report that members of the crew found cannibal villages (which were notably more sophisticated than the Arawak villages encountered on the first voyage), in which they saw human body parts roasting on spits. He also describes an encounter with a group of Indian women that he believed to be from the all-female island of Matinino because of their intelligence and strength.[46]

Dr. Diego Alvarez Chanca's account of his travels with Columbus on the second voyage is the first to be written by a trained scientist.[47] The ethnographic detail evident in Chanca's account is lacking in many of the others. However, his letter was not made widely available until the publication of Martín Fernández de Navarrete's compendium *Viages* in 1825. Therefore Chanca's letter did little to contribute to the published circulating discourse of cannibalism in early sixteenth-century Spain, but it nevertheless does demonstrate one individual's interpretation of cannibalism while reflecting the prevailing discourses. It also reveals much about how Spanish agents comprehended the actions of Indians. More popular works like Andrés Bernáldez's *Historia de los Reyes Católicos Don Fernando y Doña Isabel* from 1513 relied heavily on Chanca's writings. Thus even if the letter was not published and widely circulated it was influential for many other accounts.[48]

Chanca reports that some of the crew went to a village on the island of Guadeloupe and returned with parrots, spinning implements, food, reporting that the village also contained "four or five bones of human arms and legs. On seeing these we suspected that we were amongst the Caribbee islands, whose inhabitants eat human flesh."[49] This speaks to the prevalence of cannibalism as an explanatory trope for scattered, incomplete evidence: he assumes that the human bones are evidence of cannibalism, but this is not an obvious conclusion unless one already assumes the existence of the practice of cannibalism among the Caribs.

At another port, Chanca writes, he and other members of the crew found "a vast number of human bones and skulls hung up about the houses like vessels intended for holding various things."[50] Remarking on this same incident, the more sympathetic Las Casas, who was not present, argues that the bones must have belonged to important members of the tribe or loved ones, not victims of cannibalism, "because if they ate as many as some say, the cabins would not hold all the bones and skulls, it seems that after having eaten them there would be no object in keeping the skulls and bones for relics unless they belonged to some very notable enemies."[51] Las Casas reaches a different conclusion than Chanca from the same evidence; his sympathy for the plight of the Indians means that cannibalism is not his first conclusion for the presence of human bones. In both cases these men allowed their predisposition toward the Indians to shape their conclusions.

Modern research has confirmed Las Casas's suspicions to some degree, revealing that the presence of bones and other body parts in Carib houses was not necessarily a sign of cannibalistic practices; rather the Caribs cleaned, displayed, and venerated the bones of powerful members of their own tribe.[52] From this perspective the episode reveals a cultural misunderstanding in which the agents of Spain interpreted events based on their knowledge and experience from the first voyage as well as from historical and literary precedent. In other words, Columbus and his men reported that the Caribs were man-eaters, and classical and medieval tradition supported this assertion; thus the presence of bones in Carib homes must be evidence of cannibalism.

Fear of the Caribs guided the actions of the members of the Spanish fleet and their interactions with the Indians. They assumed that the tales about the unbridled anthropophagic appetites of the Caribs were true, and this caused them to fear for their safety and to doubt Carib motives in any exchange they had. In one case several crewmembers left the ship to explore an island, and when they did not return, their shipmates feared the worst. Chanca writes, "We already looked upon them as killed and eaten by the people that are called Caribbees; for we could not account for their long absence in any other way."[53] Embellishing Chanca's version, Bernáldez reports that the missing men were assumed to have been killed and consumed by the Caribs "since it was unreasonable to think anything else."[54] Crewmember Michele da Cuneo echoes these sentiments in a letter he wrote in 1495.[55] As it turned out, however, the men had simply gotten lost and eventually rejoined the group. The assertion that the absence of the crewmembers must be attributed to their consumption at the hands of the Caribs is a reversal of Columbus's sentiments from the first voyage; then he believed that the Arawaks may have been mistaken, that their people were merely captives among the Caribs.

Chanca appears to have fully accepted that Caribs were man-eaters and thus believed that they must have killed and eaten the men. His letter describes the constant warfare between Caribs and the peoples of neighboring islands in which they sought to obtain captives, particularly young women to be servants and concubines. Chanca records that the Caribs were exceedingly cruel to these women and that they even ate the children they sired with them. The children born to their Carib wives, however, were unharmed. In this scenario the copulation between Carib men and their captive women existed outside of the structure of Carib kinship. Children produced from these couplings were not considered members of the tribe, and as such their Carib fathers bore no responsibility for them. Despite the fact that children born out of wedlock were often shunned in medieval and early modern Europe, Chanca was horrified that Carib men engaged in sexual relations with captive women without ethical consequences or obligations toward either mother or child.

Chanca also writes that the Carib raiding parties took as many male hostages as they could, brought them to the village, and immediately killed and ate them:

> They [Caribs] say that man's flesh is so good, that there is nothing like it in the world; and this is pretty evident, for of the bones which we found in their houses, they had gnawed everything that could be gnawed, so that nothing remained of them, but what from its great hardness, could not be eaten: in one of the houses we found the neck of a man, cooking in a pot. When they take any boys prisoners, they cut off their member and make use of them as servants until they grow up to manhood, and then when they wish to make a feast, they kill and eat them; for they say that the flesh of boys and women is not good to eat. Three of these boys came fleeing to us thus mutilated.[56]

The castration of animals, which was believed to help fatten them and improve the quality of the meat, was a common practice in animal husbandry, and thus Chanca's description furthers the symbolic association of Indians with animals. Additionally castrated male animals were believed to be more docile than intact ones. In this example Chanca encapsulates all of the most important tropes that Europeans believed about cannibalism among the Caribs. The Caribs were thought to live on different islands from the noncannibalistic Indians, and they traveled widely for their conquests. Whether or not the two broad cultural groups of the Caribbean at this time, the Arawak and the Carib, were in fact two wholly different groups occupying different islands remains a subject of great scholarly debate.[57] However, this debate is less important here than it might seem; it does not matter whether or not the Caribs were a separate cultural or linguistic group, only that European invaders went to great lengths to distinguish between the "good Indians," meaning the Arawaks, and the "bad Indians," the Caribs. The extent to which their origins and languages differed mattered far less to many contemporary observers and writers than what kinds of behaviors they exhibited. The presence of man-eating signaled the presence of Caribs and vice versa. Or, as Bernáldez succinctly put it, the priority was to "distinguish the good ones from the Caribs who had worse customs than the other Indians."[58]

Chanca also discusses his belief that the Caribs consumed the males they conquered and kept the females to work as slaves, to serve as concubines, and to bear children for eventual consumption. The desire to eat the flesh of men and possess the flesh of women drove the Caribs to terrorize their neighbors. The connection between sex and cannibalism is quite evident in Chanca's example. Dominance, for the Caribs, came through different incorporative practices, according to Chanca. Male enemies were incorporated through ingestion; their flesh was consumed immediately after the battle and was the ultimate object of desire. Female enemies, on the other hand, were incorporated through forcible sex, and their labor was exploited through slavery. In Chanca's understanding, the place of Arawakan women in the cannibalistic practices of the Caribs was twofold: to produce children with their captors who would eventually be served up at cannibal feasts and to fulfill deviant sexual desires. Even though the Carib men had their own wives, they desired sexual congress with powerless women (something of which European men were also guilty).

Chanca reiterates that the Caribs castrated the young men they took captive and asserts that the presence of bones in Carib households is solid evidence of their voracious anthropophagic appetites. He indicates that they consumed the male warriors of enemy tribes, but the young men were emasculated and forced into servitude alongside the women of their tribe. This practice is quite curious, for if the Caribs desired the flesh of men above all else, why would they not imprison the young men, allow them to grow into adulthood, and consume them when they were ripe, so to speak? If this questionable practice is taken to be true, perhaps Chanca and others failed to recognize fully the importance of consuming warriors rather than passive captives (and of castrating male captives to render them passive). However, the consumption of the offspring of Arawakan women and Carib men calls this into question. What is evident is that by the time of the second voyage, Europeans were beginning to create specific gendered associations around the practice of cannibalism.

The connection between Indian women's sexuality and cannibalism was made most explicit in the letter that Michele da Cuneo sent to his friend Gerolamo Annari in 1495. Cuneo, a childhood friend of Columbus who accompanied him on the second voyage, reported on his interactions with Caribs, expressing no uncertainty that they were anthropophagous. The most widely referenced portion of his letter discusses his own sexual conquest of a young Carib woman. The crew had engaged in a battle with three or four men, two women, and two presumably Arawak captives who had recently been castrated. The crew was victorious over the Caribs, despite the latter's determination and vigilance. Those who were captured, both Carib and Arawak, were sent to Spain. In the letter Cuneo tells his friend about his interaction with one of the captured Carib women: "While I was in the boat I laid my hands on a gorgeous cannibal woman whom the lord admiral granted me; when I tried to satisfy my craving she, wanting none of it, gave me such a treatment with her nails that at that point I wished I had never started. At this, to tell you how it all ended, I got hold of a rope and thrashed her so thoroughly that she raised unheard-of-cries that you would never believe. Finally, we were in such accord that, in the act, I can tell you, she seemed to have been trained in a school of harlots."[59] This incident is an appalling tragedy to modern-day readers, but it is obvious in Cuneo's rather flippant attitude about the whole affair that he saw nothing wrong with his actions; in fact he brags about it to his friend.[60]

Cuneo explains throughout his letter that he believed there were two different kinds of people inhabiting the Caribbean: Cannibals and Indians. Their differentiating characteristics were that the Cannibals were fiercer and cleverer than the Indians and had "an insatiable appetite for that human flesh." The differences as he describes them were largely cultural, not biological. When describing their physical characteristics, he does not differentiate between the two groups. His physical descriptions focus much more on sexuality than do the accounts of Columbus. Cuneo carefully records his observations about the beauty of Native women, describing their breasts, stomach, and procreative practices. He gives detailed accounts of their orgiastic religious practices and their sodomitic tendencies. His account includes a level of detail about the practices of cannibals that is not present in Columbus's writings. For example, he writes that the Caribs gouged out the eyes of their victims and ate them immediately after killing them.[61]

The fate of the unfortunate young woman in the passage above was sealed by Cuneo's assumption that she was a cannibal or a member of the Carib tribe. It is not clear what led him to this conclusion, other than the fact that she and her companions put up a good fight, were traveling by canoe, and seemed to have captives with them, all of which were reported to be characteristics of the Caribs. The woman's body became one of the spoils of victory. Cuneo is careful to state that she was given to him by none other than Columbus himself. Based on this, in claiming the lands of the Caribbean for Spain, Columbus also claimed dominion over the bodies of its inhabitants. The fact that she was seen as a tradable commodity exemplifies the extension of European gender norms onto Native peoples, in which women's bodies were property to be exchanged and controlled. The justification for her rape was twofold: first, possession of the bodies of women on the losing side of a war was commonplace for victorious European men; second, her status as a cannibal effectively erased any limited agency that she might have possessed in the eyes of men like Cuneo. The fact that Columbus felt justified in giving the Carib woman as a gift to his friend indicates the extent of the power that he assumed was vested in him by the Crown.

The notion expressed by Cuneo that the young woman merely needed to be coerced into sex and then she would show her true colors is a window into the way the Spaniards viewed the possession of the Indies in general. Columbus, and others like him, argued that what they were doing was ultimately in the best interests of the Indians; they believed, in effect, that they were saving the Indians from themselves. The *requerimiento*, for example, simultaneously established Spanish power and presented Indians with a false choice: they could submit peacefully and happily to the will of Spain, which would ensure their protection and their ability to enter paradise, or face destruction for their refusal.

Several of the secondhand reports that circulated about Columbus's second voyage tell similar tales of cannibalism on the Carib islands. After speaking with Columbus and several members of his crew, Simone dal Verde composed an account of this voyage in 1494. He reiterates the good Indian versus bad Indian divide, which colored most discussions of life in the Caribbean. He states that while Indians were "meek and trusting," Caribs were "suspicious and cruel, for they eat human flesh."[62] Thus, according to Verde, the practice of cannibalism among the Caribs was the most important evidence of their cruelty. Beginning with accounts of the second voyage, the idea that the human-eating habits of the Carib defined them dominated. No other real evidence about their behavior or practices was necessary because their cannibalism said it all. This idea had profoundly disastrous effects for the island Caribs.

After assuring us that the Caribs were indeed cannibals, Verde mentions the evidence of cannibalism that was discovered. The Spaniards captured several Arawak prisoners of the Caribs who led them inland to a recently abandoned village. In this village they found two young girls and two young boys. The "genital member[s]" of the two young boys had been removed. Verde reports that this was done in order to "fatten them for eating." Importantly he wants to assure his audience of the truthfulness of his statements because "this is such a horrible thing to think about, let alone assert that it actually happens," indicating that no one would make up something so horrible. He also reports that the Caribs ate men and kept the women. His informants told him that they found many bones in their houses and that "in one house human flesh was roasting and a man's head was on the coals." Although Columbus did not accompany his men inland to this cannibal village, they brought him back evidence of the horrors they found there. Verde was doubtful about the stories that the crewmembers told because he did not deem mere sailors particularly trustworthy, but nevertheless he concludes that he believed this information "based on what everyone says." He also claims to have spoken with a Carib prisoner in Spain, who now exhibited shame and regret for his former cannibalistic ways. According to Verde, this Carib man was made to see the error of his ways through the power of contact with civilization, a sentiment that was echoed throughout the Americas. Finally, similarly to Cuneo, Verde reports that the Cannibals and the Indians were physically indistinguishable but that the Caribs were more "robust and clever" with a slightly more "scorched and rugged" complexion, revealing the complicated ways in which early modern European writers connected physical difference, savagery, and, status.[63]

Verde's account is one of the earliest secondhand reports of the voyage available to us. Many other writings of this period contain similar sentiments, reporting on the fierceness of the cannibals and presenting evidence of their acts. Interestingly several of these accounts go to great lengths to assure their audiences that they are reporting the truth and not slandering the Caribs without provocation. Nicolò Scillacio wrote in 1494 that some of his evidence about cannibalism came from "Pedro Margarit, a very reliable Spaniard who went to the east with the Admiral, drawn by the desire to see new regions" who reported that "he saw there with his own eyes several Indians skewered on spits being roasted over burning coals as a treat for the gluttonous, while many bodies lay around in piles with their hands removed and their extremities torn off. The Cannibals do not deny this, but openly admit that they eat other humans."[64] The grim scene highlights the excesses of the Carib cannibalism and describes practices not known before, such as removing the extremities prior to roasting. Authors like Verde and Scillacio present their indictments of Carib savagery carefully and cautiously, yet the detail that each provides both confirms and calls into question the veracity of their accounts, depending on one's views.

It was often repeated in the decades following Columbus's second voyage that the Caribs traveled far and wide to capture the Arawak, and when they did so, they killed and consumed the male warriors; castrated the young boys, whom they then fattened for eventual consumption; and kept the women as slaves or concubines.[65] Successive accounts of the voyage embellished one another. For instance, Angelo Trevisan tells a story very similar to Verde's about the discovery of the cannibal village in his *Libretto about All of the Spanish Sovereigns' Navigations to the Newly Discovered Islands and Lands* from 1504. He writes that the men discovered that while the Indians' houses contained stone vessels "like our own," they also found human flesh roasting alongside that of parrots, geese, and ducks. Additionally they saw "bones of human arms and thighs which they keep to make the tip of their arrows for they have no iron. They also found the head of a boy not long dead, which was attached to the beam, still dripping blood."[66] Marcantonio Coccio also describes this example in his report, which was written in 1500 and published in Venice in 1504.[67] From the initial rumors of cannibalistic activity on neighboring islands that Columbus received on his first journey to these gruesome descriptions of the horrors of life on the Cannibal islands, an important shift occurred.

The skepticism that Columbus initially displayed was replaced by certainty. These early authors displayed a desire to prove their horrific accusations, while simultaneously repeating the dubious tales of sailors as fact. It was certainly possible that one member of the crew described the charnel house still dripping with the blood of sacrificed victims and that this story was passed from person to person until it was published and distributed. If this is the case, it is likely that this eyewitness account is lost. What remains is a series of increasingly disturbing descriptions of Carib behavior that demonstrate the further conflating of Caribs and Cannibals.

In many accounts of the second voyage, Carib and cannibal are one and the same. Whatever term the individual author might use, be it Caribees, Canibales, or Caniba, the defining characteristics of these people is their human-eating. Curiously, however, Zorzi's letter describes a group of people who "live on human flesh, as do the Cannibals."[68] Thus while these early writings indicate a further linking of man-eating and Carib, there was still some ambivalence about these two terms.

Any ambivalence about the existence of New World cannibals would be erased by a series of laws passed by Spain, which have become known collectively as "the Cannibal Laws." Immediately after Columbus's return to Spain in 1493, the freedom of Indians (in the sense that they were free to choose to become subjects of Spain) was established.[69] However, in 1503 the Crown issued the first in a series of important pieces of legislation relating the practice of cannibalism in the New World. This law first asserted that the souls of all Indigenous Americans were redeemable, and therefore they were to be offered the chance to convert to Christianity.[70] The decree describes the conversion efforts made by Spanish representatives on the early voyages to the Americas, noting that on certain islands the explorers and the accompanying priests and missionaries were greeted kindly and treated with respect, yet on other islands they encountered vicious cannibals hostile to their presence. Based on these observations, the Spanish Crown gave permission for its subjects to use any means necessary to subdue the cannibals: "If the said cannibals should resist and not wish to receive and welcome in their lands the captains and peoples who by my command go and make the said voyages, and if [the cannibals] do not wish to listen to them in order to be indoctrinated in the things of our Holy Catholic Faith and enter my service and become subject to me, [then persons under my command] may and can capture [the cannibals] in order to take them to whichever lands and islands . . . in order that [the cannibals] might be sold and a profit be made."[71] This decree embraces a slippage of identity, as any who resisted colonization became cannibals in the eyes of the Spanish Crown. This and other such laws provided a shaky security to Native Americans who were eager to give up their freedom to serve the Spanish Crown and their religion for Catholicism. This was, of course, an ideal that would likely never have existed. How many peoples were eager to give up their freedom? Therefore, in practice, this law paved the way for the slave trade in the Americas that led to the near extinction of many of the peoples of the Caribbean, including the Caribs and the Arawaks. The slaves of the New World provided the resources and labor necessary for any large-scale settlement in the Americas. Right from the start, slavery was a fundamental part of the European endeavor, as Columbus brought back slaves on his first voyage. The success of European expansion in the Americas depended on the blood and labor of cannibals.

This legislation proved difficult to enforce, and by 1518, the Crown found it necessary to form a council to determine formally which regions were inhabited by Indians/Arawaks and which by Cannibals/Caribs. Additionally the discovery of certain natural resources, like gold, caused great concern over the appropriate division of labor. Rodrigo de Figueroa was given the task of classifying Native cultures; earlier classificatory determinations had already been made, but Figueroa's job was to come up with the definitive system. He collected testimony relating to the practices of cannibalism and sodomy, among others, and within two years produced a report that designated which regions were inhabited by Cannibals.[72] In this way the developing discourse on cannibalism in the Caribbean had a significant impact on the shift of Spanish interests in this region from exploration to colonization.

The evidence of cannibalism, which was often little more than hearsay, helped to determine the nature of the Natives' relationship to the Spanish and who was available for exploitation. Figueroa's classification system was not static but changed with economic and political developments in the Americas. In 1511, prior to Figueroa's classification, the island of Trinidad was said to be inhabited by Cannibals, but the priest and Indian advocate Las Casas convinced Figueroa to change the classification. Or perhaps the fact that gold was discovered on Trinidad in the intervening period was the reason for the change in status; maybe this was less about empathy for the inhabitants and more about preserving the Indigenous labor force for the *encomenderos*.[73] Lending credence to this theory is the fact that Trinidad's status was once again changed in 1530, this time from Arawak to Carib, when its natural resources proved less valuable than initially believed.[74] Since a larger labor force was no longer necessary to extract natural resources, the enslavement of the Indigenous population on other islands would prove more beneficial to the empire than maintaining their presence on Trinidad. Their recategorization as Caribs opened them up to the slave trade.

As these classifications and the resulting legislation sought to restrict the enslavement of Arawakan Indians while setting up the Caribs for exploitation and destruction, women and children, no matter their tribal affiliation, were initially excluded. It was not until much later, in 1569, that women's culpability for cannibalism was legally determined and they were allowed to be enslaved alongside their male Carib compatriots; the ban on enslavement of children under fourteen years old was maintained, however. Thus the official Crown position in the early sixteenth century insisted that women, although they might have been considered morally culpable for the cannibalistic actions of the tribe, were not considered legally responsible for these actions. Men like Cuneo used the Carib women's status as a cannibal as a justification for their rapacious actions, thus ensuring a kind of sexual enslavement to European men even if convention insisted that the women could not be physically enslaved. While Cuneo's disturbing actions took place before the first official Cannibal Law was in place, he provides a useful example for thinking about the presence and absence of Carib women from the perspective of imperial Spain. Because women were legally absent from the restrictions on slavery, in theory it did not matter if they were determined to be Carib or Arawak, they were not to be enslaved. Instead women were afforded the same "choice" offered to the friendlier Arawakan Indians: submit to Spanish authority willingly or face the consequences.

## Cannibalism According to Amerigo Vespucci

Vespucci has the honor of being both the namesake of the continents of the Western Hemisphere and one of its least trusted explorers. There is some doubt that he was present on all of the voyages he claimed to be on, and there are accusations that his accounts were mere fabrication.[75] Whether or not his writings contain "truth," they were popular and widely published by the early sixteenth century. Vespucci hailed from the Republic of Florence, but he sailed for both Spain and Portugal. He claimed that his first two voyages were undertaken for Spain and his last two for Portugal. He was not the captain of any of these voyages, which makes the credit given him for discovery all the more curious. After returning from his voyages he was awarded a prestigious position as chief navigator for Spain and was granted Spanish citizenship. At this time of exploration rather than straightforward conquest, one's place of origin was less important than claims of loyalty to a particular crown.

Vespucci's first published work, a letter to Lorenzo di Pierfrancesco de' Medici commonly called *Mundus Novus*, was first printed in Florence in late 1502 or early 1503 and had an immediate and lasting impact.[76] Another letter, written to Piero Soderini, was published in 1505, and a Latin edition was published in Martin Waldseemüller's important book on cosmography and geography, *Cosmographiae Introductio*, in which the term *America* was first applied to the western continents. In addition to these, several other personal letters to Lorenzo de Medici and one fragmentary letter called the Ridolfi Fragment remain.[77] Since Vespucci's published writings about his voyages to the Americas were written and published after he had returned from his four dubious voyages, they tend to describe the Indians in more general terms rather than describing his changing impressions on each successive voyage. The "Letter to Soderini" is broken up into descriptions of each voyage but makes general assumptions about Indian behavior and character throughout. As Vespucci's voyages took him to mainland South America and to lands that were likely occupied by Tupí peoples, some of his descriptions of cannibalism may refer to these groups rather than the Caribs. However, given the dubiousness of his travels, the vague way he describes Indian groups, and the blanket assertions that he makes, it is reasonable to combine his discussions of the cannibalistic practices of Carib and Tupí peoples. Indeed as the Tupínamba became the most infamous cannibal tribe of the Americas after the Caribs ceased to pose a major threat, Vespucci's writings mark the origin of two unique but similar trajectories of cannibal discourse, one in North America and one in South America.

Vespucci's writings, in contrast to those of Columbus, focus much more on the sexual behaviors and the gendered practices of the

Natives he encountered. For example, Vespucci reports, "They have another custom that is appalling and passes belief. Their women, being very lustful, make their husbands' members swell to such thickness that they look ugly and misshapen; this they accomplish with a certain device they have and by bites from certain poisonous animals. Because of this, many men lose their members, which rot through neglect, and they are left eunuchs." This explanation for the presence of eunuchs among Caribbean Indians is not present in earlier writings. As was discussed previously, the existence of eunuchs among the Carib was attributed to their practice of castrating young boys for eventual consumption. How Vespucci learned of this practice is not clear, nor does it seem that he fully understood how it worked. Regardless, he blamed the women of the community for the deformities and inadequacies of the men. It is unclear how and why the men lost their penises through neglect if the women were so lascivious. Vespucci assures his readers that their lustfulness was evidenced by their incestuous practices and promiscuity.[78] Furthermore, in this passage Vespucci hints at his own dueling fascination and disgust with Indians and their practices. While he appears to be astonished by these practices, he nevertheless is careful to report them. His cautious ambivalence is expressed in passages like the following: "They are not very jealous, and are inordinately lustful, the women much more than the men, though decency bids us pass over the wiles they employ to satisfy their inordinate lust."[79] He wants the reader to know about the strange habits of Indian men and women but does not want it to seem that he is presenting a sensational tale meant to titillate.

Without reading too much into his psyche, one could argue that Vespucci's writings reflect the competition between his desire for Native women and his revulsion at such a prospect. His descriptions of Native women are laden with contradictory terms of desire and loathing. For example, he writes, "Their women, as I have said, although they go naked and are exceedingly lustful, still have rather shapely and clean bodies, and are not as revolting as one might think, because being fleshy, their shameful parts are less visible, covered for the most part by the good quality of their bodily composition."[80] He is surprised that their breasts are never saggy and that one cannot tell the difference between the "virgins" and those who have borne children merely by their physical appearance. In his "Letter to Soderini" he gives a similar account, remarking on the women's beauty, fecundity, lustfulness, and cruelty.[81] Most interesting, however, he says, "When they were able to copulate with Christians, they were driven by their excessive lust to corrupt and prostitute their modesty."[82] This statement seems to describe a situation in which the European men are powerless against the sexual wiles of Indian women, who are driven only by their desires. However, as men of civilization they are able to be more temperate than Indian women.

Vespucci lacked the ability, or perhaps the willingness, to see cultures on their own terms; instead he based his assessments of the sexuality of Native women on his preconceived ideas of modesty and chastity. By asserting that Indian women were forceful in their lust, he seemed to be excusing the behavior of the European men who copulated with them.[83] He never indicates in his writings whether or not he engaged in carnal relations with Indian women, but he did not deny that some members of the crew did. Excessive lustfulness was an indication of savagery because it followed that a person who could not restrain his or her sexual desire would also be incapable of showing restraint in other areas of life. Caribs and Arawaks were both accused of eating improper foods (human flesh was but one of these), not abiding by consistent mealtimes, excessive laziness, and more. Vespucci even criticized Native peoples for being too generous because this trait caused them to give freely of their bodies as well as their possessions. He reports that it was a great honor for parents to give their virginal daughters as a token of friendship.[84] The trade in the bodies and "honor" of young women seemed to disturb Vespucci. Cuneo, on the other hand, showed little regard for the innocence of the young woman that he encountered. In fact in Cuneo's account, the fact that she was presumed to be a cannibal ensured that she was not an innocent, regardless of her sexual history.

In his discussion of the cannibalistic practices of the Indians, Vespucci veered from the descriptions in other accounts, insisting that the Caribs were indiscriminate in their man-eating. In *Mundus Novus* he says that victorious Caribs not only ate the vanquished Arawaks but that "human flesh is common fare among them." And he insists on the veracity of his observations: "This you may be sure of, because one father was known to have eaten his children and wife and I myself met and spoke with a man who was said to have eaten more than three hundred human bodies; and I also stayed twenty-seven days in a certain city in which I saw salted human flesh hanging from the house beams, much as we hang up bacon and pork."[85] Any pretense of uncertainty about the practice of cannibalism has disappeared.

Vespucci was confident in the fact that human flesh was a common element of their diet.

Unlike others observers who described cannibalism, Vespucci believed that Indians practiced exocannibalism as well as endocannibalism. Based on the writings about Columbus's first two voyages, it seemed that the Caribs only consumed outsiders (exocannibalism); however, the consumption of a wife and children described by Vespucci was an act of endocannibalism. If this were indeed the case, it changes much about what Europeans believed about Carib anthropophagy up to this point. The consumption of enemies, while abhorrent, could be understood in the context of the practices of dehumanizing and humiliating vanquished enemies, which was common throughout Europe.[86] The consumption of members of one's own family, however, was much less comprehensible as it implied a complete lack of community and disrespect for the sanctity of familial relations.

Vespucci's accounts are contradictory in a number of ways, not the least of which is his failure to distinguish between endocannibalism and exocannibalism. In the "Letter to Soderini" he describes the cannibalistic habits of the Caribs:

> They eat little meat, except for human flesh; for Your Magnificence must know that in this they are so inhuman that they surpass all bestial ways, since they eat all the enemies that they kill or capture, female as well as male, with such ferocity that merely to speak of it seems a brute thing—how much more to see it, as befell me countless times, in many places. And they marveled to hear us say that we do not eat our enemies, and this Your Magnificence should believe for certain: their other barbarous customs are so many that speech fails to describe such facts.[87]

Here Vespucci again directly contradicts descriptions from earlier writings, including Columbus himself, by insisting that they ate both male and female enemies. While most modern scholars recognize that all reports of cannibalism are somewhat dubious, Vespucci's are particularly questionable. He was adamant that the Caribs ate members of their own tribe as well as both male and female enemies, in spite of all previous assertions to the contrary. He also insisted on proving the veracity of his account by continuing to emphasize that he observed these behaviors with his own eyes on a number of occasions. It is interesting to note, however, that whenever specific details might have lent further credence to his reports, he hid behind a veil of civilized decorum. Additionally by emphasizing that the Carib propensity for man-eating existed alongside a range of other "barbarous customs," he symbolically linked cannibalism with other descriptors of savagery, making them inextricable.

While Vespucci's writings deviated from the established base of knowledge about Caribs in the late fifteenth and early sixteenth century, he also repeated a number of now-familiar tales. He reported on the practice of Carib castration of enemies prior to their consumption; in fact his story of this encounter is remarkably similar to earlier accounts. He also recorded the presence of the Amazon-like women but added that they were also giants.[88]

One of the most famous passages about cannibalism comes from Vespucci's description of a deadly encounter during his third voyage. The crew encountered a group of Indians with whom they wanted to communicate, but the Indians seemed reluctant to do so. When the crewmembers landed on the shore, all of the Indian men ran away; in an effort to reassure them, the crew returned to the boats, leaving just one young man on shore to converse with them. The young man approached the women, who gathered in a circle around him. All the while another woman was sneaking down from the mountain with a club in her hands. This woman then snuck up behind the young sailor and hit him; the rest of the women grabbed him and started to drag him away as the men emerged from their concealed positions and shot arrows at the ship. The ship's crew retaliated by firing on the people on the beach, causing them to flee toward the mountain,

> where the women were already hacking the Christian up into
> pieces and then eating them; and the men, indicating by their
> gestures that they had killed and eaten the other two Christians
> [who had been sent to them earlier]; which weighed upon us
> heavily, and we believed them, having seen with our own eyes the
> cruelties they committed upon the dead man. All of us considered
> this an intolerable wrong; and more than forty of us prepared to
> land and avenge such a beastly and cruel deed, but the captain
> general would not consent; and they remained unpunished for so
> great an offense; we departed from them most unwillingly and
> greatly ashamed because of our captain.[89]

Vespucci seems certain that it is the duty of Europe to change the behavior of Caribs and not to tolerate their man-eating. The cruelties that the Caribs reportedly performed on the European emissary serve as a perfect justification for their destruction. Yet the captain of the mission would not allow the crew to seek revenge, which filled Vespucci with shame and regret. Such a passage seems intended to inspire outrage and revenge against the Indians who were getting away with these cruelties as European men merely watched. The voyeuristic element of Vespucci's tale is evident; they were forced to watch Indian women kill, dismember, and consume a member of their community without being able to act effectively. How they could have seen such details from the safety of their ship is, of course, questionable. The European counterattack against the Indians did not deter them, and ultimately the captain forced the ship to turn away. The whole situation was emasculating for Vespucci: not only did the Europeans fail to protect their young crewmember, but they were also forced to retreat like cowards. He had to watch helplessly as Carib women consumed a European male body. The vulnerability of the young man at the hands of women, who Vespucci and the rest of the crew clearly underestimated, reflects masculine anxieties of conquest. Travel to a foreign land and interactions with strange people in this case led quite literally to the incorporation of "civilization" into "savagery" rather than the triumph of Europeans over Americans. The ferocious appetites of the Carib women not only threatened European men through sexual deviance and corruption but also posed a deeper menace to the very fabric of their civilization: their bodies.

## Visualizing Cannibals

Descriptions of the participation of women in cannibalistic rituals existed in the literature of the period but were even more prominent in visual representations. Visual renderings of man-eating add an important dimension to a discussion of the origin of the trope of the cannibal, allowing for a more sustained connection between gender, sexuality, cannibalism, and empire. Visual depictions of the cannibal were no more reliable than the writings they often accompanied. Simply interrogating the writings of early explorers cannot provide a complete picture of the cannibal; images of cannibalism help to fill in some of the gaps in knowledge. Additionally visual images would have been more comprehensible to a largely illiterate populace. Together text and images open new avenues for discursive exploration. For instance, the role of women and the feminization of the New World become clearer through this investigation. Women featured more prominently in the images produced about the New World than in the writings of early explorers. In such images women were often shown taking on an active role in the performance of cannibalism. Because descriptions of cannibal women in European writings of the encounter period were often contradictory, unclear, or left out all together, the combination of the visual and textual helps to create a more complete picture of the cannibal.

In the writings of Amerigo Vespucci, women, and Cannibal women in particular, posed the most significant impediment to European conquest. It was against their actions and even on their bodies that the conquest of the Americas needed to take place. Despite the obvious errors in Vespucci's accounts, including his navigational reports, the popularity of his writings was on par with those about the Columbian voyages. While Columbus's works may have set the stage for the development of the trope of cannibalism, it is through Vespucci that these ideas achieved their clearest, most lasting articulation. The gendered nature of savagery Vespucci established in his writings, in particular as witnessed through the act of cannibalism, moved with the Europeans across the vast continents of the Americas. In addition to the continuation and contestation of these discourses in written work, the circulation of visual images reflecting the voyages of Vespucci were quite popular and well-circulated. In these images the culmination of all of the elements of the trope of the cannibal was apparent. Particularly evident, more so visually than textually, is the connection between sex, cannibalism, and conquest.

The strategies employed by European explorers to make sense of the New World insisted that the inhabitants fit in preexisting categories. Thus the medieval association of women's bodies with food and consumption carried forward. In many ways women's bodies were bearers of both corruption and salvation, and the paradigmatic cannibal in visual images was a woman.[90] In the earliest decades of the sixteenth century, written and visual texts displayed a complex set of associations between savagery, cannibalism, gender, and sexuality. In visual representations of the conquest, most of which were produced decades after the event, the fear of corruption at the hands of Indians and incorporation into their lives was much more evident. While writers like Columbus and Vespucci were not devoid of political intentions, their writings, to one degree or another, attempted to describe events linearly and incorporated older heuristics for contact with radical alterity. Images of conquest, on the other hand, did not need to describe encounters with Indigenous Americans so much as represent them. This difference between description and representation highlights one of the important facets of the discourse of cannibalism. For Europeans venturing to the New World, the act of cannibalism symbolically represented the savagery of the inhabitants of the Americas and was also something to be witnessed and described.

Just as written accounts about early explorations of the Americas tell us much about the background, biases, and beliefs of their authors, the visual depictions similarly demonstrate how artists and publishers constructed the narrative of exploration and conquest to suit their particular concerns. For example, the De Bry family, who were among the most important publishers of material on the Americas in the late sixteenth and early seventeenth centuries, not only edited the texts they published to suit their desired audiences, but they also altered and embellished the artistic renderings of others and fictionalized some of their own. While they modified the texts to address the concerns of Spanish Inquisitors, the visual images that accompanied the texts were altered to emphasize the alterity of their subjects.[91] Thus the visual images are often more salacious and sensational than the texts. Images emphasized pagan religious practices as well as the nakedness and unbridled sexuality of Indians; as such, depictions of sexualized women were common.

The American landscape itself was feminized in the writings of encounter and discovery, beginning with Columbus. After landing in the Caribbean, Columbus wrote of the errors of earlier navigators. Instead of assuming that the Earth was flat, he described it as actually shaped like a woman's breast, with earthly paradise near the center that resembled a nipple. His words bring to mind the image of a man searching for sustenance, glory, and wealth from the earth through its nurturing nipple. It was not male virility and strength that this representation of the landscape asserts; rather the great discoverer appears infantilized.[92] The conqueror sought enlightenment, riches, and salvation from within the female body; from his conquest of women came his domination of the world.

The conflation of the breast with the New World is seen in many of the visual depictions created in the period of discovery and encounter, and such images were linked with representations of cannibalism. Images of cannibal women with a suckling baby in tow were common and created a strange visual resonance that indicated both savagery and humanity but, more important, pointed to the maternal character of the New World. The figure of a lactating woman was common in the writing and art of the Middle Ages. Symbolically and tangibly the breast-feeding mother linked the bodies of women with food and consumption. Breast milk was essential for the survival of infants and thus the continuation of humanity. The primal food of humanity issued from the bodies of women. Caroline Walker Bynum notes, "Medieval people did not simply associate body with woman. They also associated woman's body with food. Women were food because breast milk was the human being's first nourishment—the one food essential for survival."[93] Breast-feeding and the sustenance it provides featured regularly in medieval writings and images. Male writers often spoke of receiving the spirit and spiritual wisdom from the breast of Christ. The Virgin Mary was commonly shown as the bare-breasted, lactating provider of nourishment to Christ, and by extension Christianity at large. Religious cults that centered on the breast milk of the Virgin proliferated throughout Europe in the Middle Ages. Thus the images produced from travels to the Americas referenced the traditions of breast-feeding but also diverged from them in profound ways. While the bodies of the cannibal mothers were depicted as providing food, the sacred dimension was missing. In the absence of the Christ, conquering European men stood in as the intermediaries between truth/civility and barbarism. It was their civilizing power that would soon nourish the wanting, savage masses of the Americas.

These traditions are evident in one of the earliest images of the New World, a German woodcut from 1505 (Fig. 2.1). The image is not specifically labeled as representing Island Caribs, but based on the traditions of Carib representation in writing, it is clear that these were not the timid Arawaks of the Greater Antilles. Toward the center of the visual space is a woman with a suckling child at her breast and two other children who appear dependent on her. This family is calm and serene yet surrounded by a scene of cruelty where human flesh is being carved and hung from the rafters. In the background European ships approach, coming to interrupt the young mother from her nursing. The ships spell doom for the Carib way of life. The children who once sought their sustenance from their cannibal mother will soon be subjects of European civilization. Another woman appears to be cutting up the body of some unfortunate man, and yet another is even shown gnawing on the uncooked flesh of an arm. The men stand poised for battle in full regalia yet shockingly ignorant of the imposing ships on the horizon. Thus they appear emasculated and unable to

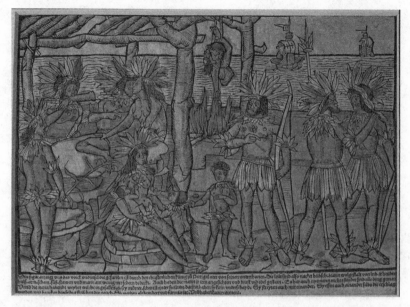

FIGURE 2.1 "Early German woodcut of a New World scene." Hand-colored woodcut, ca. 1505. (Courtesy of Spencer Collection, The New York Public Library, Astor, Lenox, and Tilden Foundations.)

protect the women and children from the advancing Europeans. This image represents the New World "savage" as feminine and maternal. The breast-feeding woman embodied the European fear of being consumed as well as the possibility of consumption. The representation of cannibal discourse in this image shifted from the ways Columbus and others depicted Caribs as masculine and Arawaks as feminine; instead it presents a more confident scene in which European civilization will be brought to bear upon the Americas and European masculinity will undoubtedly triumph.

Other images, such as a 1509 woodcut entitled "Life among the Indians" that was published with a German version of Vespucci's "Letter to Soderini," also show the maternal side of the Americas. This image depicts a village scene replete with lounging families and the preparation of a cannibal meal. The figures in the foreground are remarkably similar to one another, although one is easily distinguishable as a woman because she is breast-feeding, and another is obviously male as he is shown urinating. Toward the back of the image two individuals are engaged in the dismemberment of a body; they appear to be a woman and a man. The woman seems to be cupping her breast as the man lowers his axe toward the body splayed out before them. The image of the female breast is prominent in this image. There is a suckling infant who, once again, survives on the life-giving milk of the cannibal mother. The woman in the back of the visual space gazes at the dismembered body part and reaches toward her bosom. Her position reinforces the cyclical nature of the act of cannibalism. The sustenance provided by the human body before her will in turn be processed and redistributed to the next generation of her tribe through her breasts, thus ensuring the perpetuation of the cannibal tradition. What differentiates this image from the earlier 1505 woodcut (Fig. 2.1) is that this represents an uninterrupted cannibal scene. There were no European ships lurking on the horizon. The cannibal mothers continue to nurse their children from the blood of humans.

Images played a critical role in the "construction and maintenance of relationships of colonial power and subordination in the early modern Atlantic world."[94] The success and popularity of Vespucci's writings can be attributed not only to his literary skill but also to the illustrations printed in his published works. Columbus's works were sometimes illustrated with simple practical engravings, but despite their spotty publication record and difficult provenance, Vespucci's works were more fancifully illustrated.[95] Vespucci's penchant for exaggeration and hyperbole was quite evident in his accompanying images, which included numerous depictions of the "savages" of the New World.

By the late sixteenth century representations of the New World as a nude female had become prevalent. One famous image is an engraving by the Flemish artist Jan van der Straet, which was later reproduced by Theodore Galle and used to illustrate the influential book *Nova Reperta* (*New Discoveries*), which was first published around 1600. The images that accompanied this text documented the invention of gunpowder, the printing press, olive oil, eyeglasses, and more, in addition to the discovery of the New World. The caption added to the image in the print edition is "Americen Americus retexit— Semel vocauit inde semper excitam" (Amerigo rediscovers America—He called her once and henceforth she was always awake [my translation]). The waking figure is positioned next to a sloth, whose very name represented inactivity. On the other side of "America" is Vespucci himself. He carries the symbols of Western technological

FIGURE 2.2 "America." Theodor Galle after Jan van der Straet. Engraving, ca. 1580. (Courtesy of Print Collection, Miriam and Ira D. Wallach Division of Art, Prints, and Photographs, The New York Public Library, Astor, Lenox, and Tilden Foundations.)

innovation, progress, civilization, and conquest: "a cruciform staff with a banner bearing the Southern Cross, a navigational astrolabe, and a sword—the mutually reinforcing emblems of belief, empirical knowledge, and violence."[96] The landscape, in contrast, appears much more primitive and lacking in technology. Thus the image presents a land that, though peopled, is a blank slate on which European civilization can be placed.

Van der Straet depicts the moment of encounter in symbolic form. The image shows the meeting between a man, Vespucci, who represents Europe, and a woman, representing America. The sexual overtones in their meeting are undeniable. The depiction of a cultural encounter represented as a sexual encounter was a common trope in early modern texts. This image did more than follow in the footsteps of its predecessors; it also paved the way for depictions of America for generations to come. The art historian Michael J. Schreffler offers an insightful interpretation of the role of cannibalism in Van der Straet's images. He asserts that unlike many contemporary and subsequent images, the association of cannibalism with the allegorical figure of America occurs quite subtly in this image. The cannibal scene is relegated to the background yet remains centered and visually enthralling. Schreffler notes the juxtaposition of cannibalism with the figure of America's outstretched hand and asserts that this reveals the nature of depictions of colonial power in early modern images. He argues that the placement of the cannibal scene near the center of the composition, just outside of the grasp of the waking figure of America, establishes the preeminence of the relationship between America and Vespucci rather than America and the cannibals.[97] The image therefore foreshadows the future of American anthropophagy. It shows that the benefits of contact with the Native peoples of the Americas far outweighed the dangers imposed by their cannibalistic nature, for cannibalism was but a secondary feature of their societies. However, even though the cannibal scene is relegated to the background, it is still ever present in this rendering. Vespucci's arrival awakened the formerly sleeping figure of America, but the cannibals were already preparing their feast. They lurk in the background, present but not active in the scene.

The presence of the cannibals in this image seems to offer no danger to Vespucci, yet there is a sinister nature to their persistence in the scene. The image also represents the passing of time, with events occurring closest to the horizon representing the perceived past. The meeting between Vespucci and the figure of America, on the other hand, occurs in the present, indicating the potential of the New World.[98] Thus the cannibal scene would soon be relegated to the past. The allegorical figure of America represents the civilized version of the continent. She is what the inhabitants of the Americas are moving toward, what contact with the European explorers will bring to them. Although she appears mostly naked, with bare breasts, her modesty is still somewhat protected. She is seated on a hammock, not on the bare ground like the cannibals in the distance.

The placement of the cannibal scene in a space distinct and separate from the two central figures also indicates, according to Schreffler, the "anxiety about the practice of cannibalism as well as the ambivalence and instability of early modern discourses of colonial power." The image represents Europeans' confidence in the existence of cannibalism in the New World but also demonstrates their inability to adequately witness and document it. This pattern would continue through the centuries. The image forces the viewer to acknowledge the existence of cannibalism but allows for an understanding of its elusive nature.[99]

The image is also a compartmentalized vision of the Americas. The depiction of Europe is more cohesive and is embodied by Vespucci and his invading ships. America is represented by its flora and fauna, the sexualized reclining allegorical woman, as well as the cannibal scene. European colonial power rested on the ability to perceive the inhabitants of the Americas, and indeed the land itself, as consumable. Therefore the scene of physical consumption is pushed into the background.[100] Native peoples were primarily consumable objects and only secondarily consumers. This recasting of Native peoples was evident throughout the era of European colonization. The settlers in North America felt that it was their right, their duty in fact to consume the lands the Native peoples were letting go to waste. Europeans saw the New World as the ultimate vessel for their consumption.

The early modern literary historian Louis Montrose asserts that the image created by Van der Straet depicts the event discussed earlier, in which a young man from Vespucci's mission was killed and cannibalized on the beach as the rest of the crew looked on helplessly. Montrose offers little evidence as to why this incident may have inspired the Van der Straet image. He argues that the story is an early example of cannibal discourse that reinforced the emergent themes of cannibalism, savagery, and deceit: "Of particular significance here is the blending of these basic ingredients of protocolonialist ideology with crude and anxious misogynistic fantasy, a powerful conjunction of the savage and the feminine."[101] Thinking of the Van der Straet image as an allegorical re-creation of a real occurrence limits the power it possesses. It forces the event to remain constrained within the imagery and the implications of its real-world counterpart. The worldview of the European conquerors of the Americas must then be drawn out from the image, extrapolated, expanded, and then applied to their understandings. However, if the image is treated as an allegory for the European conception of the New World, the discourse is contained within the image itself. This is not to discount context; rather such allegorical depictions need not point to a real incident to have discursive meaning. Their meaning is created in their visual resonance. Read this way, the image indicates more than the actual fear of being cannibalized that Vespucci and his men may have experienced, but it also references anxieties about the role of women and, most important, women's bodies.

The Galle/Van der Straet image (Fig. 2.2) foreshadows the role that gender played and continues to play in the colonial project. Anne McClintock discusses this image in *Imperial Leather*. Referring to the central figure of America, she writes, "Her nakedness and her gesture suggest a visual echo of Michelangelo's 'Creation.' Vespucci, the godlike arrival, is destined to inseminate her with the male seeds of civilization, fructify the wilderness and quell the riotous scenes of cannibalism in the background." Thus the encounter itself was an act of penetration. As Vespucci penetrated the lands of the Americas, he also positioned himself as the purveyor of civilization, which he provided through his masculine dominance over the feminized figure of America. He awakened the sleeping continent and called her by name. Thus "invested with the male prerogative of naming, Vespucci renders America's identity a dependent extension of his and stakes male Europe's territorial rights on her body and, by extension, the fruits of her land."[102] It is through Vespucci's utterance of the name America that the continent woke up. Without the masculine force provided by the European conquerors, the Americas would never have awakened to realize their true potential and would have remained forever primitive and cannibalistic (and feminine).

The work of gender is evident in this image beyond the central awakening figure as at least two of the figures in the background appear to be women, although this is difficult to see without access to the original or a high-resolution version. One is clearly a male as he has a beard, and the sex of the other is impossible to determine. The most active participant in the scene, the person turning the spit containing the roasting leg, is a woman. The other woman observes from a little distance while holding a small child in her lap, possibly nursing it. McClintock presumes that the body roasting in the background is male, likely following the assumption that the neutral body was always gendered male.[103] While it cannot be proved that the figure is in fact male, assuming it is further illustrates the ambivalence of conquest and the desire of European men to be both the consumer and the consumed. Furthermore the neutral/male body in the scene demonstrates what many Europeans perceived to be the unnaturalness of gender roles in savage societies, for if the women are preparing to consume the body of a man, this places them in a position of power and dominance and simultaneously weakens their male counterparts. In this period the dangerous bodies were often those of women; thus the "savage" was not predetermined to be virile and masculine and the existence of societies in which women held varying degrees of power threatened to expose the fragility of male dominance in Europe.

Transgressing the boundaries of European gender norms caused Indians to be perceived as savages, and this savagery was in turn read as emasculating. Indian men, in this view, failed to achieve any recognizable standard of European masculinity, just as women failed to fit into existing standards of femininity. Thus Indians were perceived as less masculine and therefore less powerful than their European conquerors. The conquest of the Americas can then be read as a contestation between competing understandings of gendered norms, which, for Europeans, was expressed as a fight between their masculine selves and the emasculated people of the Americas. In this way the contact between Europeans, Caribs, and Arawaks was as an elaborate contestation for male dominance. The Arawaks were commonly represented as fearful, timid, and overly kind, all feminine traits, whereas the Caribs were depicted as fearsome, irrational, and driven only by desire, which were all masculine traits but taken beyond the limits of acceptability.

By presuming that the corpse being roasted is male, McClintock reads the image as "less about the soon-to-be-colonized 'Other,' than it is about a crisis in male imperial identity." The image portrays an idealized encounter as well as depicting what McClintock calls "a dread of engulfment." The figure of the cannibal most easily represents this fear and serves as a projection of European desires for consumption.[104] The projection of the cannibal trope onto the unfamiliar inhabitants of the Americas allowed Europeans to name their fear. By calling them cannibals, the Natives were no longer fundamentally unknown but could be categorized and dealt with accordingly. This allowed the Spanish, French, and English empires to justify their actions and establish imperial power in the New World.

# 3 / Conquering Cannibals: Spaniards, Mayas, and Aztecs in Mexico

In 1552 Juan Ginés de Sepúlveda and Friar Bartolomé de las Casas famously debated the rationality of Indians and the justification of conquest in the Spanish city of Valladolid. Las Casas, as the Protector of the Indians, argued that the Spanish conquest of the Americas was unjustifiable because it caused unnecessary suffering to innocent people and because it was not effective in bringing Indians to Christ since the brutality of the Spanish would likely cause Indians to resist spiritual and political conquest more vociferously. The Spanish humanist and philosopher Sepúlveda believed that the balance of cruelty rested firmly on the side of the Natives. He argued that the sheer scale of Indian sins and their shocking cruelty made Spanish conquest more than justifiable. In his eleventh objection to Las Casas's points, Sepulveda stated:

> Regarding his [Las Casas's] claim that by saving the lives of the innocent people who were being sacrificed, the war was just, but that it should not be done since one must choose the lesser evil, and that the evil in this war is greater than the deaths of so many innocent, his lordship calculated wrongly, because in New Spain, according to those who have returned from there and know of this, each year more than twenty thousand persons were sacrificed; this figure, multiplied by the thirty years since this sacrifice was ended would be six hundred thousand, and in the entire conquest, I do not believe that more have died than were sacrificed in one year.[1]

There are obviously a number of questions to be asked about the assertions Sepúlveda makes. First, he fails to differentiate among Indian groups and does not specify precisely who was committing these atrocities. Who was sacrificing twenty thousand people a year? Who was being sacrificed? In what part of the Americas were these sacrifices occurring? Furthermore, as he indicates, Sepúlveda himself never traveled to the New World and thus all of his estimates come from others. How could anyone, even an eyewitness, really determine how many people were sacrificed in a given year, even if one were to limit the count to one place, Tenochtitlan for example? Presumably Sepúlveda's informants got their reports from other Indians with whom they spoke. Were these informants enemies of the group they claimed sacrificed thousands upon thousands of people? Were they members of the group doing the sacrificing or being sacrificed? Either way, how would someone be able to effectively calculate the number of victims? In Sepúlveda's account we see a common sleight of hand that occurs in many conquest texts. He presents information as fact and assures us of its veracity because he learned it from those who were there, but he provides no proof that the original information is correct or trustworthy. If it were indeed true that twenty thousand people were sacrificed every year, then the population would have had to be astronomical to sustain the levels necessary for that many deaths.

Las Casas is famous, at least in part, for his creation of the "black legend" of Spanish cruelty. He is responsible for some of our most enduring images of Spanish cruelty and for advocating a more sympathetic picture of Indian life. Conversely Sepúlveda props up a narrative that rests completely on the notion of Indian cruelty. For both men, however, the implication seems to be that unnecessary cruelty is illogical, sinful, and unacceptable. While they might disagree about which party is crueler, they agree on the fact that unfettered cruelty cannot be allowed to persist. Much of the discourse of the conquest of Mexico revolves around competing narratives of cruelty and suffering. The Spanish conquistadors attempted to present themselves as men doing God's work by ridding the world of a terrible scourge bent on cruelty and destruction. The picture they painted of the conquest was one in which their actions were justified based on the activities of the peoples they encountered.

In chapter 2 I explored cannibalism as a formative trope of early imperial expansion in the New World and investigated the gendered genesis of European expansion in the Americas.[2] Drawing from these insights, in this chapter I primarily focus on the conquest of the Aztec Empire by Spain under the leadership of Hernán Cortés and the place of cannibalism in the discourse on the conquest of Mexico. Through this interrogation how the discourse of cannibalism changed in the context of conquest and shaped the nature of imperial power in Mexico will become clear. I will begin with a discussion of cannibalism in conquest and an overview of gender and sexuality in the Spanish Empire. Then I will investigate the firsthand evidence of the conquest, arguing that the discourse of cannibalism in this context drew from the precedents established in the Caribbean but also changed in order to adapt to the shifting conditions of Mexico. Finally, I will conclude with a discussion of the legacy of the discourse of cannibalism in New Spain.

The fact that the Spanish used cannibalism and sodomy, among other sins, as justification not only for their initial conquest but also for centuries of exploitation and slavery is well documented. The Spanish and Portuguese empires practiced widespread slavery and exploited Native labor to a degree not present in any other American imperial context. They supported this behavior, at least in part, by arguing that slavery was permissible and preferable for those Natives who resisted their imperial efforts and those who practiced cannibalism. The fact that those who resisted the Spanish (and the Portuguese) most vehemently were often those who were most vociferously accused of being cannibals should come as no surprise.[3] The "sins" of Natives were used as validation for their subjugation and the (attempted) erasure of Indigenous cultural practices. While a great number of scholars have investigated this very fact, few have acknowledged the important link between the practices used as justification and the differing understandings of sexuality and gender between the Europeans and the Indians. It was these differences that helped to shape the Spanish approach to the conquest of Mexico.

There are many sources available to the modern reader about the conquest of Mexico; however, most of these are secondhand accounts that drew from the writings of eyewitnesses. With the exception of the codices that detailed the conquest from the Aztec perspective and the writings of a few Spanish friars about preconquest Mexico, there is limited textual evidence from the Indians themselves.[4] In fact only sixteen pre-Columbian codices remain.[5] The early Catholic Church in Mexico systematically destroyed many of the extant Aztec and Maya texts, and few escaped the fire. Thus my focus remains primarily on European discourse and representation rather than actual Indigenous practices. Cannibalism played an important role in the gendering of conquest as well as in the ways Spanish conquistadors constructed their ideas about masculinity.

Just as Columbus and Vespucci brought earlier understandings of difference and cannibalism with them to the Caribbean, Hernán Cortés and his contemporaries inherited an intellectual legacy shaped by their predecessors. By the time Cortés and his men began traveling inland across the Yucatán, the presumptive existence of cannibals in the New World was well established. There was little debate about whether or not the Caribs were cannibals, even if there were extensive arguments about how the practice of cannibalism related to their potential enslavement. Based on this established discourse and its underlying assumptions about the existence of savagery in the Americas, it would have seemed logical to readers back in Spain that the practice of cannibalism extended inland. What did pose a challenge to the ideas about cannibalism that had been established in the previous decades was the sophistication of Aztec and Maya societies. The Caribs were believed to be uncivilized in part because of their practice of man-eating but also because of other practices such as nakedness, promiscuity, lack of a recognizable religion, and lack of centralized governmental power. The peoples of Mexico, however, did not meet many of the characteristics of savagery. The specific cultural context that the Spaniards encountered in Mexico forced them to reevaluate and rearticulate their understandings of cannibalism. Because they met more "civilized" cultures in Mexico and because they were interested in exploiting the natural resources and labor in the regions they conquered, they necessarily understood the presence of cannibalism and other aberrant cultural practices as impediments to their efforts, but not as impasses.[6]

In discussing the differences in approach to conquest and the ways power functioned in the various empires of the Americas, the historian Patricia Seed argues that control of mineral resources was of the utmost importance for the Spanish Crown. Based on this priority, Spaniards tended to be more interested in the exploitation of Native labor than their English counterparts would be nearly a century later in Virginia and New England. Spanish conquistadors needed Indian labor in order to obtain the vast riches they believed that God had placed beneath the earth for the faithful to uncover and from which they should profit. They developed a method for the division of Indian labor known as the *encomienda* system, in which Spaniards (and sometimes Indians) were entrusted with a specific number of Natives whose resources and labor were given in exchange for their protection. While this system was not explicitly slavery, it often functioned as such and will be referred to in those terms.[7]

Cannibalism and slavery had an important relationship in Spanish legal history, and man-eating was commonly referenced as one of the sins for which Indians could be enslaved without provocation. Slavery was an essential part of the Spanish imperial machine, for Native labor was necessary to obtain the riches awaiting them beneath the surface. Expansion into new territories, like Mexico, enabled the Spanish to increase their supplies of labor, resources, and converts. The *enco-mienda* system also had important consequences for the discourse of cannibalism, as men writing about the conquest years later felt the need to defend their actions in Mexico with descriptions of the atrocities that Indians committed in order to preserve their economic rewards.[8]

The Spanish hoped to bring religion and civilization to the peoples of the Americas, but they also hoped to bring back wealth to support the growing mercantilist economy of Castile. The islands of the Caribbean proved useful in enriching Spanish coffers through the exploitation of Indigenous labor and the extraction of natural resources. However, the Native peoples of the Caribbean did not possess great wealth, and their numbers were rapidly declining from disease and overwork. The discovery of the Yucatán peninsula by Francisco Hernández de Córdoba in 1517 spurred interest in the lands to the west and encouraged the voyages of Juan de Grijalva in 1518 and Hernán Cortés in 1519. Córdoba's expedition was filled with violence and tragedy, but witnesses brought back tales of cities of stone and large populations. For enterprising men like Cortés, who were stifled by the existing power structures and eager to make a name for themselves, the allure of great wealth to the west was irresistible.

On February 18, 1519, Cortés set sail from Cuba with ten ships and 530 men. His mission defied protocol and was a direct affront to the governor of Cuba, Diego Velázquez de Cuéllar, who had explicitly ordered Cortés to conduct a mission of trade and diplomacy, not conquest. His mission was, in one way, a test of the extension of imperial power and the ability of an individual to justify his possession and conquest of a sovereign people. But Cortés's plan was both conquest and settlement, as he believed that without both the Spanish could not succeed and prosper. He also recognized the importance of converting the Native populations in order for Spain and Spanish civilization to triumph in Mexico.[9]

## Spanish Precedents and Traditions

Cortés embodied all of the characteristics of a masculine hero, expanding the empire and exploiting the bodies and labor of the Native women he encountered. His successes portended not only the erasure of the customs of cannibalism and sacrifice among the Aztecs but the establishment of a stratified society in which power was constructed as masculine and women's participation in political, social, and religious matters was eliminated. Conquistadors like Cortés employed the trope of cannibalism in order to make sense of and demean Indigenous bodies and cultures. This does not mean that Natives did not in fact practice ritualized cannibalism, but rather that Europeans specifically interpreted Native culture in order to support their imperialist desires. Beyond the fact that accusations of cannibalism helped to justify acts of conquest for men like Cortés and Bernal Díaz del Castillo, cannibalism also epitomized the anxieties of imperial masculinity and served as a representative trope through which they understood Native lives and bodies.

Unlike the people the Spaniards came upon in the Caribbean, the Mayas and Nahuas of Mexico appeared to be more civilized by European standards. They possessed empires and cities that were organized in ways that, though decidedly foreign, were nonetheless legible as civilizations. Unlike the Arawaks and Caribs of the Leeward and Windward Islands, the Chontal Maya and Nahuas lived in permanent houses and practiced a recognizable religion.[10] They possessed great caches of gold, engaged in the exchange of material goods, and had a hierarchical political and social order.[11] In other words, they did not appear to be living in a state of nature; they were not the atavistic savages that Europeans imagined in the Caribbean. Therefore the encounters between Europeans and Indians took on a decidedly different character on the mainland.[12] Rather than being able to construct these interactions in terms of masculine civilization and feminine savagery, the Spaniards faced circumstances on the mainland that forced them to rearticulate how power would function in their interactions with Native peoples. The encounters between Europeans and Natives in the Caribbean did not take place in the context of a full-scale invasion. European intervention in the Caribbean began not as an invading force but rather as an exploitative, sporadic economic system. Although colonies in the Caribbean developed quickly, Columbus did not arrive as a conqueror or a colonist.

FIGURE 3.1 "Brazilian cannibals dressed in Moorish fashion."
Woodcut. Title page of Hans Staden, *Warhafftig Historia
vuud Beschreibung einer Landtschafft der Wilden, Nacketen,
Grimmigen Menschfresser Leuthen, in der Newen Welt America
gelegen . . .* (Frankfurt, 1557[?]). While it depicts a group of
cannibals in Brazil, this fanciful representation of Staden's
captivity among the Tupínamba demonstrates the continued
association of Native Americans with Moors. (Courtesy of the
John Carter Brown Library at Brown University.)

Spanish expansion into the New World came on the heels of the successful elimination of Moorish power from Spain in 1492, when the country became united under the banner of the kingdom of Castile. In many ways the Spanish expansion into the Americas was an extension of the Reconquista. From the conquest of Al-Andalus the Spaniards learned valuable lessons about conquest and colonization, which they brought with them to the Americas. In fact they often referred to Indians and Moors in similar ways, and their descriptions of Indian culture and objects were based on Moorish traditions.[13]

D. W. Meinig characterizes the Spanish model of imperialism as an incorporative system, in which Spaniards inserted themselves into preexisting hierarchies. There was a place for Indians, albeit a subordinate one, in this system. Despite the inequalities that existed between the Spanish and their Indian subjects, there was still a great degree of dependency. The Spanish conquest of Mexico would not have succeeded without the help of a large number of Indian allies. In simple terms, groups who were disaffected with Aztec control were willing to cast their lot with the Spanish in order to rid themselves of their oppressors. For this reason, and later because of their dependence on Indigenous labor, the Spanish needed the Indians; the Spanish presence in Mexico was not sustainable without them. In the early years of conquest and settlement, Spanish men relied on Indian women as cultural intermediaries and for sexual gratification, marriage, and procreation. From these unions came a large population of *mestizos* who would greatly influence early imperial policies in Mexico. The relatively small population of Spaniards in Mexico in the first half of the sixteenth century forced them to rely on Indian resources and to associate more directly with their Mexican subjects and allies than would occur in the English colonies in North America. This level of intimacy between the Spanish population and the Indians made the elimination of the practice of cannibalism that much more important to the conquerors.

Meinig also argues that while the Spaniards brought with them from Europe the idea that humanity was innately hierarchical, they were not inflexible. Rather "it would appear that different local circumstances, and especially basic differences in imperial objectives, were critical."[14] In other words, it is important to take into account the circumstances that Spaniards encountered in the Americas in order to understand fully how the discourse of cannibalism took shape. Meinig indicates that based on what they encountered in

Mexico, Spaniards developed a stratified society that included racial and cultural hybridity to varying degrees. Therefore it is only logical to assume that the way Spaniards thought about cannibalism was, at least in part, influenced by the local circumstances they encountered.

The idea of the cannibal hinged on negotiations between differing notions of masculinity and femininity and stressed that travel to new lands and contact with strange people posed a threat to masculine order. Thus European representations of cannibalism among the Caribs often emphasized the participation of women and the threat to the European male body. Cortés and his men were greatly influenced by these precedents. However, the Mexican mainland posed its own unique challenges and forced them to understand cannibalism in different terms. The belief that the Aztecs and Mayas practiced cannibalism forced the conquistadors to develop new strategies for eliminating their anthropophagic appetites while still incorporating them into the empire as allies and subjects. Furthermore, in the accounts of conquest women were far less likely than men to be accused of participating in acts of cannibalism. Spaniards wrote about cannibalism among the Aztecs and Mayas as a predominantly masculine ritual that took place on the battlefield and in temples, traditionally male spaces.

The Spanish also brought ideas about the gendered nature of power to the Americas. Sexuality and gender were inextricably intertwined in sixteenth-century Spain as they were everywhere. Power was expressed through sexuality, which was manifested in the assertion of masculine dominance and feminine submission. In the context of warfare, Spaniards viewed their defeated enemies as effeminate and weak. However, in order for their victory to be meaningful, they had to rearticulate the feminized losers as masculine, for victory over women was no real victory at all. Spaniards believed that deviant sexual practices were more common in certain geographic regions, and because of this they expected to encounter homosexuality, polygamy, and cross-dressing in the Americas.[15] They also believed that what they perceived as deviant sexual practices indicated savagery. Thus the success of Cortés's conquest of Tenochtitlan hinged not only on military victories but also on the remaking of Native worlds and the imposition of Spanish ideas about gender and sexuality. In fact "the Iberian discourse on the character of conquest was itself unmistakably gendered, indeed phallic in character."[16] The gendered contestations of power in Mexico took place both on and off the battlefield; the battles pitted differing masculinities against one another, while the civilizing mission of Cortés challenged Aztec and Maya gendered and sexual norms. Aztec and Yucatecan Maya societies were structured around gender complementarity and gender parallelism, as opposed to the male-dominated arrangement of European society.[17] However, in the gendered configurations of both Spaniards and Mexica, the separateness of male and female spaces was paramount; to turn one into the other was a breach of norms and a humiliation.

It is difficult to encapsulate the norms of gender and sexuality in early modern Spain, especially given that the dominant discourses of gender and sexuality espoused in the legal discourse, both royal and ecclesial, and public discourse cannot be said to represent accurately the practices of everyday Spaniards. Rather these general norms represented ideal Spanish gendered and sexual practices. Thus it is important to be mindful of the disparities that existed between discourse and practice when making general statements about the gendered and sexual practices of early modern Spain, just as we must keep in mind that not all Spaniards thought or felt the same way.[18] According to Catholic doctrine and royal law, women's virtue and honor depended on their virginity and purity. However, in practice, women's lives and their positions in Spanish society were far more complicated. By the time Cortés was heading toward Tenochtitlan, the social status of women in Spain had begun to decline because of increasing social emphasis on religious and ethnic purity. These concerns about Spanish identity and national culture led to an increased policing of women's sexuality in order to ensure the homogeneity of the Spanish population. The more rigid definitions of appropriate behavior for women, which emerged in the wake of the Reconquista, insisted upon domesticity, obedience, and silence.[19]

At the same time that the bodies of women and female sexuality were being increasingly regulated in Iberia, understandings of masculinity were also changing. Spanish literature of this period was intensely concerned with defining masculinity. The historian Edward Behrend-Martínez argues that being a man in early modern Spain generally meant "keeping one's word, supporting one's family, heading a patriarchal household, demonstrating sexual prowess, sobriety, maintaining one's independence of thought and action, and defending family and personal honor." Thus in 1519 being a man was predominantly defined by a set of behaviors, not strictly by biology.[20] Based on this understanding, conquistadors judged the masculinity of Indian men by how they performed their gender according to

Spanish standards, and the same was true for Indian women and their femininity. Differing understandings of gender and sexuality shaped the interactions between Europeans and Americans and affected the discourse of cannibalism.

Discussions of Native American gender roles, sexual practices, and cannibalism featured prominently in early Spanish imperial writings. The body of the Other was an important site for the assertion of imperial dominance and the enactment of imperial fantasies. The medievalist Merrall Llewelyn Price notes that the cannibal as Other "paradoxically depend[ed] on both a hyperdelineation and a blurring of categories of gender, under which the indigenous women were represented as voracious and sadistic sexual aggressors and the men as sexually perverse and malformed monsters, each of whom practices a bestial and bloodthirsty cannibalism deserving only of enslavement and extinction." Thus the conquest of Mexico depended on the idea that Native bodies and their practices were somehow out of order with the natural ways of the world. While this was established to some degree in the Caribbean, it was not until the conquest of Mexico that the link between cannibalism, sex, and conquest was fully articulated. Price argues that Cortés established the connection between cannibalism and sexual practices in his first letter from Vera Cruz: "From this point on, cannibalism and various acts interpreted as sodomy travel hand in hand in New World narratives."[21]

Through the bodies of women the conquistadors negotiated their understanding of both sexuality and cannibalism. Their accounts reinforced that even though neither Native nor European women typically participated in the military actions of conquest, their bodies played a fundamental role in it. They served as translators, wives, mistresses, servants, and property to be exchanged. Women were often given as gifts to Cortés and his men by local caciques as they traveled across Mexico, and while these women may not have fought and died on the battlefield, conquest was negotiated through their bodies, quite literally in the case of Malintzin.[22] Spanish textual sources indicate that conquistadors defined themselves against Native men and women, emphasizing difference over similarity in order to reinforce their perception of European superiority. Spaniards believed that men who fought and lost on the battlefield were symbolically emasculated and were able to be incorporated into the winning society in a subordinate position; on the other hand, Spanish men sought to incorporate Indigenous women through sex and servitude.

The bodies of Indigenous women were one of the many stages on which the conquest was enacted. The interactions, both on and off the battlefield, between Spanish conquistadors and Native peoples were gendered in nature. As the historian Karen Vieira Powers argues, "Considering that human sexuality is, universally, the most powerful instinctual behavior, it is probably in this arena that gender collisions of the Indian-Spanish encounter took its most drastic form."[23] Gender and sexuality were not only the most pervasive metaphors through which both Europeans and Indians understood warfare, but sexual acts, as both punishment and a negotiation of power, were integral to the success of a given military endeavor for both. The historian Peter Sigal notes that "the Maya viewed the winning group as masculine and as penetrators in sexual acts. The losers were viewed as feminine and as those who were penetrated by the penises of the opposing warriors. This distinction formed one core of the cultural matrix around which the Maya organized their perceptions of sexual desire."[24] Conquest and domination were gendered affairs for Mayas, Aztecs, and Spaniards.

Iberians understood politics, religion, and war in gendered terms as well. The monarch (whether male or female) was like a father who headed a masculine social structure that gendered dependency as female. Warfare for the Iberians was a masculine space; even on the battlefield it was important for masculinity to be defined against femininity, and these ideas extended to the conquered Aztecs and Mayas. From the thirteenth century on, Spaniards began persecuting acts of sodomy and foreigners were most commonly accused of this crime.[25] In previous centuries Spanish wartime practices may have involved sodomy and male rape, but as the Crown and Church began to police masculinity more strongly, they discouraged soldiers from engaging in penetrative punishment and erotic relationships with one another. To compensate for the restrictions on male wartime sexuality, Spanish military commanders often brought prostitutes with them to serve as a more acceptable outlet for sexual urges. These women, along with family members of soldiers, accompanied the group and performed an array of nonsexual and sexual tasks. Thus upon arrival in Mexico, the conquistadors fully expected to include women in their camps. Because of this tradition, the women who were given to them as diplomatic gifts by the Indians they encountered on their journey were easily incorporated into their procession. For Cortés and his compatriots the presence of cannibalism and sodomy among an enemy group not only justified conquest; it also granted them access to the bodies of Native women. Indian men were castigated for their "sins" on the battlefield, whereas Indigenous women's bodies were threatened with rape, coercive sex, and enslavement. Thus the cultural "crimes" committed by the Aztecs and Mayas were corporally punished. Spaniards took it upon themselves to "correct" the wrongful practices of Indians, and the body was the locus of their imperial discipline. However, the extent to which sins like cannibalism and sodomy actually justified the conquest varied across the records. For Bernal Díaz del Castillo, Hernán Cortés, Juan Ginés de Sepúlveda, and Alonso de Zuazo, the fact that the Native peoples of Mexico were believed to be heathens, cannibals, and sodomites easily justified the Spaniards' actions. Zuazo asserted, "These people follow the 'trifecta of sin' as the Italians say: they do not believe in god, they are almost all sodomites, [and] they eat human flesh."[26] However, Las Casas and other writers more sympathetic to the Indians tended to downplay both the practice and the importance of cannibalism and sodomy.[27]

## Narratives of Conquest

In the conquest narratives of Cortés, Díaz, and others, many of the earlier Caribbean patterns continued. For example, the assumption that Indians practiced cannibalism and other "inappropriate" cultural practices that were believed to accompany it, such as promiscuity, polygamy, and effeminacy, persisted often in the absence of evidentiary support. These writings did not support the notion that being a cannibal made one irredeemable, even if they argued that the practice of cannibalism made one ripe for conquest.[28] In other contexts, such as in Iroquoia, human-eating was believed to transform the practitioner physically and psychologically into an insatiable monster.[29] Copulating with a cannibal monster would certainly have been unacceptable to Cortés and his men; therefore they represented the Indians they encountered as humans who practiced cannibalism, not as inhuman monsters.

Cortés's version of his adventures was recorded in a series of letters written while he was in Mexico. There were originally five, but one has been lost. These letters served the dual purpose of narrating events and justifying the conquest. Cortés devoted a great deal of space to convincing Holy Roman Emperor Charles V of the necessity of his actions. He went against the direct orders of his nemesis and superior,

Diego Velázquez de Cuéllar, the governor of Cuba, whose fears that Cortés was overly driven by ambition proved correct. Velázquez was more interested in establishing trade with the Natives in order to enrich his own coffers than in funding permanent settlements on the mainland. The rivalry between these two men would eventually have disastrous consequences, resulting in Cortés's abandonment of Tenochtitlan to fight Velázquez's forces, led by Pánfilo de Narváez.

In his letters Cortés is driven to justify his brash actions. He often does this by recording the atrocities committed by the peoples he encountered. Indeed he repeatedly writes of the horrific sacrifices and idolatry practiced by the Aztecs and Mayas, whose aggression provides evidence of the necessity of using force to conquer and convert. He understood the people of Mexico as already subject to the Crown of Castile through God's divine providence, and the reading of the *requerimiento* cemented this authority.[30]

Díaz, who was a soldier in Cortés's force, wrote his version of events many years later, and his motives, while quite different from those of Cortés, were nonetheless just as political. Díaz began writing his account in 1551 and continued to work on it for almost two decades. He had accompanied Córdoba and Grijalva on their respective voyages before joining Cortés. His account is widely reputed to be the most definitive and trustworthy version of the conquest. Throughout his narrative Díaz humbly admits his own weaknesses in style and acknowledges his inability to remember certain events. However, he also had very clear motives for writing his account of the conquest. He directly confronts the writings of other more educated and respectable men, like Francisco López de Gómara and Las Casas. Díaz was offended that Gómara's writings had received such recognition and praise, which he attributed solely to Gómara's higher social status. Thus Díaz wrote his narrative of the common soldier in order to correct more sophisticated writings. But even more than his anxieties about class and status, Díaz was very concerned with the legacy of the conquest. He was disturbed by Las Casas's indictment of the actions of the conquistadors, particularly about the massacres at Cholula and at the Templo Mayor in Tenochtitlan. He wanted to defend the actions of the soldiers and justify the conquest in order to preserve the economic privileges that the conquest had afforded them as well as their newfound reputation and status. Because of this, Díaz actively insisted that the actions of Cortés and his men were acceptable based on the horrific practices of the Indians.[31] He supported the arguments of Sepúlveda, who used natural law to rationalize the conquest of Mexico. Thus while Díaz's account is perhaps the most extensive and trustworthy primary record of the conquest, it was not without political purpose. Perhaps because of his motivations, it contains more frequent references to cannibalism among the Indians than the works of either Las Casas or Gómara.

An individual known only as the Anonymous Conqueror penned another eyewitness narrative. Scholars question whether he was an actual eyewitness or if he merely based his accounts on the writings of others, like Zuazo.[32] Overall his account is far less detailed than Díaz's, although it does contain an important discussion linking the practices of sodomy and cannibalism. The Anonymous Conqueror's account does not survive in its original Spanish, only an early Italian translation, and later Spanish versions exist. The Italian version was first published in the third volume of Ramusio's *Navigationi et Viaggi* in 1556.

There are several other, less well-known accounts of the conquest. The brief account of the officer Andrés de Tapia focuses on military exploits and provides less insight into Indigenous culture.[33] His account covers only the first stage of the conquest and ends with the arrival of Narváez's troops. Tapia had great respect for Cortés and held his actions in high regard. In fact his account "Relation of some things that happened to the Very Illustrious Don Hernando Cortés, Marqués de Valle . . . " is based on a deposition he was asked to give in the 1540s during an investigation of Cortés's actions in Mexico. It was not published until the nineteenth century.[34] The writings of Francisco de Aguilar (also known as Alonso Aguilar), which remained unpublished until 1900, contain a very clear and concise version of the events, making only minimal reference to cannibalism.[35] Aguilar, a soldier like Díaz, also wrote his narrative in 1560, many years after the conquest. Finally there is the brief account of Ruy González, who recalled his version of the events of the conquest in a letter to Emperor Charles V in 1553.[36] González feared the growing ill will toward the conquistadors and was concerned about their legacy in a fashion similar to Díaz, who wrote his account several years later. Tapia, Aguilar, González, Díaz, and the Anonymous Conqueror recorded accusations of cannibalism and used its presence, along with other sins, to justify what they had done in Mexico. For the most part, none of these accounts contains substantive criticism of the conquest itself or of Cortés.

There were also a number of important writings by men who were not directly involved in the conquest. The most important of these for our purposes is the work of Gómara and Las Casas. Gómara served as Cortés's chaplain and secretary in Spain but never traveled to the Americas himself. He began writing his account in 1552, more than thirty years after Cortés landed on the Yucatán peninsula.[37] Although his writings never directly challenged the morality of the conquest, they nonetheless greatly offended Díaz, who lampooned the inaccuracies in Gómara's account. Despite Gómara's errors, the writings of Las Casas were far more controversial. Las Casas was not interested in glorifying the events of conquest in order to preserve the legacy of the conquistadors, nor did he have to justify his actions, as Cortés did. Rather Las Casas questioned the very foundations on which other accounts rested: the assumption that the conquest was morally justified because of the atrocities that the Indians committed. Therefore, while Las Casas did not ignore the existence of acts such as cannibalism and sodomy, he minimized them and referenced them only as occasional aberrations, not as indicators of a cultural pattern of barbarity. In addition to Las Casas and Gómara, the chronicles of Gonzalo Fernández de Oviedo y Valdés and Peter Martyr D'Anghiera also feature important discussions of cannibalism in the conquest of Mexico.

The legacies of the discourse of Carib cannibalism are evident in all of these accounts. The reputation of the Caribs was already well established, and their perceived practices were often extended to other inhabitants of the Americas.[38] Cortés remarked that in one province of the Yucatán, the Natives killed a handful of Spaniards because they had "always been very warlike and rebellious." "They are all cannibals," he writes, "of which I send Your Majesty no evidence because it is so infamous."[39] Because of their actions he enslaved them, setting aside the royal fifth: the 20 percent of all proceeds of conquest that had to be paid to the Crown. Cortés assumed that the rebelliousness of the Indians and their cannibalism justified their conquest and subsequent enslavement and that their cannibalism was so well-established that he need not provide any further proof. How their actions could have been understood so thoroughly when their previous contact with Europeans was so limited is obviously questionable. It seems that many Spanish visitors to the Americas made few distinctions among groups of Indians and that the habits of one were extended to all. Thus the anthropophagic habits of the Island Caribs and their cousins in modern-day Venezuela were used to support the existence of cannibalism throughout the Americas.

Cortés felt that he needed no evidence to back up his claims of cannibalism among the Mayas; in fact he seemed to imply that their rebelliousness was an indication of their cannibalistic ways, which is supported by imperial legislation that linked rebelliousness with cannibalism. In his writings he does not display a great degree of sensitivity to cultural differences. These discussions are limited to the writings of chroniclers like Oviedo and Martyr, who were not present during the actual conquest and had the benefit of distance and hindsight.[40]

According to Gómara, Cortés was quite explicit that eliminating cannibalism was one of his primary goals in Mexico; in fact he referred to it as an obligation.[41] Interestingly, in a *cédula* (royal decree) from 1523, the Spanish Crown charges Cortés with the elimination of cannibalism.[42] In this instance the discourse of cannibalism had a direct impact on imperial policy. Cortés convinced the monarchs of the necessity of his actions, and most important, he employed the trope of cannibalism in order to sway imperial power in his favor. It appears that Cortés echoed Columbus's belief that the existence of cannibalism would provide justification for conquest and control. Whenever Cortés encountered a new group of people, he reportedly told them that the Spaniards had come to save them from idolatry and the sins of sacrifice and cannibalism.[43] Díaz repeatedly states that the primary goal of their mission was to stop "abominable practices" like cannibalism, sacrifice, and polygamy.

While all of the firsthand accounts make it clear that Spaniards believed that human sacrifice and cannibalism were widespread and prevalent, they also accuse the Indians of breaking other taboos of Western Christendom. Again following the example set in the Caribbean, charges of sodomy, bigamy, lasciviousness, and other acts that challenged the established gender norms of Europe are common in Spanish accounts. The Anonymous Conqueror accused Indians of treating their women inappropriately and having little regard for their purity, arguing that "there are no people in the world who hold women in less esteem, for they never tell them what to do, even though they should know that by doing so they would be benefited."[44] This quote reveals much more about gender roles in Spain than practices in Mexico. The Anonymous Conqueror makes it clear that he believes that because of the nature of women they must be told what to do in order to maintain order and civilization. In this twisted logic, allowing women more freedom and self-determination is damaging not only to women themselves but to society as a whole. This of course only makes sense if one presumes that society and civilization should exist for the benefit and comfort of men or that true happiness and freedom can be found in submission and constraint. It is also clear from the Anonymous Conqueror's comments that Indian women were considered more equal to men than they would have been in Spain. This equality was perceived as a weakness that the Spaniards could exploit in their conquest as well as a catalyst for conquest. The Anonymous Conqueror also indicates that Indian men possessed many wives, "like the Moors," but only the sons of the principal wife inherited the father's property. By asserting that Indian men were not capable of controlling their women, the Anonymous Conqueror questioned Indian masculinity and virtue. Spanish imperial discourse insisted that women needed to be controlled because of their "proclivity to disobedience."[45]

The Anonymous Conqueror ends his account with a description of the vices of the people of Mexico: "All of this province of New Spain and of those other provinces eat human flesh, which they have in greater esteem than any other food, so much so that many times they go to war and place themselves in peril only to kill someone to eat. They are commonly sodomites as I have said and drink without moderation."[46] He does not distinguish among the different Indian groups that inhabited Mexico. One might suspect, given the patterns established in the Caribbean, that the Spanish would discuss the cruelty and cannibalism only of their enemies, the Mexica, and would glorify the innocence of their various Native allies. However, this is not the case. While there are many more references to cannibalism and sacrifice among the Aztecs, such references are certainly not absent among descriptions of other groups. This highlights one of the key differences in the discourse of cannibalism in the context of the conquest of Mexico. Rather than making clear distinctions between good/noncannibalistic and bad/cannibalistic Indians, the sources reveal the presence of the vice of cannibalism among a wide variety of groups; because of this, the accusation of cannibalism could not be used to divide Indians into clear-cut categories. Group distinctions were often erased in descriptions of cannibalism and sacrifice in Mexico, and the practice was assumed to be prevalent throughout the region. Thus Spaniards shifted their perceptions from cannibalism as a polarizing characteristic among Indian groups to a strategy that emphasized the differences between Europeans and Indians but nonetheless made space for the possibility of Indian acculturation into a more European way of life.

The Anonymous Conqueror closely linked cannibalism, sexual practices, and gender roles. According to Spanish sources, another key indicator that a group's gendered practices were out of order was the presence of the practice of sodomy. As mentioned previously, Zuazo believes that Indians engaged in the *tria peccatela*: atheism, sodomy, and anthropophagy.[47] These three sins made the Indians targets for conquest on religious grounds. In order to protect Nahuas and Mayas from themselves and their vices, Spaniards insisted that they had to bring Catholicism to them, by force if necessary. Sodomitic Indian men had failed to live up to their responsibilities as *men*; if they were engaging in sex with other men, especially as the passive recipient, they were making themselves like women, an unforgivable offense according to religious and legal standards. The practice of sodomy indicated not only failed masculinity but failed femininity as well, for women must not have been properly performing their duties as the presumed passive sex for men to be driven to one another. Indian woman were sometimes accused of being too masculine by performing men's work, highlighting that Indian gendered practices were perceived as out of synch with European expectations in a number of realms.

Scholarly debates continue about the actual practices of homosexuality and sodomy among preconquest Mexicans; however, Spanish sources consistently mention its presence. Much like cannibalism, it matters less for my purposes whether or not Indians actually engaged in sodomy; my concern is what accusations of such practices meant to Spanish writers. Sodomy captured the imagination of Spanish observers and chroniclers in the initial years of conquest, but after a time it was rarely mentioned.[48] The same was true of cannibalism; accusations of cannibalism played an important role in the justification of conquest, but once domination had been achieved, it was not a common subject for writers.

Indian men were guilty of abusing their women by either not telling them what to do, as the Anonymous Conqueror said, or forcing them to work like slaves. Many Europeans saw the grinding of corn, an important female duty in both the Aztec and Maya traditions, as a metonym for their oppression under Mexica rule. Despite protests that Indian women were veritable slaves to Indian men or too free for their own good, Spanish writers described feminization as a process achieved through coercion and force. In other words, women needed to be put in their proper place within civilized society through force if necessary, while Indian men needed to be emasculated and forced to recognize their own failed masculinity. Rape and coercive sex in war "were designed to denigrate and feminize the enemy, declaring that enemy to be unable to protect the women and even the men of that society."[49] The battlefield thus extended to the body, and Spanish warfare insisted upon the superiority of European cultural norms. The literature of justification relied on the trope of bodily disorder; it was assumed that the role of the European man was to correct the bodies of Indians. These accounts reflected differing notions of sacrifice and incorporation for Europeans and Indians. Each demanded the sacrifice of bodies, whether through ritual or on the battlefield. Spaniards incorporated Indian bodies through sexual congress, just as they appropriated and incorporated land and treasure.

Throughout the Spanish narratives of the conquest, Indian women were traded as commodities. The Aztec system of government was based on the payment of tribute, which included both goods and labor.[50] The status of the women exchanged by the Nahua varied according to the context; for example, slave women were typically gifted as a gesture of submission after losing a battle or to fulfill tribute obligations. The daughters of caciques and other important women were given as potential marriage partners in the hopes of establishing an alliance.[51] Thus local caciques followed protocol and provided Cortés and his men with goods, including women, whose bodies provided a physical and political link between the two groups of people. For example, Gómara remarked, "They [the Tlaxcalans] provided them [the Spanish] with everything for their means, and many offered their daughters as a token of true friendship, so they might bear children by such valorous men and bring into the world a new warrior caste."[52] Diplomacy in the accounts of conquest rarely took place without the exchange of goods, and women were almost always among the commodities presented. This was not a two-way trade, however; Native women were given to the Spaniards as gifts, but Spanish women were not offered in return, nor would they have been even if they were present in the Americas. The Spaniards did sometimes offer goods in return; however, by Spanish reckoning their worth was always significantly less than what they had been given. According to Spanish understandings of relative value, Indian groups held women in low regard as commodities or they would have demanded a greater exchange rate. This understanding misses the fact that by local tradition, the women offered in these diplomatic exchanges were often held in high regard as cultural ambassadors. For both groups, these women were an integral part of what I am calling "sexual diplomacy." They were not traditional diplomatic envoys, but through their interactions with the Spanish, both sexual and nonsexual, they enhanced cultural understanding. But most important, through their intimacy with Spanish men and the progeny produced from these unions, they produced long-lasting kinship ties and obligations.

After receiving women through gift-giving diplomacy, Cortés inconsistently applied the rule that these women had to be converted to Christianity before being taken as mistresses or wives. Indeed the very thing that caused these women to be perceived as sexually available commodities was threatened by their conversion to Christianity. In order for them to become respectable women, Cortés contended that they must be converted to Christianity. And in order for this conversion to be achieved, they first had to give up the practices of sacrifice and cannibalism. The control of bodies became a fundamental aspect of the conquest as Cortés moved toward Tenochtitlan. The bodies of women served as mediators between two groups of people, and through them were forged sexual, kinship, and political ties. Through their children these women fostered bonds that would forever tie the peoples of Mexico to those of Spain and reshape traditional hierarchies and lines of descent.[53]

Nearly twenty-five years earlier, in the Caribbean, when Michele da Cuneo used a young women's perceived status as a cannibal as justification for her rape, enslavement, and torture, he asserted a right to sovereignty over her body. On the other hand, Cortés declared that unless the women he had been given ceased to be cannibals, sexual diplomacy was unavailable, though sexual relations were not necessarily out of the question. Díaz recalled a moment when they were given a series of gifts, including women. After receiving them kindly, Cortés told the caciques that he could not accept the gifts unless they agreed to put an end to their idolatry and sacrifice. "He added that these damsels must become Christians before we could receive them. Every day we saw sacrificed before us three, four, or five Indians whose hearts were offered to the idols and their blood plastered on the walls, and the feet, arms, and legs of the victims were cut off and eaten, just as in our country we eat beef bought from the butchers. I even believe that they sell it by retail in the *tianguez* as they call their markets." Again the commodification of women's bodies and the link between sexual congress and cannibalism was explicit, and both sexual diplomacy and cannibalism were depicted as ubiquitous. This exact same exchange of bodies, goods, and words occurred repeatedly on the march to Tenochtitlan, linking the sexual availability of Native women with the practices of sacrifice and cannibalism as part of a larger imperial fascination with controlling Indigenous practices and bodies and reshaping Native hierarchies and gender and sexual norms.[54] Thus the subjugation of women's bodies served as an implicit goal of the conquest and sexual coercion was an important tactic of conquest. The historian Susan Kellogg writes, "The frequency of sexual violence and the willingness of military leaders such as Cortés and Pizzaro to distribute indigenous women among their close lieutenants suggests that conquerors indeed used 'the phallus as an extension of the sword.'"[55]

The women given to the Spaniards in the earlier example were quickly baptized and distributed by Cortés. Their acceptance as part of the Spanish entourage cemented the filial bonds between the Indians and the Spaniards. Obviously the speed of baptism brings to mind the question of the sincerity of conversion. It is unlikely that these women had any real idea of the meaning of baptism or the restrictions that conversion would place on their lives. Accepting these shallow conversions to Christianity as evidence that these women had given up their "savage cannibalistic" ways reinforces the superficiality of the cultural transformation that was expected of Indians in general. During times of conquest the mere pretense of abiding by the rules of Spanish civilization was enough for Indians to fight alongside Spaniards or to become their sexual partners. The role that these women played in the invading force is difficult to determine. Some, like Malintzin, were important cultural mediators. Based on Iberian precedent, it was likely that many of the women Cortés was given functioned as prostitutes like those who accompanied the soldiers back in Europe. There were also instances in which the Indians gave Cortés women not for the purpose of sexual diplomacy but in order to sacrifice their bodies and consume them, their bodies literally objects for European consumption.[56] We can reasonably assume that Cortés and his men did not eat the corpses of these women, but their bodies were consumed through forcible sex, servitude or slavery, and the erasure of their former identities.

From a European perspective, the practice of cannibalism was fundamentally threatening to a corporeal order that insisted on wholeness, purity, and the sanctity of the body. Sexual relationships with

Indians were an undeniably attractive possibility for the conquerors according to their own writings. Díaz openly discussed his desire to obtain a Native mistress. He asked a Spanish page working for Motecuhzoma to request "a very pretty Indian woman" for him. To which Motecuhzoma replied, "Bernal Díaz del Castillo, they tell me that you have quantities of cloth and gold, and I will order them to give you to-day a pretty maid. Treat her very well for she is the daughter of a chieftain, and they will also give you gold mantles."[57] This unfortunate woman was a commodity to be traded along with other goods to the highest bidder. Díaz never mentioned her again.

On another occasion Cortés consulted a friar before deciding what to do with the gift of women he had been offered. He believed that by accepting the gift, he might be able to convince the women to become Christians and reject their heathen ways. The friar told him, "Sir, that is true, but let us leave the matter until they bring their daughters and then there will be material to work upon, and your honour can say that you do not wish to accept them until they give up sacrifices—if that succeeds, good, if not we shall do our duty."[58] What he meant by "do our duty" is unclear. Perhaps their duty was to punish these women for the sins of their people, or perhaps they were to be killed. Based on the available evidence, it was likely that this punishment would have involved forcible sex and/or slavery. Thus the bodies of these women became the site of moral persuasion, material to mold into a fantasy of imperial womanhood for which the admonition of sacrifice and cannibalism was a prerequisite. Since the thirteenth century the Spaniards had been moving away from punishing men on and off the battlefield with rape and had begun instead to extend the battlefield to women's bodies. While the conquerors did not acknowledge that theirs was also a conquest of women's bodies, they demonstrated implicitly through their actions that a successful conquest must control the bodies of its subjects.

Indigenous women played an important role as cultural representatives, as was most famously recorded in the case of Doña Marina, more commonly known as Malinche and perhaps more correctly known as Malintzin.[59] At times both Cortés and Doña Marina were referred to as Malintze, a title that belonged to her, but since she was the mouthpiece for the Spanish, her title extended to him.[60] In this way she symbolically and literally represented the Spanish and became one of them, blurring the line between conqueror and conquered. She was an enormously valuable and valued resource for Cortés and his men. Malintzin's value, according to Díaz, rested with her masculine virtue: "Let us leave this and say how Doña Marina who, although a native woman, possessed such manly valor that, although she had heard every day how the Indians were going to kill us and eat our flesh with chili, and had seen us surrounded in the late battles, and knew that all of us were wounded and sick, yet never allowed us to see any sign of fear in her, only a courage passing that of a woman."[61] For Díaz, Malintzin's worth went beyond her role as a sexual object, although she was married to a captain and became a lover of Cortés, because she disavowed and confronted the "abominable customs" of her people. As the practice of anthropophagy represented a threat to Spanish civilization, the Spaniards countered with overt assertions of the supremacy of Spanish masculinity and masculine virtues. Natives were able to ape European masculinity but never truly achieve it, and attributing manly valor to a woman like Malintzin points to the absurd. In her role as lover and spokesperson of the conquest, she embodied European virtues but was nevertheless denied access to the respectability afforded to the women who fulfilled the hegemonic definition of Spanish womanhood, which stressed piety, submissiveness, and *limpieza de sangre* (cleanliness of blood). She is most remembered as a conduit for exchange.

For Cortés and his men it was easy to perceive the exchange of women as reinforcing the ill treatment assumed by the Anonymous Conqueror. Indigenous conceptions about gender and sexuality cannot be understood adequately by simply reading about them from a European perspective, and we should not deny that Native women may have had agency in these exchanges simply because European authors erased it. The constructions of gender complementarity and parallelism that existed in preconquest Aztec society were not the same as gender equality. Women in Aztec society were powerful within their own spheres, but the pinnacle of the parallel system was always a man. However, kinship and succession were determined by both parents, and oftentimes an individual would claim status from whichever side of the family held more prestige. Kellogg argues that, prior to the Spanish conquest, there is evidence of the increasing use of images of female subordination to bolster Aztec imperial power. Furthermore it is important to recognize the diversity of cultures and experiences in Mexico. In certain regions women's work was valued more highly and governing structures were more equitable.[62] Thus it is extraordinarily difficult to determine how much power these women had over their own destinies. In the case of Malintzin, throughout much of her life she was traded as a commodity outside of her control; she was reportedly sold into slavery to the Mayas by her Nahua mother and later was given to Cortés and his men by the Chontal Maya. She was passed around among the Spanish men as well: first she was given to the aristocrat Alonzo Hernándo Puertocarrero; she then became Cortés's most trusted translator and bore him a son, Martín; finally she married Juan Jaramillo, a union that some considered a farce, as the groom was drunk throughout the ceremony. Despite all of this, however, Malintzin was able to accrue a fair amount of power and influence, which exemplifies the complexities of Native diplomacy and women's agency.[63]

Accounts of the conquest describe it as a constant struggle of desires: for power, souls, sex, gold. Spaniards accused the Indians of sins like polygamy, but Díaz writes admiringly of the great majesty of Motecuhzoma and the number of his wives. Díaz was thus torn between revulsion and the fantasy of sexual freedom. In the same description he accuses Motecuhzoma of desiring to eat the bodies of young boys for dinner.[64] Here an inconsistency emerges, for Díaz had earlier asked a Spanish page given to Motecuhzoma to help him obtain an Indian mistress. Díaz accuses Motecuhzoma of performing lewd acts with young boys and also of eating them, yet Cortés was willing to place one of his Spanish men in Motecuhzoma's service. Either the Aztec ruler did not truly pose a threat to young men, or Cortés put a young Spaniard in great danger and supported Motecuhzoma's supposedly savage appetites. Obviously we cannot take Díaz completely at his word; instead these anecdotes reveal that the male body was considered far more valuable and desirable than the female, making the threat of cannibalism a threat to men's bodies. Women do not seem to have commonly been the victim of cannibalism, and thus it appears that the flesh of men was far more desirable.[65] European accounts often indicate that the male body was the object of cannibalistic lust, while the female body was reserved for sexual desire.

While Cortés and his men might have desired to exterminate the Native practices of sacrifice and cannibalism, their conquest itself depended on the sacrifice of Indian bodies: the men who died on the battlefield, the women who became their lovers, slaves, and mistresses, and the countless thousands who died from their unseen army of germs. In the Caribbean the prevailing pattern insisted that all cannibals were Caribs and all Caribs were cannibals, thus erasing tribal differences and disregarding the burden of truth, but in Mexico accusations of cannibalism fell in line with those whose conceptions of gender and sex failed to match Spanish norms. In other words, the conquered body had to be remade according to Spanish customs in order to become a civilized member of New Spain. The desired body was one that accommodated Spanish wants. The value of the women that Cortés was given linked directly to their relationships to sacrifice and cannibalism. The anxieties embedded in acts of cannibalism, what Ann McClintock refers to as a "dread of engulfment," shaped the events of conquest and demanded the sacrifice and incorporation of the bodies of Indian women, not as a part of a religious ritual but in order to assert power through sexual diplomacy, violence, and warfare.

The act of cannibalism represented a fear of infection and corruption through contact with Others in a fashion similar to the perception of homosexual or sodomitic infection.[66] Cuneo believed that the Arawaks had "caught" man-eating from the invading Caribs. In Spanish discourse the presence of sodomy among a particular group of people was seen as a dangerous and contagious practice, for "once indulged in, it will prove too pleasurable to ever be resisted again, resulting in permanent and polluted emasculation."[67] These same fears were expressed about cannibalism. Any indulgence in cannibalism or sodomy opened the doors to depravity, savagery, and damnation.[68]

The Spanish believed they faced a multitude of terrifying and infectious challenges to their civilization in the Americas. In order to ensure what they were certain was the inevitable victory of civilization, they presumed that it was necessary to fight the Indians on the battlefield and in their homes. It was their duty to help Indians along a path toward civilization and away from the disease of barbarism. In order to properly civilize Indians, it was necessary to eliminate taboo sexual practices and cannibalism. Sacrifice, though certainly not accepted by the Spanish conquistadors, did not evoke the same fears of infection and subsequent descent into barbarism.

The path from barbarism to civilization was a difficult one, and writers disagree about the best way to go about it. The sixteenth-century Jesuit missionary and writer José de Acosta, for example, argued that the shift from savagery to civilization was a tiered process, in which a group first abandoned cannibalism and sacrifice and then practices like sodomy would follow.[69] According to Acosta, there thus existed a linear path from barbarism to civilization. Along this path were certain practices that had to be abandoned or overcome in order to achieve the ultimate goal of emulating the Catholic cultures of western Europe. Cannibalism and human sacrifice were among the first practices that needed to be abandoned, followed by inappropriate sexual behaviors. While Acosta may have believed cannibalism, sacrifice, and sexuality to be mutually exclusive cultural practices that could be abandoned piecemeal in a process of gradual cultural reformation, those directly involved in the conquest, like Cortés and Díaz, emphasized their interconnectedness and the importance of ridding Native societies of all of these barbarous vices in one fell swoop.

Spaniards denigrated the Other through accusations of cannibalism, for such accusations called the humanity of the Other into question.[70] Interestingly, however, none of the eyewitness accounts of the conquest of Mexico strongly indicates any doubt as to whether or not the people they encountered were indeed human.[71] For example, the eyewitness accounts of Cortés, Díaz, Tapia, and the Anonymous Conqueror accept that the inhabitants of Mexico are human. They may be a lesser kind of human, a natural slave or a barbarian, but they are human nonetheless. Just as in the Caribbean accounts, however, these writings are full of assumptions about cannibalism and sexual indecencies. The historian Anthony Pagden points out that in many of the accounts of cannibalism from throughout the New World, sexual rites are a part of the cannibal ritual. Acts of cannibalism dissolved borders and boundaries, created instability in social categories such as "male/female, young/old, kin/non-kin."[72] Thus cannibalism threatened the masculine order of Spanish imperialism and Spaniards' ability to incorporate Indigenous bodies into the empire.

## Legacies of Conquest

The Iberians who wrote about the New World held often contradictory, unclear, and ignorant views about Indigenous practices, in particular about sex, sacrifice, and cannibalism. By the mid-sixteenth century men like Las Casas were arguing that sacrifice and cannibalism did not serve as a justification for conquest; however, this view was most certainly held by a minority. For many sixteenth-century Spaniards it was clear that cannibalism did provide justification.[73] Las Casas, Martyr, and Oviedo each argued (to varying degrees) that cultural practices were not static, nor were they representative of an innate nature. None of these men was present during the conquest of

Mexico, and Martyr never even traveled to the Americas. Las Casas's writings were not widely circulated during his lifetime even if his ideas were well known; in fact Juan de Ovando, head of the Council of the Indies, ordered his writings to be stored by the Council and all access restricted.[74] Well-known sixteenth-century scholars of the Salamanca school such as Francisco de Vitoria supported Las Casas's positions. For these men the cultural practice of cannibalism among the civilizations of Mexico was not enough for them to be seen as inhuman, but it did represent a fundamental violation of natural law. Vitoria argued that by consuming other humans, Indians not only violated the sixth commandment, but they also denied the body a proper burial and thus jeopardized its eventual resurrection. Cannibals cut a body into pieces and distributed it, thereby denying it the wholeness so important for resurrection. Yet although cannibals most certainly violated natural law, according to Vitoria, this did not make them inhuman or without natural rights.[75] Rather the cultural practices of Indians had blinded them to rationality and thus natural law.

Although by the time of Cortés's march across the Yucatán in 1519 there was little doubt about the humanity of American Indians, there was still much debate then and in the centuries to come about the rights of non-Christian populations. As mentioned, Las Casas and Sepúlveda engaged in a heated and long-winded debate about the rights of Indians and the justification for conquest.[76] Participants in the conquest like Díaz and Ruy González sided with Sepúlveda in their writings and railed against the apologetics of his nemesis. In his refutation of Sepúlveda's claims, Las Casas described four types of barbarians. The first was a "cruel, inhuman, wild, and merciless man acting against human reason." These tended to be people driven by anger and lack of reason, existing primarily as isolated individuals and not part of a cultural system of barbarity. The second type did not have a written language and, according to the reasoning of the time, was uncultured and unlearned. Barbarians of this second type were not "natural," but victims of circumstance. True barbarians, the third kind, were those who,

> either because of their evil and wicked character or the barrenness
> of the region in which they live, are cruel, savage, sottish, stupid,
> and strangers to reason. They are not governed by law or right,
> do not cultivate friendships, and have no state or politically
> organized community. Rather, they are without rules, laws,

and institutions. They do not contract marriage according
to any set forms and, finally, they do not engage in civilized
commerce. . . . Indeed, they live spread out and scattered, dwelling
in the forests and in the mountains, being content with their
mates only, just as do animals, both domestic and wild.[77]

Sociality was an important aspect of civilization. The polis was the
center of learning and culture, and rural life was less civilized. Thus it
was easier for Europeans to see the city-dwelling Mexicas and Mayas
as semicivilized and denigrate the Arawaks and Caribs as mostly barbarous. The fourth and final type of barbarian was ignorant of Christ.

Las Casas refuted the argument that Indians of the New World, and
in particular those of Mexico, met the standard for any kind of barbarism. He argued that although they might have been bestial, they were
nonetheless subject to law and order and with proper training and
education could come to accept God and escape such ignorance. He
further stated that it was impossible for the omnipotent God to have
erred and filled the world with true barbarians. Las Casas acknowledged that there were plenty among them in the "old world" who by
some definition qualified as barbarians, including the so-called wild
men of the forest but also heathens and foreigners. He referred to
both the Turks and the Moors in this context. He argued that while
everyone understood that the Turks, for example, had a well-orga-
nized political system and a philosophical nature, they were not to be
lauded for their civilization because "they are an effeminate and lux-
ury-loving people, given to every sort of sexual immorality." For the
friar even if the Turks met all of the other qualifications to be labeled
civilized, they could not be afforded moral equality with the societies
of western European Christendom because their sexual practices pre-
cluded it. He argued that even if Indians practiced human sacrifice or
even cannibalism, this did not justify the conquest, indicating that he
considered sexual deviance comparatively worse. The death of many
in the process of saving a few from sacrifice and consumption was a
prohibitive cost for Las Casas.[78]

Las Casas hinted at the way discourses of sexuality, barbarism,
cannibalism, and sacrifice intersected.[79] He understood that interactions between disparate cultures had to include some kind of recognition and respect for difference, even if the ultimate goal was to
create conformity through adherence to Christianity. He called the
Turks "scum" because of their refusal to accept Christianity, but even

more important than their paganism were their sexual proclivities. Las Casas was willing to see that the infidels of the Americas were redeemable because they could be converted. However, their conversion necessitated pulling them out of a state of near barbarity (as he argued that Indians were not actually true barbarians) and the denial or erasure of seemingly aberrant sexual practices. Las Casas almost (but not quite explicitly) seems to argue that the sexual vices of Turks were relatively "worse" than the widespread practices of cannibalism and sacrifice among the Mexicas and Mayas. When compared to other chroniclers and eyewitnesses, Las Casas tended to downplay and overlook Indigenous homosexual and sodomitic practices.[80]

Writing in the early seventeenth century, Bernardo de Vargas Machuca, a veteran of Spanish conquest in the Americas, took up Sepúlveda's mantle and confronted the decades-dead Las Casas in his *Defense and Discourse of the Western Conquests*. He drew from classical knowledge, citing Pliny, Cicero, and Democritus, for example. He first tells the reader that the lands of the Americas are not nearly as populous as people have been led to believe, which calls into question Sepúlveda's assertion of twenty thousand sacrifices a year. For Vargas Machuca the lack of people gave credence to Spanish claims that the land was unused and deserved to be improved. He describes an event in a Venezuelan colony in 1519–20 where Spanish soldiers were accused of cruelty toward the Natives. Las Casas was so incensed by the behavior of the Spaniards under Gonzalo de Ocampo that he asked for leave to remove Ocampo and settle peaceful colonists among the Indians. As soon as Las Casas left to go to Santo Domingo to round up more settlers, Vargas Machuca reports,

> the Indians gathered and cruelly attacked them [the Spanish soldiers and settlers], killing them and eating most of them. . . . But at this time there was no lack of people to imitate the religious ceremonies, bringing the breviary by hand, for all [the Indians] wore the clothes and dresses of the villagers, taking the place of their owners; they made a thousand martyrs of them and their wives, so grave that when [the soldiers] went to punish them, they found the villagers rotting on the beaches with horns stuck in their lower parts, and this would have been after making [sexual] use of them. All of these people died, and not a creature escaped.[81]

Vargas Machuca drives home what he believed to be Las Casas's profound naïveté. As soon as the "sincere Bishop" left, the Indians returned to their true state. They cannibalized and raped the colonists, seemingly without reason or rationale.

After this evocative introduction, Vargas Machuca proceeds to counter the conventional narrative of the Spanish conquests espoused by Las Casas, beginning with Hispaniola. On this island, he argues, the initial view that Indians were a peaceful, tractable people was shattered almost immediately as the Indians got over their confusion about exactly who or what the Spanish were and revealed their true "evil intentions." The Indians who were not made to submit by the Spanish on Hispaniola

> caused inhumane cruelties, setting Spanish towns afire, first burning the churches and the Holy Sacrament within, making martyrs of the religious with many and varied torments and deaths, eating them cooked and boiled, taking many men and women whose eyes were torn out to dance in their drunken revelries and gatherings on leashes they attached through a hole pierced under the lower jaw. Some of these they fattened up in order to be eaten . . . others are burned and made into ash in order to drink in *chica*. . . . They make war flutes of the bones, and eat on plates made of the crowns of the skulls, triumphant. In effect, at every turn they are the most cruel people in the world, as brutish as they are cruel, and it is my opinion (and that of many who have dealt with them) that in order to paint a perfect picture of cruelty one must paint a portrait of an Indian.

Just a few sentences later he says that he does not know why he bothers to tire himself relating such tales of cruelty since "as we know that those who eat human flesh eat their own children and vassals; and so their barbarity may be seen, I can say that they disobey and break the laws of nature itself."[82] Thus, more than a century after the first Europeans landed in the Caribbean, the ubiquity of cannibalism in the Americas remained a powerful assumption.

In spite of his suggestion that it is a waste of time to describe the cruelties of Indians as they are so obvious, he spends the next few thousand words doing just that. He describes their laziness, their stupidity, and their sexual improprieties. It is obvious to him why Indian women are so eager to have sex with Spanish men as they are treated with such cruelty and disdain by their own men. He also justifies removing Indian women from their Indian husbands (unless they were properly wed in Christian matrimony), for if a cacique has more than one wife or commits incest then "it would be meritorious to take her and separate her from him."[83]

For Spaniards cannibalism was more than simply a sign of savagery; it was a fundamental violation of the natural order, and wars of conquest made the elimination of cannibalism extremely important. Sodomy, incest, promiscuity, and cross-dressing were among the other sins that rounded out this category of barbarous practices. Spaniards often framed their conquests, of both Americans and Muslims, as a contest over morals. They believed in their own religious and therefore moral superiority, and this superiority afforded them the right to conquer and humiliate their enemies. This belief enabled them to project their own fears of inadequacy and effeminacy onto their enemies. The conquest of Mexico was fundamentally a clash of cultures, neither of which had a thorough understanding of the other. The Spaniards observed and interpreted Indian behavior based on preexisting cultural understandings of barbarism and difference. The cannibalism and sacrifice that they saw reinforced the necessity of conquest and shored up their sense of their own masculine heroism. Just as Indians were perplexed by horses and speculated that they might be large deer, Cortés was not privy to Aztec cosmology and thus understood Indigenous rites within a framework developed from Christian ideology and Muslim influences. These cultural misunderstandings played out on the battlefield and in the sexual encounters between European men and Native women. Women were subjugated through sexual violence and servitude, while Native men were killed in battle. The accusations of cannibalism both justified the conquest and helped to establish the gendered order of Spanish imperialism. With a thorough understanding of the intersections between cannibalism, sex, and gender, the development of imperial power within the conquest of Mexico becomes clearer.

# 4 / Converting Cannibals: Jesuits and Iroquois in New France

Given the number of topics that appear in the Bible, it should come as no surprise that cannibalism is mentioned several times.[1] Most references to man-eating are found in the Old Testament and describe the punishments and deprivations experienced by nonbelievers. Cannibalism appears as both a punishment for misdeeds and a reason to punish. For example, the prophet Jeremiah proclaimed that God was going to punish the people of the Valley of Ben Hinnom by "mak[ing] them eat the flesh of their sons and the flesh of their daughters and all shall eat the flesh of their neighbors in the siege."[2] Chapter 3 of the book of the minor prophet Micah describes a group of people who consume others not out of desperation but simply out of wickedness, as they have rejected all that God offered and now eat the flesh of believers:

> You who hate the good and love the evil,
> who tear the skin off of my people,
> and the flesh off their bones;
> Who eat the flesh of my people,
> flay their skin off them,
> break their bones in pieces,
> and chop them up like meat in a kettle,
> like fish in a cauldron.
>
> Then they will cry to the LORD,
> but he will not answer them;

> he will hide his face from them at that time,
> because they have acted wickedly.[3]

Micah prophesied that God would punish those who did not treat believers with dignity. The implication is that the act of cannibalism could cause God to turn away from an entire group of people; loving God and practicing cannibalism are incompatible. In chapter 3 we saw that for some conquistadors in Mexico, the practice of man-eating was irreconcilable with conversion to Christianity. When Christian missionaries went to the Americas they confronted this issue repeatedly. In Canada, Jesuit missionaries struggled to make sense of the supposed cannibalistic practices of the Natives and attempted to develop strategies to convince Indians to give up their ways in exchange for the promise of heavenly rewards. These missionaries expected cannibalistic Indians to exchange the body of their enemy for the body of Christ in their proverbial kettles.

This chapter examines discourses of cannibalism in French North America, adding conversion to the layers of exploration and conquest that I have already discussed. I focus on the discourse established in the vast records of Jesuit missionaries in New France, which contain the most prolific descriptions of anthropophagy in Canada.[4] There are several general themes about the discourse of cannibalism in Jesuit writings: the fear of cannibalism as a catalyst for and impediment to imperial and missionary expansion, the connection between cannibalism and animality, and the way the ritual of cannibalism functioned as a discursive trope for the negotiation of masculinity. Together these overlapping themes help us to better understand the place of cannibalism within the religious arm of imperialism.

## The Jesuits and Their Relations

Between 1896 and 1901 the historian and librarian Reuben Gold Thwaites led a project that compiled and translated the huge numbers of extant Jesuit writings from New France between 1610 and 1791 into the seventy-three volumes collectively called *The Jesuit Relations*.[5] The seventy-one textual volumes (the other two contain the index) include the yearly digests of Jesuit activities in New France, which were published annually from 1632 until 1673 by Sébastien Cramoisy in Paris, after which they were published sporadically. Thwaites also included many documents that would have been less widely available to the reading public in seventeenth- and eighteenth-century Europe, such as personal correspondence between missionaries and their families and friends as well as the original letters written by field missionaries to their superiors. The latter documents were edited by the superiors and compiled into the yearly digests. The earliest account is that of Marc Lescarbot, originally published in 1610, followed by Father Pierre Biard's from 1611. The documents in *The Jesuit Relations* were written by a wide range of individuals, including priests and lay members of the order known as *donné*. Initially the *Relations* were not intended to be public documents, but as the mission efforts progressed and public interest in New France increased, they began to be written and published for a general audience.[6]

As an organization, the Society of Jesus grew rapidly from its founding in 1540 by Ignatius of Loyola to thirteen thousand members throughout the world by 1615. The Protestant Reformation, which began in 1517, had an enormous impact on politics and culture in western Europe. For my purposes, one of the important effects of the Reformation was the redefinition of masculinity that developed in its wake. In Protestantism the seat of patriarchal masculinity shifted from the Church Fathers to the male head of household. This shift led to an unspoken challenge to the masculinity of celibate Catholic clergy, as they were the leaders of their flocks but not of families. By the mid-sixteenth century Jesuit masculinity seemed at odds with the new ideas of manhood that were emerging in many parts of Europe.[7] However, despite these rapid social and political changes, the Society of Jesus grew quite substantially.

The peculiar ways in which Ignatius expressed his masculinity provided an enticing model for his followers and drew many toward the society that he founded. In light of the ongoing gendered theological crisis, Ignatius modeled a brand of masculinity that was neither anxious nor threatened. Prior to founding the Jesuit Order, he had been a soldier, which greatly influenced his philosophy and practices. Drawing inspiration from the life and works of Ignatius, the Society of Jesus stressed self-reflection and homosocial intimacy that was unbridled by the hierarchical social norms that permeated other aspects of interaction between men. To join the order one had to take vows of humility, poverty, and chastity. The dictates against acting on one's carnal desires were rigid.[8] Indeed Jesuits had to redirect their sexual desires into acts of charity and compassion.

Ignatius's autobiography modeled the process of turning a soldier into a chaste and self-sacrificing member of the clergy—a soldier for

God. In his autobiography he directs men to also protect the chastity of others.[9] Rather than exhibiting bravery while facing an enemy on the battlefield, Ignatius and his followers did battle against the sinful forces of sexuality and violence. Ignatius took it upon himself to remove the corrupting influences of men's basest desires in order to harness their power in a new direction. The Jesuits stressed sexual purity and spoke out against the lax enforcement of dictates against concubinage. While Protestants sought to recenter the naturalness of sexuality and procreation by allowing ministers to marry, the Jesuits challenged this new definition of masculinity and remained steadfastly chaste. Thus while many in the early modern period saw reproduction and fatherhood as natural, masculine traits, the Society of Jesus challenged this assumption and sought to create a new model of masculinity that relied not on the flesh but on the spirit.[10]

At the center of Jesuit understandings of masculinity was piety, but Ignatius also displayed a number of characteristics that were typically associated with female spirituality, such as fasting and excessive spiritual suffering. He combined traditions of male and female mystics and became at once father and mother to his followers. He urged his followers to allow their bodies to be open to the divine but not weak; they had to be physically able to fight for souls in far-off lands. For example, crying enabled the soul to be open, but only strong men shed tears.[11] Jesuit men were trained to be strong in spirit and body. They had to practice restraint in all aspects of their lives. Thus the model of Jesuit masculinity was one in which men were deeply emotional but also exhibited the strength and self-restraint of the soldier.

In dealing with people of different backgrounds and faiths who exhibited divergent understandings of masculinity, the Jesuits demonstrated their masculinity through words, not weapons. However, the Iroquois often ignored the missionaries' words and they were forced to fight for God by suffering on the scaffold. Ignatius and the members of the Jesuit Order provided an alternative model of masculinity to that of the conquistador.[12] Unlike Cortés, the Jesuits did not come to New France poised to incorporate women into their camp through sexual diplomacy, nor did they arrive prepared to fight on the battlefield. Instead they fought their war against the spirits, not the bodies, of the Indians they encountered.

Women were officially barred from entering the Society of Jesus in 1547. They were able to support the men of the order and to serve them, but they could not play a spiritual role. Ignatius believed that the presence of women in the Order would have been burdensome and would have prevented the priests from successfully completing their missions abroad. They did not want to be tied down by women in any capacity. Excluding women symbolically strengthened the bonds between men. Ignatius's teachings effectively incorporated the feminine aspects of spiritual life in order to physically exclude women from their ranks. Thus the Jesuit Fathers did not need the physical presence of women in order to lead others to the path of salvation.[13] The Virgin Mary was considered the only ideal woman, and the Jesuits were able to channel her power through their male bodies. Women were not entirely absent from the lives of Jesuits, however, as members of the Order were encouraged to cultivate spiritual and emotional attachments with them. Jesuit masculinity was not cloistered, and men were allowed to engage freely with women so long as the homosocial bonds that existed between the members of the order remained centered.[14]

New France was not the first major evangelizing effort taken up by the Order of Jesus. Prior to arriving in North America, the Order had sent missionaries to many parts of South America as well as Japan and Goa in modern-day India. They faced different challenges in Canada than in Japan, and historians confront greater difficulty analyzing Jesuit accounts in New France as Indians left few written records. Thus the Jesuit accounts must serve as both ethnography and religious documents. A further consequence of the lack of written records is that the Jesuits themselves had to rely only on the experiences of missionaries in other parts of the Americas coupled with their own powers of observation as a guide.[15]

The Jesuit missionaries in South America reported incidents of cannibalism among the tribes they encountered. In 1549 six Jesuits, led by Manuel de Nóbrega, arrived in Bahia, Brazil. Nóbrega and his compatriots wrote prolifically about their experiences and often expressed horror at the Portuguese mistreatment of Indians and the cruelties of slavery. However, their writings also discussed cruelty among the Indians, the Tupínamba in particular. Chief among these was cannibalism. Thus at the same time that the missionaries were concerned about Indian treatment by their colonial leaders, they indicted them for horrific acts.[16] The Jesuits in North America tended to express less frustration with French cruelty, but, like their Latin American counterparts, their relationship with the colonial leaders was often strained.

The way the Jesuits constructed their masculinity played an important role in their interactions with Native peoples in New France. The contest between the Jesuits and the Iroquois for dominance and influence in New France can be characterized to some degree as a contest between differing understandings of gender, and masculinity in particular. Furthermore the threats to their masculinity that the Jesuits faced in Europe helped to shape their actions in North America as they sought to establish the Catholic faith in the region. Unlike Columbus or Cortés before them, the Jesuits did not typically engage in sexual relations with their conquests. This does not mean that they were not concerned with Native sexuality; rather they enacted their civilizing agenda to the spirit rather than the body. The discourse of sexuality played a vital role in encounters between Europeans and Natives in the Caribbean and in Mexico; in New France the discursive intersection between cannibalism and sexuality worked differently, but was no less important. Jesuits focused significantly less on the intersection of cannibalism, sodomy, and other practices that were at odds with prevailing norms of gender and sexuality. Rather they wrote about cannibalism as a practice that demonstrated the existence of real savagery and evil among the Indians. Much like Columbus and Cortés, however, the Jesuits used the discourse of cannibalism to demonstrate the necessity of their intervention in Canada, and the presence of cannibalism drew people to the region armed with tools for its eradication. For the Jesuits these tools were words and faith rather than guns, swords, or sexual violence.

The writings of Jesuit missionaries in New France reveal a complicated relationship with the emerging French Empire.[17] Their published accounts served to reinforce Jesuit interests in converting Indians to Catholicism, and to varying degrees they also supported the desires of the French monarchy. By saving Indian souls, the Jesuits were actively preparing New France for colonial status, for colonists, provincial governments, and economic expansion. The representation of Indians in the *Relations* reflects conflicting goals: the Jesuits needed to make the French reading public understand the necessity of their efforts, which they did through rich descriptions of the savagery of the Indians; however, they simultaneously needed to demonstrate the importance of New France to the empire in order to garner funds and encourage colonists. Thus Indians were generally represented as savage but redeemable. The horrific accounts of torture and sacrifice of Frenchmen at the hands of the Iroquois may have been a deterrent to colonization efforts, so these negative representations had to be tempered with miraculous tales of savage Natives who became pious Christians. The French public was eager to read stories about the experiences of missionaries and neophytes and quickly came to view the missionaries as saintly.[18] The Jesuits depended on royal favor and private donations in order to sustain their work in New France; to maintain this support Jesuit writings demonstrated a balance between condemnation of Indians and tales of redemption.[19]

Pierre Biard, one of the first two Jesuit missionaries in New France, emphasized the importance of colonization, but not outright conquest, to French successes in the Americas. He positioned the work of the Jesuits as fundamental to such a cause because it was necessary to Christianize Indians in order to pave the way for French colonists. Biard appealed to the vanity of the French monarch by assuring him that if he gave up in Canada after having devoted so many resources to these efforts, France would appear effeminate and weak to its imperial competitors back in Europe.[20] Thus, nearly from the outset, the French presence in Canada was constructed in gendered terms. In order to earn a place among the other great imperial powers of the sixteenth and seventeenth centuries, France had to establish its ability to compete with other men. By playing to the fears of being cast as feminine and weak, Biard encouraged French expansion as a matter of masculine pride. Biard saw the work of the Jesuits as essential to the success of French imperial expansion and thus positioned them as representative agents of imperial masculinity. His mission in North America did not last long, and the Jesuits were forced to leave in 1613 after some scuffles with the English. They attempted to establish a solid missionary base several times but were not successful until 1632. In addition to questions about whether or not the Jesuits were the best religious order to send to New France, they also found themselves in the middle of growing absolutism in the French monarchy, which affected support for the order.[21]

The expansion of the French Empire in North America was decidedly religious in nature, as both conversion and colonization were integral to economic success. As a whole the French were less interested in conquest than in colonization and conversion.[22] Unlike the Spaniards who came before or the English who followed, the French Crown was not able to move large populations of their subjects to the Americas, although they did attempt a variety of other models. In Canada the population of French men and women remained relatively low, and Indians significantly outnumbered Europeans. However, the influence of France was felt throughout the region, often through traders and missionaries who traveled between far-flung settlements. The French Empire in Canada was mostly a series of small settlements, traders, and missionaries spread thinly over a relatively large region. There was no large-scale conquest of Canada like that which occurred in Mexico, nor was there an organized effort to incorporate Indians into the French Empire. Rather the French Empire was generally more commercial and spiritual in nature. The French used their influence to gain economic power in the Americas and to convert Indians to Catholicism.

The Jesuits were unique among most of the proselytizing groups in the North America as they tended to be more sympathetic toward the suffering experienced by Native peoples after the coming of Europeans, and they were more sensitive toward Indigenous cultural practices.[23] Rather than simply discounting Indigenous beliefs, Jesuit missionaries were careful to try to incorporate these traditions into their sermons. They studied Native beliefs and utilized this knowledge in their conversion efforts. Unlike the Protestant missionaries of New England, the Jesuits in New France learned and instructed Indians about Christianity in their Native language. Protestant missionaries in general expected Indians to first become civilized according to their standards, which often included sedentary agriculture, modest dress, and the guarding and policing of sexual practices.[24] The Jesuits were more willing to allow the Natives freedom to worship God and live as they desired (within certain constraints of course).

For the Jesuits faith was the most important thing; from faith in God civilization would come. They understood certain Native beliefs, such as the worship of the Sun, as simply misguided and misdirected efforts to worship the true God. In fact some believed that Indians had simply lost their way on the path to God, and they sought evidence of preexisting Christian beliefs in Native cultures. Even if the minions of Satan had intervened in Indian cultures and led them to corruption, the Jesuits believed that Indians were not beyond salvation. Years of experience in missions throughout the world had taught them that day-to-day practices were less important than the possession of an unwavering belief in God and the adherence to certain principles of Catholic morality.[25] This adaptive style allowed the Jesuits to be more successful than their Protestant counterparts in New England at converting and baptizing Indians. The Jesuits were particularly successful in these efforts among the Hurons and Montagnais.[26]

In spite of their willingness to accept and incorporate Native beliefs and practices into their proselytizing efforts, the Jesuits could not condone, look past, or incorporate cannibalism, torture, and sacrifice. Additionally, while the Jesuits believed that Indians were redeemable and human, they nonetheless recognized distinct differences between tribes. The differences between the Huron and the Iroquois, for example, shaped the way the Jesuits went about their conversion efforts but did not affect their overall faith in Indian humanity and redeemability. Throughout the New World up to this point, Europeans who encountered Indians vacillated between viewing them as undifferentiated Others and making unsupported distinctions between tribes, as in the Carib and the Arawak example.

The protocultural relativism of the Jesuit missionaries in New France was evident throughout the extensive published records of their exploits. However, inasmuch as the Jesuits were comparatively complimentary toward Native peoples and practices, their writings were nonetheless filled with innumerable examples of perceived Native savagery, cruelty, and heathenism. The most laudatory references to Indians were reserved for Christian converts.[27] Thus while the Jesuits believed that Indians were fully human and completely capable of receiving God's divine grace, they regarded their cultural practices as savage and believed that without Christian intervention, Indians would remain forever savage and damned.[28]

The earliest records of the Jesuits in New France tended to include more damning descriptions of Indians than the later documents, singling out the Iroquois as consummate villains.[29] In these earlier records, not only did the Jesuits have to justify their presence in New France, but they also had to entice new priests to come join them. Thus they presented Indians as being in great need of spiritual guidance, using descriptions of their horrific practices to demonstrate this. French power was less firmly established in the initial years of the missions and the region was experiencing a great deal of political and social unrest.

Jesuit writing reflected the intellectual traditions of the time. Scholars have located two primary motivations for French colonial writings. The first was the simple transmission of new information to a desiring audience. These communications were constructed according to the prevailing cultural frameworks of the time, and they often invoked classical and medieval traditions. Although these tropes were less common in the writings of Jesuits than in those of early explorers like Columbus and Vespucci, they did persist. The second important goal of French colonial writings was to use descriptions of the New

World and its inhabitants to draw conclusions about life in Europe.[30] At times Jesuits admired Indians for what they perceived as the simplicity of their cultures and the lack of artifice in their interactions, which in turn reflected Jesuit opinions on the lavishness of French aristocratic society. The Jesuits prefigured the tropes of both the noble and the ignoble savage Indian, which would dominate after Rousseau. While the Jesuits believed that Indians were devoid of "true culture" and "true religion," they nonetheless exhibited some qualities worth emulating. The Jesuits' comparative relativism as a whole enabled the creation of a corpus of writings that afforded its audience important insights into both sides of the Atlantic.

The volumes of *The Jesuit Relations* contain more than 130 references to acts of cannibalism. Given the vast number of topics covered in these volumes, cannibalism seems to be only a minor concern; there are far more numerous and detailed accounts of the flora and fauna of the region as well as innumerable descriptions of the conversion and martyr experiences of individuals. While there is significant evidence that the Iroquois of New France were anthropophagous, it is the way French observers interpreted this practice that is at issue here.[31] The fearsome reputation of the Iroquois was developed in part as a response to terror tactics they employed, which led to widespread mistrust of the Iroquois and exaggeration of their inhuman savagery. Their reputation preceded them in a fashion similar to the Arawak stories about Carib cannibalism. Not much is known about the practices of the Caribs before the Europeans came and whether or not their anthropophagous repute preceded this encounter, but from a European perspective, it was clear how the Iroquois became infamous.[32]

The torture and cannibalization of captives likely occurred among many tribes of New France.[33] However, the Jesuits singled out the Iroquois for their cannibalistic ways. Throughout the seventy-one textual volumes of the *Relations*, the Iroquois appear to be the most consistent threat to the Jesuit efforts in New France. More than 50 percent of the references to cannibalism in the *Jesuit Relations* relate to the Iroquois.[34] Just as in the Caribbean and Mexico, the Jesuits first encountered a group, the Hurons in this case, from whom they learned about a neighboring tribe who terrorized them and practiced cannibalism, in this case, the Iroquois.[35] According to the Jesuits' own records, both of these groups engaged in anthropophagous practices, yet the Hurons, who were more closely allied with the French, were not indicted to the same degree as the Iroquois, echoing the Maya-Aztec pattern in Mexico.

Members of the Society of Jesus began witnessing to Iroquois tribes in 1653, after a particularly tumultuous period of Iroquois-Huron relations. The Iroquois agreed to accept the Jesuits and made a tentative peace with the French, in part because of increasing pressure from the Dutch. Father Simon Le Moyne traveled to Iroquoia in 1654, but hostilities broke out again and the Jesuits were forced to abandon the mission in 1658. Over the next several decades the Jesuits maintained a sporadic yet persistent presence among the Iroquois but achieved only limited success in their conversion efforts. The majority of interested converts were captives of other tribes then living among the Iroquois.[36] The first reference to cannibalism among the Iroquois is from 1640, and the last is in a letter from October 1683.

The Jesuits described a number of circumstances in the Americas in which they believed that man-eating occurred, including among starving shipwrecked sailors and even among French fugitives. These events were always described as isolated incidents, however.[37] Jesuit priests did not assume that starving French sailors who consumed one another would repeat their horrific actions. Descriptions of the practice of cannibalism among Indians suffering the ravages of starvation were also quite typical. Indian starvation cannibalism was not presented as quotidian, yet Jesuits assumed that when starvation cannibalism occurred among Indians it represented their degenerate cultural practices and indicated their savagery. In other words, when European individuals turned to cannibalism out of desperation it was an unfortunate occurrence but was not representative of European norms, but when Indians ate other humans to survive they did so because they were savages. For much of the time that the Jesuits were with the Hurons, the Iroquois were laying siege to Huron villages. According to the Jesuits, these circumstances disrupted traditional migration patterns, causing widespread starvation that drove some to desperate acts of cannibalism.

Describing the sufferings of the Huron that resulted from famine, plague, and war, Father Paul Ragueneau chronicled the depths to which they were forced to go in order to sate their hunger. He wrote that they were digging up corpses with little regard to kinship. Mothers were eating the bodies of their children, and brother consumed brother. Ragueneau remarks, "It is true, this is inhuman; but it is no less unusual among our savages than among the Europeans, who abhor eating flesh of their own kind. Doubtless the teeth of the starving man make no distinction in food."[38] Ragueneau is willing to recognize that all humans, when faced with the horrific circumstances that were experienced by the Huron, might become cannibalistic. This demonstrates the Jesuits' ability to put cultural practices in context and judge them accordingly. By their own accounts, they were willing to concede that cannibalism in times of extreme deprivation was a disturbing but sometimes necessary act, reinforcing their belief that Indians were not beyond redemption.

According to Ragueneau, although the starving Hurons were driven to cannibalism, it was the Iroquois who were the villains. Without the aggravations caused by the Iroquois raids, Ragueneau did not believe that the Hurons would have become "dying skeletons eking out a miserable Life," nor would they have been driven to perform heinous acts of endocannibalism. The desperateness of the Hurons' situation led them to consume carrion and even to consume one another in secret. This, Ragueneau claims, was solidly against Huron practice. Although they may have consumed the bodies of their enemies, eating a fellow Huron was deeply taboo and elicited the same horror that the consumption of human flesh would have in France.[39] Ragueneau reiterates the sentiments he expressed earlier, that "famished teeth ceased to discern the nature of that they ate" and that extreme starvation caused kin to consume kin. While the Jesuits reported that the Huron did sometimes kill and cannibalize their enemies, they did not readily consume their own, and it was only desperation that drove them to it.[40] The mania induced by extreme starvation forced the Hurons to deny their kinship relations, a practice that in normal times would have been a terrible violation of cultural norms. In this example Ragueneau hints at the importance of Jesuit intervention among both the Huron and the Iroquois, for he makes clear that the Huron were a suffering people in great need of help, just as his villainizing of the Iroquois urged greater French intervention among them.

One remarkable feature of the accounts of Iroquois cannibalism in *The Jesuit Relations* is that, in all of their descriptions of starving Indians driven by their hunger to commit acts of anthropophagy, the Jesuits do not indicate that they too participated in acts of starvation cannibalism, though it is certain that the missionaries and the *donné* did suffer alongside their potential converts. This obviously begs the question of what the Jesuits were eating while the Native peoples were driven to consume one another. Three possible scenarios emerge.

First, the Jesuits had food that they chose not to share with the Indians or shared only with converts, which would make them somewhat culpable for Indian man-eating. Second, the Jesuits were also driven to eat their fellow man but did not record it. Third, perhaps their religious convictions and the discipline of *civilization* enabled the Jesuits to resist the temptation to consume their fellow man. Each of these scenarios is possible; however, the only one even hinted at by the writers themselves is the third. Even if they were on the brink of death, their faith in God allowed them to persevere.[41] In this way the Jesuits were clearly setting themselves above their potential converts. While they could conceive of why the Indians might be driven to consume one another, they themselves were above these base desires. Jesuit masculinity insisted on control and self-sacrifice, two traits that might explain their lack of participation in starvation cannibalism (or at least their refusal to mention it).

## Inhumane Humans

Even when the Jesuits described Huron acts of ritualized cannibalism against their enemies, the Iroquois were still portrayed as the real adversary of Catholic France throughout the *Relations*, and their bellicose tendencies were blamed for forcing the starving Hurons to consume one another (never mind that the diseases brought by the French were to blame as well). One priest accused the Iroquois of cruelty greater than anything else the Indians endured, including famine. Describing the period of terror that followed the tortures of Fathers Jean de Brébeuf and Gabriel Lalemant, Father Ragueneau said that the Hurons fled their villages "in order to escape the cruelty of an enemy [the Iroquois] whom they feared more than a thousand deaths. . . . Many, no longer expecting humanity from man, flung themselves into the deepest recesses of the forest, where, though it were with the wild beasts, they might find peace."[42] In this passage Ragueneau simultaneously declares the pitiful state of the Hurons and the inhumanity of the Iroquois. This assertion of inhumanity is a common theme in descriptions of the Iroquois in the *Relations*, especially in those volumes that focus on the Huron missions.[43]

The Jesuits probably gave little credence to the idea that the Iroquois were actually something other than human. Rather their descriptions of inhumanity positioned the Iroquois as the biggest threat to their efforts in New France as well as the richest field for missionary work.

The supposed inhumanity of the Iroquois seemed to result from cultural differences, not innate characteristics. In a fashion similar to the Aztecs and Mayas of the Yucatán, the Iroquois presented a conundrum to the Europeans who came into contact with them. The Iroquois had the most sophisticated governing structure in the region, yet they seemed to be cruel, bellicose, and unyielding. Both the Huron and the Iroquois were always willing to share with members of their own tribe; in fact the ability to give things away signaled one's power far more than the possession of wealth.[44] However, this kindness resulted from an intense preoccupation with group loyalty and cohesion. In modern terms this might be thought of as an extreme version of an "us versus them" mentality. Thus the Huron found it abhorrent to consume members of their own society but not their enemies, and the Iroquois exhibited similar characteristics. Early European visitors found the Iroquois well organized, powerful, and unimaginably cruel. These kinds of dualistic characterizations of Indians represented some of the contradictions of empire and civilization: if the Indians were capable of rationality, then France had no right to conquer them. Jesuit writings demonstrate this ambivalence and position the French presence in the New World as essential for the religious conversion necessary to make Indians viable subjects. The fundamental contradiction at the heart of European expansion in the Americas was the question of equality: If Indians were capable of being converted and civilized, did they deserve equal treatment and consideration?

The violent tendencies of the Iroquois were infamous throughout much of North America.[45] At times the terms *cannibal* and *Iroquois* are used interchangeably in the *Relations*, an interesting shift from the use of the word *cannibal* to signify *Carib* more than a century before. Their reputation for ruthlessness in battle led one Jesuit to observe that despite the horrific conditions of starvation faced by the Hurons, the wrath of the Iroquois was more feared. The Hurons were "still too happy not to have fallen into the hands of an enemy a thousand times more cruel than the wild beasts, and than all the famines in the world."[46] During the period of Jesuit intervention in New France, the Iroquois engaged in nearly constant warfare with their neighbors, both Indian and European. They took advantage of the chaos caused by the massive depopulation from disease, the disruption of trade routes, and territorial realignment, among other causes, to carve out a tenuous niche for themselves in a new world and enhance the Great League of Peace and Power.[47]

The Jesuits and other visitors to New France had difficulty understanding the nature of Indian warfare as it differed significantly from how war was practiced in Europe. As soldiers for God, the Jesuits expected to suffer greatly in their war for souls but to emerge victorious, having successfully defeated Indian heathenism. They expected to gain control over the losers and to enforce their will upon them. However, Indian warfare was not fought for the same reasons or with the same end in mind. Rather than fighting for access to resources, for which most European wars were fought, the motives of Iroquois warfare were more complicated.[48] What they did have in common, however, was an understanding that battles were fought for masculine domination and that war was the domain of men. For example, it was common among eastern Native tribes and western Europeans to employ gendered language to insult enemies.[49]

War among the Iroquois, especially after the European invasion, was often fought in order to assuage the grief of those who had lost a loved one, creating an almost self-perpetuating cycle of warfare. The grieving process was potentially disruptive to the order necessary for Iroquois life. The bereaved might experience periods of intense despair or rage that could threaten the community. In order to prevent these kinds of disruptions, members of another clan would attempt to "cover the grief" of the mourners. This could be done by a variety of means, including bestowing gifts, making payments, or giving a feast. If these efforts failed, however, the female members of the decedent's clan could call for action that was more drastic. They actively discouraged violence against members of their own tribe, and thus they sought to fulfill their violent desires in battle with enemy tribes. Members of the decedent's clan did not typically participate in the mourning war; rather "young men who were related by marriage to the female survivors of the deceased but who lived in other longhouses were obliged to form a war party or face the women's public accusation of cowardice."[50] Thus the women urged the men to raid enemy tribes. The role of women in Iroquois warfare eluded the Jesuits, who were fighting to prove their masculine dominance over others and understood war as a contest only between men. Indian warfare, however, was as much about manhood as womanhood. The Iroquois men who fought battles did so to prove their bravery but also to reaffirm female power in the village. While the Jesuits were trying to save souls in order to protect their definition of chaste femininity, their direct exclusion of women meant that they failed to understand the full spectrum of their gendered encounter with the Iroquois.

By framing the interactions between the Jesuits and the Iroquois as a contest between competing ideas about masculinity, the Jesuits went to great lengths in their writings to describe the Iroquois as a formidable enemy since victory over such an enemy carried great value. For members of the Society of Jesus victory probably did not mean the same thing that it did for French bureaucrats. Instead of calculating their success in economic or political terms, success for the Jesuits was counted in souls saved. The practice of cannibalism among the Iroquois, then, made them appear even more terrifying. Father Paul Le Jeune remarked in 1641 that the presence of fifty Iroquois was enough to drive two hundred Frenchman from Canada: "If these Barbarians become enraged at our Frenchmen, they will never let them sleep soundly; a Hiroquois [sic] will remain for two or three days without food behind a stump, fifty paces from your house, in order to slay the first person who shall fall into his ambush. If he be discovered, the forest serves him—for an asylum; where a Frenchman would find only a hindrance, a Savage will bound as lightly as a deer."[51] Le Jeune seemed to find Iroquois skill in forest warfare both admirable and distressing. The ability of Native Americans to hide in the forest disturbed Frenchmen and heightened their general sense of uneasiness and mistrust of the American landscape. Despite all of these seeming advantages that the landscape provided the Iroquois, Le Jeune assured his readers that they would not have been successful without the intervention of Dutch and European weapons.[52] In this way Le Jeune subtly emasculated the Iroquois by making them appear dependent on the Dutch.

The assumption that the forest was a favorable place for the Iroquois but a dangerous hindrance for the French highlighted the way Europeans tended to see Indians as firmly connected to the landscape. Le Jeune's description of the Iroquois attack calls to mind an image of an animal stalking its prey, thus reaffirming the animality of the Iroquois. Le Jeune and other Jesuit missionaries reinforced this supposed animality further in their descriptions of what they presumed to be illogical and inhuman rage. The Jesuits did not understand the roots of Iroquois anger, nor did they understand the cultural meanings of anger in a society that favored group conformity.

When reporting incidents of cannibalism, Jesuit priests often employed animalistic metaphors, referring to the warriors as both wolves and tigers.[53] For example, in the following passage from 1642, Barthélemy Vimont dehumanizes the victorious Iroquois through his description of their cruelty and fury:

> They [the Iroquois] dismembered those whom they had just slaughtered, cut them in pieces, and threw the feet, legs, arms, and heads into the pot, which they set to boil with joy as great as the sorrow felt by the poor captives who remained alive, when they saw their countryman serving as the quarry of these Werewolves. The women and children wept bitterly, and those half Demons took pleasure in the hearing their doleful chants. When the supper was cooked, these wolves devoured their prey; one seized a thigh, another a breast; some sucked the marrow from the bones; others broke open the skulls, to extract the brains. In a word, they ate the flesh of men with as much appetite as, and with more pleasure than, hunters eat that of a Boar or of a Stag.[54]

By referring to the Iroquois as wolves, Vimont strips them of their rationality and reduces them to beings of pure emotion and instinct. However, the strength of this pronouncement is lessened somewhat by the use of the words *werewolf* and *half-demon*. Both of these creatures retain something of their humanity.[55] The werewolf might be overcome by its animal nature at certain times or situations but otherwise exists as a rational, thinking person. These descriptors demonstrate some of the ambivalence that the Jesuits felt toward the Iroquois; they knew that the Iroquois were human beings, but they struggled to make sense of what they perceived to be depraved actions.

Comparing humans to animals is one of the common tropes employed to deem someone a savage, and cannibalism "still remains probably the most powerful symbol of savagery."[56] The fact that the Iroquois acted like animals and consumed their fellow man justified European interventions and positioned Indians as functionally inferior savages. Jesuits feared death "by the claws of these tigers, and by the Fury of these demons."[57] As the missionaries struggled to make sense of the cruelty of the Iroquois, they employed older metaphors of monstrosity to express their anxiety. Unlike Columbus or Vespucci, the Jesuits did not wonder whether or not the cannibalistic Iroquois were actual monsters in the classical sense; they perceived them as flawed human beings whose cultural practices led them astray. In order for French expansion into the Americas to succeed they had to find common ground on which to communicate and negotiate with one other. The Jesuits hoped that through their culturally sensitive mission efforts, they could entice Indians away from savagery and toward recognizable (even if inferior) civilization. The Iroquois practice of cannibalism stood in the way of imperial and religious expansion in the North America. However, the Jesuits neither explicitly stated that the elimination of cannibalism was a primary motivator, nor did they stress that it had to be eliminated prior to the onset of their civilizing agenda, as Cortés did in Mexico.

At the same time that they feared being eaten by the Iroquois, some missionaries expressed a perverse thankfulness for their cruelties. The superior at Quebec, Barthélemy Vimont, recalled the capture of twelve canoes full of Huron people, along with Father Isaac Jogues and several other Frenchman, by the Iroquois in 1642. He wrote, "If those tigers burn them, if they boil them, if they eat them, they will procure for them sweeter refreshment in the house of the great God, for love of whom they expose themselves to such dangers." He further remarked that sacrifice was what enabled souls to be saved, for through his death Jesus brought barbarians to civilization and salvation. The practice of cannibalism among the Iroquois, then, appears to be both an impediment to the Jesuit missionaries and a catalyst for their actions. In fact Father Ragueneau remarked in his yearly relation, "Up to the present time, the Hiroquois have done almost more good than harm in New France. They have delivered many souls from the fires of Hell, while burning their bodies in an elemental fire."[58] Even if thousands of Hurons were dying on Iroquois scaffolds, the Jesuits felt confident that they had given the sacrificial victims a gift. The terror wrought by the Iroquois encouraged many deathbed conversions and baptisms and brought Indian souls to God.[59]

The ferocity of the Iroquois attacks against neighboring tribes prevented the missionaries from making much headway into Iroquoia. Yet such cruelty and the possibility of martyrdom was a strange enticement to the priests. Father Chaumonot wrote of his desire for martyrdom in 1649, following the sacrifices of Fathers Brébeuf and Lalemant: "We all, as many Fathers as we are here, have never loved our vocation more, than after having seen that it can raise us even to the glory of martyrdom; there is nothing but my imperfections which can make me give up my part. . . . If Your reverence ask it for me from the good Jesus, through the merits of his four great servants, Fathers Jogues, Daniel, de Brébeuf, and Lalemant, I hope that you will obtain it for me; and then the good Jesus might indeed give me the grace to die for the advancement of his Kingdom."[60] Chaumonot saw his missionary work as a path to martyrdom, and he desired to follow in the footsteps of other Jesuits who had been killed by the Iroquois. The possibility of martyrdom drew others like Chaumonot to New France. They demonstrated their commitment to God through their ability to withstand the horrific conditions and constant threat of torture and death in order to assure Indians a place in Heaven (which would lead to the missionaries' salvation as well). Catholic tradition would not have allowed the priests to seek out martyrdom for their own personal benefit; rather, as Chaumonot indicated, the difficulty of their work among the Iroquois and the possibility that they might be killed for their faith made their desire to "save" the Iroquois stronger. The more difficult the challenge, the greater was the reward. While the Iroquois fought bitterly to keep the Jesuits out of their territory and to obtain economic dominance in the region, their persistence acted as a draw to masochistic Jesuit priests. Suffering and dying for one's God was the ultimate sacrifice that proved one's commitment to the faith. With their torture and sometimes death and cannibalization, the Jesuits sought to prove their masculine valor to both the public back in Europe and the Indians they encountered.

Both Jesuits and Iroquois were well aware of the power of suffering. For the Jesuits, their suffering on Earth was the key to eternal salvation in heaven. For the Iroquois, however, the suffering of others could directly benefit their tribe. The power of captives was extracted through their torture, execution, and occasionally consumption. According to Jesuit writings, not all captives were cannibalized, but it was not uncommon. It is difficult, if not impossible, to figure out exactly how often and for what reason captives were cannibalized, but evidence suggests that the attainment of the spiritual power of the victim had a great deal to do with it. Throughout the drawn-out process of torture to which the captive was subjected, he was expected to maintain composure and exhibit the stoic bravery of a true warrior. The victims of torture and cannibalism were most often male, but the Jesuits did mention the occasional female victim.[61] Often victims were made to sing throughout their torture. According to Jesuit records, those who endured the torture most admirably were the most desirable bodies to consume. The consumption of the body of a warrior imbued the tribe with all of his symbolic power and bravery. Thus although the Jesuits were not warriors in any traditional sense, by suffering and dying on Iroquois scaffolds they were able to obtain access to the symbolic power of warrior masculinity. Whether or not the Iroquois viewed them as such was not as important as the reputation for warrior-like martyrdom that the Jesuits presented in their digests for audiences back in Europe.

The ritual of torture was carefully calculated and designed to extract spiritual power by prolonging the life of the victim. These periods of torture were followed by brief periods of respite, in which the victim was revived as much as possible. Nuance often escaped the Jesuit observers; they tended to describe the ritual as more impulsive and savage as they did not fully comprehend its complex social, religious, and political aspects. They did observe, however, that there was some significance to the way the captive acted during his extensive torture. The more stoically a given captive handled his torments, the more fervent his torturers became and the greater their desire seemed to be to consume his flesh.

The Jesuits understood that there was a connection between the suffering inflicted upon a prisoner and the bravery and stoicism he exhibited, as these were qualities that were important for masculine warriors. Vimont's text of 1642 describes an incident in which "the Hiroquois were furious with rage on observing" the stoicism of a particular captive. Vimont writes that the Iroquois believed that the composure of this warrior was a bad omen, and so they asked the man why he remained so silent. He replied, "I do . . . what you could not, if you were treated with the same cruelty that you show me. The iron and the fire that you apply to my body would make you cry out very loud, and weep like children, while I do not flinch."[62] According-ing to Vimont, this overt challenge to the masculinity of the Iroquois warriors resulted in a marked increase in the severity of the torture. Vimont describes the torture inflicted on this man in vivid detail. The "tigers" removed the top of the victim's scalp and applied hot sand to the wound. They then took him down from the scaffold and dragged him through the village until "he looked like a monster." "Such a sight, which would have caused horror to men, rejoiced those Demons, who, as their final act of cruelty, cut open the breasts of those whom they wish to kill, tear out their hearts and their livers, which they roast; they cut off their feet, and their hands, which they cook partly under the embers, partly on a spit before the fire; in short, they roast and boil them, and then they eat them with delighted rage."[63] The more stolid the Huron captive remained, the more furiously the Iroquois tortured him. Vimont saw this response of the Iroquois as one of fear, but even if this captive did make the Iroquois afraid, the heightened the spiritual power they could draw from his torture, death, and consumption. While Vimont may not have fully understood the gendered significance of the ritual for the Iroquois, he did interpret it as a contest for masculine dominance.

Vimont ends his description of these events by comparing the Iroquois to wolves and insisting that they were under the control of demons: "*Homo homini lupus*; man becomes a wolf to other men, when he allows himself to be governed by Demons." This sentiment nicely encapsulates the general Jesuit views on the relative humanity of the Iroquois. They were not *actual* wolves or monsters or otherwise nonhuman, but the presence of demons among them had corrupted them to the degree that they were *like* nonhumans. The corrupting nature of the devil cast a veil over the humanity that the Iroquois inherently possessed and caused them to act without human reason or compassion. The Jesuits believed that without their intervention, the Iroquois would continue to lose their humanity to the devil. For example, in 1645, remarking on the potential peace between the Iroquois and the Hurons, Vimont wondered how people who had been so lost in cruelty could "find enough gentleness to agree together."[64] He believed that it was beyond his skill as a mere human to change their savage behavior and that without the intervention of God (and his representatives on Earth, the Jesuits) they would be lost.

## Bravery, Masculinity, and Suffering

Just as the Jesuits struggled to find ways to deal with the level of sophistication and savagery they perceived in the Iroquois, these conflicting representations were also common in their descriptions of cannibalistic torture rituals. They wrote of these events as disordered, lustful, demonic affairs, but they also sometimes hinted at the possibility of greater cultural significance. The numerous descriptions of torture demonstrate the importance of the behavior of the captive in determining the trajectory of his torture. The most worthy captives, those most deserving of a terrible death, were those who demonstrated remarkable composure on the scaffold, and this practice seems to have been extended to the Jesuit martyrs as well. The description of the torture and death of Father Jean de Brébeuf shows the importance that the Jesuits ascribed to bravery during the ritualized torture and cannibalism: "Another one of those barbarians, seeing that the good Father would soon die, made an opening in the upper part of his chest, and tore out his heart, which he roasted and ate. Others came to drink his blood, still warm, which they drank with both hands,—saying that the Father de Brébeuf had been very courageous to endure so much pain as they had given him and that, by drinking his blood, they would become courageous like him."[65] It was the priest's ability to withstand the extremes of Iroquois torture that made his body more desirable for consumption. Despite the tortures he endured, Brébeuf was reported to have remained stoic and even to continue to missionize to the other captives throughout his ordeal.[66] This act reinforced the masculinity of both the Iroquois and the Jesuits involved. Just as the Iroquois used the ritual torture of captives to establish their dominance over a feminized enemy, Brébeuf also reinforced his masculinity through stoic bravery and through his commitment to proselytizing, right up until the end.

The events of Brébeuf's martyrdom were also significant because they revealed the adaptive strategies of Iroquois ritual torture as well as the connection to Catholic religious discourse. At one point during his torture, a man who had previously been taken captive by the Iroquois and remained with them performed a mock baptism on Brébeuf. The man remarked, "Echon [Brébeuf's name in Huron] . . . thou sayest that Baptism and the sufferings of this life lead straight to Paradise; thou wilt go soon, for I will baptize thee, and to make thee suffer well, in order to go the sooner to thy Paradise." The man then proceeded to pour boiling water over Brébeuf's head three times, remarking each time, "Go to Heaven, for thou art well baptized."[67] According to the Jesuit observers, this mock baptism demonstrated not only the depravity of the Indian but also the profound impact that their missionary work was having. Even if the Huron and Iroquois had not fully accepted Catholic teachings, the fact that they were familiar enough with the ritual of baptism speaks to the influence of the Jesuit missions.[68] This incident reveals that besides using the torture ceremony to obtain the spirit of the most worthy victims, the Iroquois, and the foreigner adoptees living among them, also used it to vent their anger against the French and their Jesuits.[69] The captured man, who had previously been the recipient of Brébeuf's Christian wisdom, directed his anger toward the priest as a representative of an enemy tribe, a warrior whose death would assuage the anger and sadness of the bereaved and prove the superiority of Indian masculinity. This particular torture experience was calculated to extract the maximum

P. Ioannes de Brebeuf, et P. Gabriel Lallemant Galli Soc. IESV. exco
riato vertice, subulis sub ungves infixis, ferventibus aqvis baptizati in locum
evulsorum oculorum ardentibus prunis inditis, ignitis appensis securibus, toto cor
pore ustulati, ac demum plurium hararum tormentis rescissis undiq, et voratis
eorum carnibus membratim pro Christo discerpti, ab Iroqvæsis in nova Francia.
A. 1649. 16. 1147 Mart.

majorenè animarum zelo, an moriendi pro
Christo desiderio, meritò ambigas, ùt cujus
in scriptis nihil crebriùs occurrat, quàm,
similia verba: *sentio me vehementer impelli ad
moriendum pro Christo, Ardentissima decem
continenter diebus in me persensi Martyrij desi-
deria.* Quibus demum scilicet incitatus,
hisce verbis Martyrij exequendi votum con-
cepit: *quid retribuam tibi Domine mi IESu, pro
omnibus quæ retribuisti mihi? Calicem salutaris
accipiam, & nomen tuum invocabo. Voveo ergo in conspectu æterni Patris tui, sanctique Spiri-
tùs, in conspectu Sanctissima Matris tuæ, castissi-
mìqs ejus Sponsi Josephi, coram Angelis, Apostolis,
& Martyribus, Sanctisq, meis parentibus Ignatio
& Francisco Xaverio: voveo, inquam, tibi Domine mi IESu, si mihi unquam indigno famulo
tuo Martyrij gratia misericorditer à te oblata*

*fuerit, me huic gratia non defuturum: sic, ut
imposterum licere mihi nunquam velim, aut qua
sese offerent moriendi pro te occasiones, declinare
(nisi ita fieri ad majorem tuam gloriam judica-
rem) aut jam inflictum mortis ictum non acce-
ptare gaudenter. Tibi ergo Domine mi I E S U
& sanguinem & corpus, & spiritum meum jam
ab hac die gaudenter offero, ut pro te, si ità dones,
moriar, qui pro me mori dignatus es. Fac ut
sic vivam, ut ità mori tandem me velit. Ità Domine, calicem tuum accipiam, & nomen tuum
invocabo, JEsu, JEsu, JEsu.*

Cùm verò persæpe deinde mors illi à
barbaris decreta, & dies etiam necando indi-
ctus esset, ipse decretoriam horam impavi-
dus expectans, & interim eventûs securus,
inque animarum quæstum toto conatu in-
tentus, meruit sæpius Christum IEsum vi-
dere

FIGURE 4.1 "Martyrdom of Jean de Brébeuf and Gabriel Lalemant." Engraving. In Matthias Tanner, *Societas Jesu usque ad sanguinis et vitae profusionem militans in Europea, Africa, Asia, et America* (Prague, 1675). (Courtesy of the John Carter Brown Library at Brown University.)

suffering from Brébeuf and was likely intended to humiliate and demoralize him. Back in France this incident would likely have horrified readers and supported the necessity of the overseas missions.

Despite the horrible tortures inflicted upon him, Brébeuf remained steadfast: "During all of these torments, Father de Brébeuf endured like a rock, insensible to fire and flames, which astonished all the bloodthirsty wretches who tormented him. His zeal was so great that he preached continually to these infidels, to try to convert them."[70] Although he may not have intended his preaching to enrage his captors further, it reportedly did, and he played the role of the brave, long-suffering captive quite well. The records indicate that his refusal to capitulate and give in to the pain and suffering was what made his torture and ensuing consumption that much more satisfying to the Iroquois.

Iroquois cannibalism appears primarily in two manifestations in the Jesuit records. The first type took place on the battlefield immediately after the completion of the battle or raid. Only the male warriors of the tribe were involved in this exocannibalistic event.[71] This was a solely masculine affair that occurred outside of the prevailing structures of female power in the village. In these instances the Jesuits did not record the presence of any particular power structures that might have dictated who received the spoils of war (in this case, human flesh). Rather the warriors were represented as only lustful and furious, incapable of rationality, more ravenous monsters than participants in a carefully calculated ritual event. For example, Vimont described the aftermath of an Iroquois attack in 1644: "They then threw themselves on the body of the man whom they had killed; they tore his heart out of his breast, and scalped him; they cut off his lips, and the most fleshy parts of his thighs and legs, which they boiled and ate in the presence of the captives."[72] This cannibalistic act was not a carefully crafted ritual event; rather, in the eyes of the Jesuits, it was a crime of passion and fury and evidence of dangerous uncontrolled masculinity.

The other representation of Iroquois cannibalism in the *Relations* presents anthropophagy as the dénouement of the choreographed ritualized torture of captives by the whole tribe. These acts of exocannibalism occurred within the confines of the village, and women, children, and the elderly were all active participants. A Christian Huron captive of the Iroquois escaped in 1659 and described the conditions of his torture in the Iroquois village of Onnontagué. In fear for his life, he contemplated using a knife that he had hidden to slit his own throat, but the teachings of the Jesuits reminded him of the sinfulness of this act. He tossed his knife aside, committed his life to God, and marched toward his captors ready to accept his fate. He described the torture inflicted upon him: "All leaped upon me in a crowd on every side, some cutting off my fingers, others lacerating my flesh. . . . My poor hands were insufficient for all the women tugging at them on every side, while one of the boldest of the men tried to cut off one of them entirely."[73] The effects of the Jesuit presence are made clear here: without their influence, the unfortunate man in this example would have suffered the same torture but would not have been able to achieve eternal salvation.

While the missionaries may not have been able to stop the torture and cannibalization of captives, they were able to save the souls of many of the victims. After facing the gauntlet, this Huron captive was taken to a cabin, where his death sentence was pronounced. The headman of the village set forth the conditions of his execution and instructed the villagers to leave the arms and heart of the victim unmolested as they were reserved for a man "who had dreamed some months before that he was to eat them."[74] Just as the convert was about to face torture on the scaffold, a fierce storm began that belayed his death. He remained on the scaffold and watched as dogs devoured a recently sacrificed Frenchman's body, and he hoped that he would soon join the man in heaven. No explanation was given as to why the convert's body was to be eaten by the tribe (excepting the parts set aside for the prophetic dreamer) but the Frenchman's was not. Fortuitously the storm continued to rage, preventing the Iroquois from using firebrands, so the convert was taken to a cabin until the ritual could be resumed.

During this storm-induced delay, an Iroquois man returned to the village from a hunt. His family was afforded the right to determine whether the captive should be killed or adopted into the tribe. The Iroquois man decided that "his family was not under greater obligations to avenge the public wrongs than the others, who had, despite these injuries, spared their prisoners' lives." So the Huron convert's life was spared; he eventually escaped and fled to the French.[75] This might have been an inspirational tale for the European readership. Not only were the lives of the Jesuits in danger among the Iroquois, but the lives of Indian converts were as well. The success of French imperial efforts in Canada hinged upon the successful conversion of Indians and the protection of French interests. The anthropophagous practices of the Iroquois threatened to symbolically emasculate France. Examples that demonstrated Catholic triumph over cannibalistic incorporation supported the expansion of masculine imperial power in the Americas and indicated the willingness of the French to face even the most savage enemy.

The act of cannibalism as described by the Jesuits was perpetrated predominantly by men and represented an important facet of how the Jesuits perceived Iroquois savage masculinity. Iroquois warriors killed and consumed their enemies in part to frighten them into submission, but also in order to assert masculine dominance and to emasculate their enemies. The importance of bravery and valor on the scaffold was necessary for the exchange of power, which was at the center of the mourning war and its rituals. Male captives were expected to brave the tortures without showing signs of weakness, which to the Jesuits meant effeminacy. In 1647 Jesuit superior Jerome Lalemant recorded the experience of Isaac Jogues in which his masculinity was called into question. Jogues was unable to hold back his tears at the treatment of "that worthy and valiant Christian Eustache," who received worse treatment than other captives. On seeing Jogues's tears, Eustache cautioned him against showing weakness for fear that the Iroquois "should regard him as effeminate." Eustache then spoke to his tormenters: "Do not suppose that those tears proceed from weakness; it is the love and affection that he feels for me, and not the want of courage, that forces them from his eyes. He has never wept in his own torments; his face has always appeared dry, and always cheerful. Your rage, and my pains, and his own love are the theme and the cause of his tears."[76] The Huron captive Eustache went to great lengths to assure the Iroquois that Jogues was not crying like a woman, that his tears were an acceptable presentation of masculinity.[77] Jogues displayed the measured combination of emotion and physical strength that Ignatius of Loyola modeled a century earlier. Since the Jesuits did not come with swords and guns, they had to prove their masculine dominance over their subjects in a different way from the conquistadors. Thus they linked Iroquois masculinity with the acts of torture and cannibalization that they committed. By suffering through the horrors that the Iroquois inflicted upon them, the Jesuit priests were able to fashion themselves as spiritual warriors.

The participation of women in practices such as cannibalism was perceived as singularly aberrant and presented a unique kind of anxiety for European men. The fear of the powerful woman who would quite literally consume men with her lust was a terrifying prospect for early explorers of the Americas. The Jesuit missionaries of New France, however, had a different focus when it came to Indigenous sexuality. The competing impulses of desire and repulsion so evident in the writings of men like Cortés, Columbus, and Vespucci were far less common in the works of celibate Jesuit priests. Catholic missionaries were deeply concerned with policing Native sexuality and eroding women's power and self-determination. In fact they found women more difficult than men to convert. They consistently remarked on the vehemence of women's refusal to accept their ideas.[78] In Jesuit discourse women were obstinate, lewd, lascivious, untrustworthy, and unchaste, but they were not likely to be anthropophagi.

There are only a few examples in *The Jesuit Relations* in which women are reported to be the specific victims of cannibalism. (In many instances the gender of the victim is not clear.) In one case a young woman escaped the kettle and was not actually killed. What is perhaps most interesting about her story is that it is the only occurrence of nonstarvation endocannibalism among the Iroquois in these records. In the village of Oiogoen, a man dreamed that he gave a feast of human flesh; He then invited the local chiefs to his cabin and asked them to guess his dream.[79] Finally, after many speculations, one man guessed correctly. This man then offered his brother for sacrifice and placed him in the dreamer's hands "to be cut up on the spot, and put in the kettle." The chiefs were frightened by this turn of events, until the dreamer told them that it was a woman that needed to be sacrificed. This caused the people of the village great anxiety, but they believed that they had to follow through with the dreamer's predictions. They adorned an unsuspecting young girl with riches and led her to the place of sacrifice: "All the people attended to witness so strange a spectacle. The guests took their places, and the public victim was led into the middle of the circle. She was delivered to the Sacrificer, who was the very one for whom the sacrifice was to be made. He took her; they watched his actions, and pitied that innocent girl; but, when they thought him about to deal her the death-blow, he cried out: 'I am satisfied; my dream requires nothing further.' Is it not a great charity to open the eyes of a people so grossly in error?"[80] This passage makes it clear that the Jesuits believed the act of consuming a member of the tribe was almost unheard of among the Iroquois. Whether or not the episode was more disturbing to the Iroquois because the potential victim was a woman cannot be determined, but it clearly caused the Jesuits more anxiety. In the descriptions of Carib cannibalism in chapter 2, the role that women played in acts of cannibalism was emphasized. However, this was not the case in Jesuit writing. The

Jesuits did not claim dominion over their lands and resources, and, as such, the existence of female cannibals could not be easily mobilized in discourse to justify their actions.

In November 1668 Father Étienne de Carheil journeyed to the mission of St. Joseph in Oiogouen. A slave woman from a village called Andastogué accompanied him part of the way. During their two days together, Father Carheil taught the young woman about Christianity. Upon their arrival the unfortunate woman was "offered to Heaven, as first-fruits of his labors." She was baptized before being "burned and eaten by those barbarians, on the sixth of November." Despite her death, her time with the priest was apparently well spent as "this journey that they made together was put to use by him in making her enter on the road to Paradise."[81] The lack of compassion for the fate of this woman is obvious, for her conversion had assured her a place in Heaven and her death brought her salvation, offering no impediment to the priests as they prepared their mission. In both the Caribbean and Mexico, where accusations of cannibalism were used as a justification for conquest, the presence of cannibalism was also cause for hesitation, but this was not the case among the Jesuits. While they believed that they had to get rid of cannibalism in order for Indians to be fully civilized, they also showed less fear of being cannibalized. They desired martyrdom and did not see cannibalism as an impediment to their efforts to the same degree.

Despite the Iroquois' perceived propensity for cruelty, the Jesuits do not record any sexual violence toward female prisoners. The connections between sodomy, cannibalism, and castration seen in other contexts do not exist in the Jesuit records. However, there are a few examples of implicit discursive links between sex and cannibalism. For example, one young woman who had escaped the Iroquois related her observations of a cannibal feast. As she approached the village of Onon-ïoté with her captors, she overheard them talking around a bonfire they had made from her countrymen. She feared what they were going to do to her, and the conversation that she heard gave her little comfort: "She had also heard, at her departure, some young men, who, not supposing that she understood their language, were asking one another which part of the body they would find the most dainty. One of them, looking at her, answered that the feet roasted under the ashes were very good."[82] Although their language is not explicitly sexual, the young woman was greatly disturbed that her body was symbolically violated. For the members of the Society of Jesus who sought to teach Indians about the importance of chastity and self-restraint, this incident highlights the dangers posed by Iroquoian savagery. The act of cannibalism, especially the consumption of a woman, was a violation of the purity of the body. Thus while most Jesuit representations of cannibalism focus on masculinity and the warrior, the incidents involving women were particularly troubling to the writers.

Another description of the cannibalization of a woman by the Iroquois comes from the account of Jean de Lamberville in 1682. Two female prisoners from Maryland were tortured, killed, and consumed after being afforded religious instruction by the Jesuits, who had not attempted to stop their cannibalization. In the same letter Lamberville describes the cruelty of the Iroquois. He records that they had brought seven hundred Illinois captives back from battle; they had also killed and eaten "over 600 others on the spot." Those children who were old enough to survive without their mother's breast milk were kept alive, but "the others were cruelly roasted and devoured." Furthermore, Lamberville says, "they tied living men and women to the stakes, and, as fast as their flesh became roasted, they cut it off, and ate it."[83] This is likely a gross exaggeration for it would take an enormous number of people to eat six hundred humans, but as a discursive example in the *Relations*, it effectively demonstrated the depths of Iroquois depravity to an astonished French audience.[84] It seems unlikely that the Iroquois would have killed and consumed a large number of women of childbearing age, as typically these women would have made up the majority of those the Iroquois took back with them. Since they most often chose to adopt women and children, it is reasonable to assume that if this event happened at all, the women were likely a small minority of the victims cannibalized that day.

Jesuit missionaries argued that acts of cannibalism were linked to success in battle, indicating a direct connection between masculinity and man-eating. In addition to valuing the flesh of the bravest captives most highly, cannibalism and masculine prowess were connected in other ways. For example, after requesting to be baptized, an old Iroquois man recounted an interesting story to a Jesuit. He recalled that in his youth, after fasting in preparation for a ritual, he experienced a dream apparition in which a man came down from the sky. This sky-man assured the dreamer that he would take care of him and guaranteed him success in life. Then "he held out to him, a piece of human flesh, quite raw. The youth in horror turned away his head. 'Eat this,' said the old man, presenting him with a piece of bear's fat."

The young man ate the bear meat and the sky-man departed. As the years went on, all of the predictions made by the sky-man came true; the Iroquois dreamer had great successes in hunting and a prolific family. "He attributes this excellent fortune that he has always had in the chase, to the piece of bear's fat that the Demon made him eat; and he judges from this that he would have achieved equal success in war, had he eaten the piece of human flesh that he refused."[85] In this example the consumption of human flesh was clearly linked to the prowess of a warrior. Consuming flesh literally gave men the ability to succeed in battle.

*The Jesuit Relations* reveal a great deal about European perceptions of the practice of cannibalism among the Iroquois. Despite the Jesuits' attempt to view Indian practices on their own terms, cannibalism was a cultural practice of which they struggled to make sense. Rather than relying on simple observation and objective determination, Jesuit missionaries fell back on earlier tropes of animality when speaking about the practices of torture and cannibalism. They compared the Iroquois to animals, demonstrating the tension between their belief that Indians were flawed yet redeemable humans. The Jesuits faced conflicting understandings of the nature of Indians: they were both generous and unimaginably cruel. The missionaries' negotiation between their ethnographic observations and their beliefs about human nature is evident in their descriptions of the inhuman actions of the Iroquois. They expertly balanced rich descriptions of Indian life and New World landscapes with inspirational tales of conversion and martyrdom. Detailed descriptions of cannibalism in the *Relations* served to reinforce the necessity of the Jesuit presence in Canada, just as they indicated the difficulty of the work among the Indians. Reports of the horrors faced by missionaries enabled them to gain support for the cause from within the constraints of French imperial interests, and they drew some priests to the New World with the promise of martyrdom. Descriptions of cannibalism demonstrated how the Jesuits negotiated their masculinity and constructed themselves as warriors for God. Since they did not go to New France armed with guns or swords, they engaged with Iroquois warriors on the scaffold and not the battlefield. Through their torture, sacrifice, and cannibalization the Jesuits proved that even as celibate clergy, they could still compete as men.

# 5 /    Living with Cannibals: Englishmen and the Wilderness

In 1729 Jonathan Swift anonymously published his now famous work, *A Modest Proposal for Preventing the Children of Poor People From being a Burthen to their Parents or the Country, and for making them Beneficial to the Publick*, in response to the growing deprivation and desperation of the Irish. In this satirical essay Swift suggests that the Irish eat poor children as a way to solve both population problems and hunger. Swift was quite aware of the tropes of cannibalism and the tendency to denigrate peoples and cultures through anthropophagous accusations. He insists that he learned about the supposed deliciousness of young children from "a very knowing *American*" acquaintance, underscoring the connection between the Americas and cannibalism. He proposes not simply to consume poor children but also to regulate procreation and breed humans for food; of the roughly 120,000 poor children, twenty thousand were to be set aside as breeders. Swift argues that only one fourth of the breeders need to be male, "which is more than we allow to sheep, black cattle, or swine, and my reason is, that these children are seldom the fruits of marriage, a circumstance not much regarded by our savages, therefore, one male will be sufficient to serve four females."[1] While Swift is not accusing poor Irish of being cannibals, he does satirically indict them for their sexual improprieties and links them to animals. Thus even as it uses cannibalism to satirize eighteenth-century society, *A Modest Proposal* deftly demonstrates the pervasiveness of the discursive connections between cannibalism, savagery, sexuality, and animality.

While the preceding chapters interrogated cannibalism in the discourses of exploration, conquest, and conversion, this chapter explores the relationship between cannibalism and settlement in the English overseas empire in North America. The British Empire differed in many ways from earlier French, Spanish, and Portuguese models, as did the discourse of cannibalism that was established in English texts. One important divergence is in the number of references to Indigenous cannibalism, as English sources contain far fewer descriptions of Native American anthropophagy. Interestingly among these limited references are a striking number of accounts of European individuals engaged in anthropophagous acts. There are also several accounts written by women, which are exceedingly rare in other imperial contexts.

In this chapter I uncover how English understandings of cannibalism served to support the development of an emerging frontier masculinity that defined itself through contact with, immersion in, and victory over savagery. While firmly entrenched in early modern notions of difference, in which Europeans believed themselves to be innately superior to Native Americans, the accounts of cannibalism in British writings from Jamestown to the Seven Years War reveal that Englishmen also expressed their superiority in relation to their European competitors in the New World. Cannibalism in many English accounts served as a metaphor through which colonists articulated their authority over the lands and peoples of North America. The nature of English imperialism and cultural beliefs about gender and hierarchies of humanity enabled English men to develop a uniquely American masculinity, which would see its full expression in the frontier heroes of the nineteenth century. In these texts cannibalism served as a counterpoint to masculinity because the reckless savagery that English writers saw in Indian anthropophagites contradicted the measured manliness expressed by Englishmen. Additionally contact with and triumph over cannibalism were both essential in establishing the supremacy of English civilization. Not only did English settlers articulate their encounters with Native peoples in decidedly gendered terms, typically representing Natives in terms of feminine weakness, but these gendered relationships also affected the imposition of imperial power in North America and helped to shape the nature of English expansion in Atlantic North America.

## English Patterns

Earlier Spanish accounts of cannibalism stressed the stark dichotomy between the civilized and the savage, which translated most commonly into a racialized (in that these ideas would eventually come to be defined in terms of race) dynamic in which Europeans were "civilized" and Native Americans (and Africans) were "savage" and inferior. While this dynamic was still at play in English texts, the representative dichotomy between Indian savage Otherness and European civilization changed slightly. This change is particularly evident in narratives of captivity among the Indians. Rather than simply underpinning the cultural divide between the European and the Indian, English writers emphasized the superiority of the English over all others. During the Seven Years War accusations of cannibalism were lodged against Indians as well as Frenchmen; this reinforced English cultural superiority and their claim to the North Atlantic coast, both of which helped to define a new kind of Anglo-American masculinity. The French were accused of being nearly as savage and bloodthirsty as their Indian allies, and in some cases pious English settlers believed Catholicism itself to be cannibalistic.[2] Thus the settler dynamic created a new paradigm of cannibal discourse that reinforced English supremacy. Because English settlers were faced with a set of circumstances in which they were competing for dominance among not only a variety of bellicose Indian tribes but other European empires as well, cannibalism functioned as a rhetorical strategy for establishing an Anglo-American identity. In the case of Englishmen driven to desperate acts of human consumption, the records of their cannibalism simultaneously assert their dominance over the land by demonstrating the lengths they will go to ensure their success in the New World and reinforce a developing Anglo-American masculine ideal that emphasized strength, sacrifice, and piety.

There are several possible reasons why English records mention acts of cannibalism less often than other records. First, large-scale English efforts of conquest and colonization in North America tended to begin later than Spanish expansion: in the seventeenth rather than the sixteenth century.[3] By the seventeenth century millions of Native Americans were dead from foreign microbes, resulting in incalculable disruptions of cultural patterns and traditions. It is also possible that the Native people the English encountered were not anthropophagous.

The years that elapsed since Columbus's initial encounter with the peoples of the Americas allowed both groups to become more familiar with one another. Europeans learned about the New World, just as Native peoples learned about Europeans, through trade and physical encounters. This greater awareness of one another was not always beneficial for Indians, however. Longer exposure to Native peoples did little to change many of the stereotypes that Europeans believed about them. The time that elapsed allowed for discursive tropes to take hold and further cemented the idea that Indians were savage. In other words, because of the circulation of stories in Europe that were filled with sensationalized depictions of savage, cannibalistic Indians, visitors to the Americas fully anticipated Indian savagery. These assumptions shaped the way encounters unfolded and enabled English settlers to prefigure their expectations of their Indian neighbors. The knowledge Indians gained about European visitors helped them to interact in ways that were more effective. Whereas the Arawaks might have believed that Columbus and his men were gods (although this is certainly debatable), no one welcomed Christopher Newport to Virginia with such adulation. Groups of Natives in the interior of North America were familiar with Europeans and their goods well before they ever met them. This familiarity allowed for the interaction between these groups to be more carefully crafted and enabled European observations of Indian life to be far less exaggerated and fantastical. English settlers did not record that they saw mermaids, Cynocephali, or Cyclopes in North America. The fantastical elements that permeated the earliest accounts of cannibalism in the New World were not substantively present in seventeenth- and eighteenth-century English texts. The passage of time also allowed English settlers to familiarize themselves with the New World by reading published accounts, making the idea of cannibalistic Indians in the Americas more deeply entrenched.

Englishmen were not the only Europeans competing for dominance in seventeenth-century North America. The presence of French and Dutch settlers, missionaries, and soldiers also provided Native peoples with the opportunity to engage in diplomacy and negotiation to impact the balance of power. Despite all of this, one of the most important effects of the passage of time was the ravages of disease on Native communities. The massive depopulation and social reorganization brought about by European diseases played a significant role in altering earlier Indigenous power relationships and caused rapid changes to Native societies.[4]

It is not as easy as it might initially appear to determine whether Native North American groups actually practiced cannibalism. As we have seen, descriptions of cannibalism were always about power, and there is not a simple correlation between textual evidence and practice. Accusations of cannibalism did not necessarily reflect the actual practices of Indigenous peoples. Furthermore it is nearly impossible to determine to what degree cannibalism was employed as a denigrating rhetorical strategy without concern for actual practice. For example, although both French and English sources contain references to the practice of cannibalism among Iroquoian peoples, the English sources do not exhibit the same preoccupation with this practice that Jesuit writings do. Therefore there is more to the dearth of references to cannibalism than merely differences among Indian groups. Additionally English authors did not always provide enough information to determine the tribe to which a particular anthropophagic individual belonged, as their interests in the New World did not always necessitate a keen understanding of tribal differences. The sources about cannibalism that are discussed in the following pages tend to present a homogenized view of Indians, and authors were not careful in distinguishing one group from another. Thus it became easy for English captives, for example, to assume automatically that their captors were cannibals, whether or not they had any evidence for this. Generally English writers present Native peoples as undifferentiated Others who are simply an impediment to expansion and success, which contrasts with the discourses discussed in earlier chapters.[5]

English colonists took cues from earlier published documents; they learned tactics for survival in the Americas from these texts, but they also inherited certain legacies of stereotypes.[6] Because of this English writers often based their assessments of Native groups on empirical observation as well as prior knowledge obtained from different imperial contexts. Most English settlers in the New World were familiar with the accusations of cannibalism lodged against Native Americans by earlier writers. By the late sixteenth and early seventeenth century educated Englishmen had ready access to scores of tales of New World cannibals, and because of this many English writers presumed the existence of cannibals without needing to prove it. For example, in his account of his voyages to New England in 1638 and 1663, John Josselyn writes that he obtained information about Indian cannibalism from Spanish accounts.[7] He believed the Spanish stories about the practices of cannibalism in the Americas, but he understood these practices in relation to other English ideas about alterity.[8] He believed Indians to be "of disposition very inconstant, crafty, timorous, quick of apprehension, and very ingenious, soon angry, and so malicious that they seldom forget an injury, and barbarously cruel." He thought that they were prone to violence, melancholy, thievery, and lechery. Additionally he reports, "Both Men and Women [are] guilty of Misoxenie or hatred to strangers, a quality appropriated to the old Brittains, all of them Cannibals, eaters of human flesh. And so were formerly the Heathen-*Irish*, who used to feed upon the Buttocks of Boyes and Women Paps; it seems it is natural to Savage people so to do."[9] Josselyn's statements are quite revealing regarding the intellectual legacies of cannibalism that seventeenth- and early eighteenth-century Englishmen inherited. Not only did he read about cannibalism in Spanish accounts, but he took them to be true. Furthermore he equated New World cannibals with the Celtic inhabitants of early Britain. The English conquest of Ireland was a precursor to conquest in the Americas, and men like Sir Walter Raleigh gained knowledge about how to proceed with settlement in the New World through trial and error.[10] English descriptions of the Irish and their perceived savagery parallel the descriptions of Native Americans. Interestingly Josselyn also hints at a connection between sexuality and cannibalism. In his example of ancient Irish anthropophagy, it was the buttocks of boys and the breasts of women that were consumed. Thus the cannibalization of individuals was itself a sexual act of incorporation. The consumption of the buttocks of boys could also be seen as a subtle reference to sodomy, which, as I discussed in chapter 3, was another common denigrating strategy employed in conjunction with accusations of cannibalism.

Tales of Indian cannibalism had been in circulation for quite some time. Therefore, at least discursively, cannibalism continued to be an important force in shaping imperial attitudes toward Native people, as well as the quotidian interactions of settlers in North America, even if it did not function as a primary catalyst for expansion, conquest, or conversion by this time. English writings took the presence of cannibalism for granted and did not always heed the burden of truth.

English colonists tended to assume that American lands already belonged to them, so it was their duty to occupy North America, in spite of the people who lived there, not because of them.[11] By the eighteenth century the practice of cannibalism was not a primary justification for English settlement in the New World. Nor was the desire to convert the heathen Indians to Christianity the most important driving force behind English colonization of North America.[12] Rather, especially in the case of the Puritans in New England, colonists assumed that the land was rightfully theirs because they would make proper use of it. Therefore it is important to consider the particular goals of North American English colonization (which were shaped by the lands and peoples they encountered) when determining the place of cannibalism in their accounts. There is little doubt that the English would have loved to find another Tenochtitlan. Early English entrepreneurs like Raleigh were quite interested in establishing an Indigenous labor force and exploiting the natural resources of their lands, much like the Spanish. Unfortunately for them the vast majority of the lands that they were able to acquire did not contain the necessary ingredients to create another New Spain.[13] The enormous profits obtained from the slave labor and sugar production of the Caribbean colonies rendered mainland North America a virtual frontier, whose European settlers were more often than not outcasts in their home country. Americans tend to assume that Jamestown was established for farming and plantations, and while this is not wholly untrue, it is clear that the Jamestown patriarchs were ill prepared for farming life and were preoccupied partly by the search for riches.[14] John Smith devoted a significant amount of space in his writings to the search for gold. Even as he tried to convince others of the viability of the planter colony, he nonetheless dangled the temptation of vast riches below the surface.[15]

The English were not uninterested in the presence of Native peoples, but unlike the Spanish, they were never able to place themselves within local power structures and form a more cooperative (but still quite unequal and exploitative) system.[16] Once the fabled riches failed to appear in Virginia, the focus quickly shifted to planting. In 1588 Thomas Hariot traveled to Virginia and wrote a popular account of life in the New World that was meant to correct the slanderous reports of others.[17] His text emphasizes the potential for agriculture, and he devotes much of the work to describing the different types of plants and natural resources to be found in Virginia. His descriptions of the Indians are generally quite favorable, as his work was meant to entice new settlers and investors. He makes no mention of Indian cannibalism or sacrifice but instead focuses on their potential to be civilized and brought under submission.[18] Hariot's words were published with a series of engravings by Theodore de Bry that were based on the drawings and watercolors of John White and detailed Indian life in

Virginia.[19] Together Hariot's text and the images of De Bry present Virginia as a relatively unspoiled landscape ripe for English intervention. Unlike the descriptions of the Caribs or the Mexica written by early explorers to inspire Spanish intervention by describing the horrors of Indian practices and the necessity of civilized intervention, Hariot's account of Virginia tries to catalyze settlement by describing an idyllic landscape inhabited by tractable people.

In their northern settlements, such as Plymouth, the English were set to establish more self-sufficient and independent colonies that were distinct from their homeland.[20] The Plymouth settlers certainly received help from the Natives, but they were less interested in incorporating them into their society, even in a subordinate role, than were the Spanish. It seems New Englanders would have simply preferred the Indians to move out of their way.[21] The Puritans of the Massachusetts Bay Colony brought with them a philosophy epitomized by John Winthrop's famous pronouncement that Puritans should create a "city upon a hill," a shining example of industriousness, piety, and virtue for the entire world to see. Strict rules were imposed, especially regarding women's sexuality, and fraternization with Indians was discouraged.[22] They came to the New World bearing with them an understanding of their own perfection and preeminence in the eyes of God, which could not easily be taught. While *métis* and *mestizo* individuals played important roles as mediators, translators, and local leaders in New France and New Spain, this was not as much the case in the English colonies on the mainland of North America, where such hybridization was discouraged.[23]

English views about physical and biological differences in this period are complex, but typically English writers believed that variations in skin color were due to the biblical curse of Ham or climatic differences.[24] Implicit in their understandings of racialized difference was the assumption of the superiority of white skin over darker skin. Josselyn, for example, believed that underneath an external darker skin lay an uncorrupted layer that resembled European skin.[25] Given this belief, all humans could become civilized once the corruption and its physical markers were removed. However, skin color was not the primary determinant of acceptance into proper society; civility played a much larger role in English views on Native peoples, for an individual's actions and behaviors were of equal importance. The only appropriate sexual and marriage partners were those who were comparably civilized.[26]

In *American Pentimento* Patricia Seed argues that both the English settlers and the Spanish colonists distinguished themselves from the Indians they encountered by establishing their superiority through a hierarchical understanding of humanity (the Great Chain of Being). Each possessed an understanding of Indians as not fully human.[27] This did not necessarily mean that Indians were perceived as fully inhuman; rather behaviors, norms, and practices determined one's access to the benefits of the highest levels of humanity. Indeed Indians were *human*, but they were not acceptable humans. For the Spaniards one's moral worth as a human being was determined by religion. In order to access God's grace and therefore the proper form of human existence, one had to be Catholic. For Englishmen, however, the defining characteristic of humanity, according to Seed, was labor. Only through farming and hard work could one become a "real" human, so access to the land was of preeminent importance. Just as God placed minerals under the surface for deserving Spaniards, God created arable land upon which Englishmen could toil. Seed argues that these two fundamental ideas shaped the ways Englishmen and Spaniards interacted with the Native peoples of the Americas. In turn both empires developed discursive tropes through which they most commonly represented and understood the Indian Other. She explains that the idea of the cannibal was an ideological construct for the Spanish against which they defined themselves. Through their understanding of Indians as cannibals, they justified their conquest and their desire for the exploitation of Indian labor.

Englishmen, according to Seed, defined themselves in relation to the trope of the Indian as hunter. Hunting in England was a privilege of the rich, and owning a vast hunting preserve was an important rite of passage for English aristocrats. Respectable hunting was not for subsistence but for sport. Those who needed to hunt to survive were denied access by the creation of private preserves and the elimination of public lands. The noblemen who first went to the Americas understood hunting to be something other than work. Despite the fact that under English law Indian hunting grounds would have rightfully belonged to the Indians, Englishmen represented Indian hunting as characteristic of lazy, nomadic individuals who did not understand the importance of proper labor.[28]

Seed argues that the processes of English and Spanish imperialism in the Americas were profoundly shaped by these two general understandings of the Indian Other. Both of these stereotypes, the cannibal and the hunter, were intensely gendered ideas. Whereas Spanish ideas about New World cannibalism indicated their particular preoccupation with bellicose masculinity and Indian sexuality, the English were more preoccupied with the natural world, and hunting in particular. Indigenous hunting practices, according to Seed, challenged English conventions of both class and gender. Among Indian groups of the North American Atlantic coast, hunting was almost exclusively a male practice, which meant that farming was predominantly the realm of women. Since Englishmen valued farming and one's relationship to the soil most prominently, it greatly disturbed their sense of order to see women performing these tasks.[29] While Seed makes a convincing argument about the importance of the idea of the hunter to the British Empire in the seventeenth and eighteenth century, her assumption might lead one to the conclusion that the cannibal was not important in English expansion in the Americas. But even if the discourse of cannibalism was not an obvious catalyst for English imperialism, it nonetheless played an important role in developing notions of race and gender in North America. An investigation of cannibalism in English discourse about continental North America reveals that such discourse was used to create and reinforce Anglo-American masculinity.

## Cannibal Colonists

In sixteenth- and early seventeenth-century English writings about settlement in North America there are comparatively few references to Indigenous cannibalism. In the large collection by John Smith, for example, the members of the Powhatan confederacy are never directly accused of cannibalism. Smith's writings do reveal that the early years of the Virginia colony were largely a disastrous failure. There were too many gentlemen among the first group of Jamestown settlers who expected someone else to labor for them. They anticipated receiving tribute from the Indians, just as Powhatan appeared to receive tribute from surrounding groups, and they expected to insert themselves into this hierarchical system at the top. Unlike during the Spanish conquest of Mexico, however, the Chesapeake Indians were not so readily disposed to substitute their old master for a new one. The Spanish model of conquest and colonization was unsuited for Virginia.

Smith wrote the most famous record of early Jamestown, but he was actually in Virginia only for part of the time that he described.

He filled in the details of events that occurred in his absence with the help of eyewitnesses, but he nonetheless wrote about these events as if he were there. During one of his absences the colonists faced a period of extreme deprivation. Smith describes a dire situation in which they had run out of food and begun trading everything they had to "the Salvages, whose cruell fingers were so oft imbrewed in our blouds, that what by their crueltie, our Governours indiscretion, and the losse of our ships, of five hundred within six moneths after Captaine Smiths departure, there remained not past sixtie men, women and children, most miserable and poore creatures."[30] Smith attributes the colonists' misfortunes in part to his own absence and the cruelty of the Indians (whose bloodlust apparently required no provocation) but primarily to the ineptitude of the governors of Jamestown. He does not blame their situation on the quality of the soil but on English failures and Indian machinations. Although he does not directly accuse the Indians of being man-eaters, the language he employs ("cruell fingers," "imbrewed with our blouds") reinforces their savagery. His descriptions of their cruelty are visceral, making use of a variety of bodily metaphors, but stop short of actually accusing them of anthropophagy.

This time of starvation occurred just two years after the founding of the colony, during the winter of 1609–10. By the time the cold receded, only sixty colonists in Jamestown still lived. The reasons for this period of extreme deprivation are still a matter of debate, but things were so desperate that by the time the resupply ships finally arrived on June 9, the remaining colonists were already sailing down the James River, prepared to abandon their settlement.[31] The archaeological evidence indicates that the colonists faced extreme circumstances and that they consumed cats, dogs, horses, and rats. The textual evidence suggests that some of the colonists went so far as to eat one another. A recent forensic investigation uncovered the telltale cut marks of butchering on the bones of a fourteen-year-old girl, leading the research team to conclude that cannibalism among the English settlers at Jamestown is fact, not fiction.[32]

While all forms of available evidence indicate the presence of cannibalism, the details of what may have happened do not match neatly. In the five accounts of the "starving time" from the first quarter of the seventeenth century, not one mentions the consumption of a fourteen-year-old girl. In fact they disagree with one another on other points as well.[33] Smith describes the deplorable situation as follows: "Nay, so great was our famine, that a savage we slew and buried, the poorer sort took him up again and ate him; and so did diverse one another boiled and stewed with roots and herbs: And one among the rest did kill his wife, powdered [salted] her, and had eaten part of her before it was known; for which he was executed, as he well deserved: now whether she was better roasted, boiled or carbonadoed [broiled], I know not; but of such a dish as powdered wife I never heard of."[34] Two different acts of anthropophagy are described here. First, the starving colonists dug up the recently buried corpse of an Indian man and ate him. It is probable that the colonists caused the death of the unfortunate Indian but unlikely that they killed him only with the intent to consume his body or they would not have bothered burying him in the first place. Their act of cannibalism was an innovative act of survival, not a premeditated crime. The man who killed his wife, on the other hand, did so in order to consume her. As soon as she was dead the murderer began preparing her body for consumption by salting it. This, according to Smith, was unforgivable. Despite the seriousness of the situation, the passage ends with a joke, making light of the act of anthropophagy and the death of the nameless wife.

Following Smith, the most familiar account is that of George Percy, who wrote in response to the blame Smith assigned him for his poor management of the colony. Unlike Smith, Percy was actually present during the "starving time." He begins his account by relating the terrible circumstances that other European conquerors and settlers faced in the Americas. He even reports that some Spanish settlers in far southern South America mutinied against their commander because of the horrific starvation conditions they faced. The mutineers were hanged, but some of the desperate men cut down their corpses in the night and consumed them.[35] Percy places the actions of the Virginia colonists within a larger context in an attempt to lessen the weight of judgment. If extreme deprivation was simply part of the colonial experience, something that happened even in the wealthiest, most powerful overseas empires, then their actions might seem less deplorable. Describing the events at Jamestown, he says that the colonists were forced

> to do those things which seem incredible as to dig up dead corpses out of graves and to eat them, and some have licked up the blood which has fallen from their weak fellows. And among the rest this was most lamentable, that one of our colony murdered his wife,

ripped the child out of her womb and threw it into the river, and after chopped the mother in pieces and salted her for his food. The same not being discovered before he had eaten part thereof, for the which cruel and inhumane fact I ajudged him to be executed, the acknowledgement of the deed being enforced from him by torture.[36]

Since Percy was the president of the colony during this time, although he was ill and delegated almost all of his duties, he is quick to point out that the perpetrators were punished and insists that the conditions were unavoidable and that the most horrific acts were confined to one individual. One might wonder why the murderous man would have thrown the baby away instead of eating it if he acted out of madness from starvation. But as to their descriptions of cannibalism, Percy's and Smith's accounts are fairly consistent with one another.

Thomas Gates's account was the first to refute the tale of cannibalism. Given that his text influenced Shakespeare in the writing of *The Tempest* we can reasonably conclude that the tale of cannibalism at Jamestown had spread quickly. Gates argued that the man who reportedly killed and ate his wife was, in fact, simply a murderer who disarticulated his wife's corpse to hide his crime and that an investigation of his house turned up significant stores of food. He blamed the rumors of cannibalism on the colonists who abandoned Jamestown in the summer of 1610. He believed that they intended to become pirates and invented the story of their deprivation to hide their crimes. Gates swore that he took depositions from a supply ship captain who claimed that when he left the colony just before winter in 1609 they had three months' worth of food and sufficient cattle, making starvation virtually impossible.[37] Two other sources, composed by the Virginia Assembly and William Strachey, were both written later and were intended to defend the actions of the colonists; thus both mention the cannibalism, but merely as evidence of the desperate and unavoidable position the colonists faced.[38]

Even though there is significant disagreement between the various textual accounts and the forensic evidence, the one thing they all have in common is that each describes the consumption of a woman's body. English women were scarce in early Jamestown, yet it was a woman that was most likely sacrificed and eaten during the period of starvation. Indeed while the forensic evidence of the consumption of the fourteen-year-old girl likely represents a separate incident from that of the woman killed by her husband, each event involves the death and probable consumption of a woman. As in life, women performed the role of life-giving nurturer and provider. In each of the two acts of cannibalism recorded by Smith, the dominant white male consumed the body of a presumed inferior: an Indian and a woman. Through their deaths and cannibalization, the Indian and the nameless wife supported the power of the Jamestown patriarchs' ambitions. Their consumption reinforced their inferiority. For English men to consume other English men was nearly unthinkable (but not impossible).

## Captives and Cannibals

The vast majority of references to North American cannibalism in English writings occur in eighteenth-century captivity narratives (only a small number were published in the late seventeenth century), most of which detail the experiences of captives in the Northern Atlantic region and the Great Lakes. There was a significant increase in the number of accounts during the French and Indian War. Captivity narratives of this period tend to fall into two camps: those written by Puritans and those composed by soldiers. They differ in a number of ways, especially regarding to whom the authors give credit for their redemption. Puritan writers emphasized divine providence and reserved their harshest judgments for the character of Indians. The later narratives of soldiers were more likely to recognize personal cunning and individual effort as keys to their redemption rather than assigning all glory to God. These soldiers also pondered the relationship between the settler and the wilderness, positioning themselves as a part of the landscape rather than struggling against its maddening and corrupting influences like earlier captives.[39] Often soldiers published their accounts with profit in mind, not extolling the glories of God.[40]

Captivity narratives provide a fertile field of investigation not only because of their pervasiveness but also because they contain consistent themes and experiences. For example, a great number of captivity narratives open with a scene of colonial domestic tranquility that is suddenly disrupted by an unprompted Indian attack, destroying buildings and breaking up families. In almost every captivity narrative the author endures long periods of starvation and grueling marches through unfamiliar wilderness. Finally most narratives contain a tale of redemption and the restoration of domesticity.

Published in Philadelphia in 1699, Jonathan Dickinson's narrative of his captivity among several different groups of Indians in Florida is a lurid tale of shipwreck, kidnapping, and redemption and one of the earlier captivity accounts. While it is atypical in some ways, it contains themes that appear in other writings of this genre, including cannibalism. Dickinson interlaces elements of the captivity narrative with a tale of rescue infused with Quaker religious sentiment. In 1696 Dickinson left his wealthy plantation in Jamaica to move to Philadelphia with his family. The ship on which they were traveling wrecked on Jupiter Island, on the eastern shore of Florida, and soon they were discovered by the Jaega Indians of the nearby town of Jobe. On board the ship was a motley group of sailors, slaves, and other passengers, including the Dickinsons' kinsman Benjamin Allen and the prominent Quaker elder Robert Barrow. The majority of the drama unfolds on their journey north toward redemption at the hands of the Spanish at St. Augustine. Rather than captors, the Indians seem to play the role of hostile escort.

Right from the start Dickinson makes his views on Native Americans quite clear. His preface is full of references to their "fury," "savagery," and "cruelty." He also emphasizes their status as cannibals: "Yet are these *Man-eaters* as cowardly as cruel." Referring to Barrow, he notes, "He was *more than a Conqueror* over those bloodthirsty *Canibals.*" Barrow's virtue and piety are important features of the narrative, as he provides the voice of godly reason and confidence. Dickinson records Barrow's words of wisdom and advice: "*That he desired of the Lord, that he might not dye by the hands of those* Barbarians; *For* (said he) *They thirsted, or longed as much after our flesh, as ever I did after Victualls.*" In the preface Dickinson establishes not only his ignorance of Native practices and beliefs but, more important, his stubborn refusal to understand more. Before being shipwrecked in Florida, Dickinson already knew that it was populated by ferocious man-eating Indians; he confirms this by observing, "Their Countenance was very Furious and Bloody."[41] He needed no other evidence than a visual affirmation of their barbarity.

Dickinson's account was given the sensationalized title *Gods protecting providence, man's surest help and defence in the times Of the greatest difficulty and most Imminent danger; Evidenced in the Remarkable Deliverance Of divers Persons, From the devouring Waves of the Sea, amongst which they Suffered Shipwrack And also From the more cruelly devouring jawes of the inhumane Canibals of Florida.*

FIGURE 5.1 "Native Americans threaten Europeans." Engraving. In *Naaukeurige versameling der geden-waardigste zee en land-reysen na Oost en West Indië . . .* (Leiden, 1707). This image shows Native Americans threatening a group of castaways, including Jonathan Dickinson, after their ship wrecked off the coast southeast Florida. (Courtesy of the John Carter Brown Library at Brown University.)

*Faithfully related by one of the persons concerned therein; Jonathan Dickenson.* Despite its provocative title, which was likely the creation of the publisher, not the author, no act of cannibalism actually occurs in the narrative. On their journey to St. Augustine, Dickinson and his group were quartered in a town where the Spaniards informed them that not twelve months earlier a group of Dutch were cast upon those shores "and were here devoured by these *Cannaballs.*" Despite this one vague reference to an occurrence of cannibalism, Dickinson weaves accusations of it throughout his narrative. Even when not directly mentioning anthropophagy, he litters his account with metaphors of consumption. Although he often excludes himself from feeling fear when he describes the acts of the Indians (though he does not hesitate to say that others were afraid), he mentions that they quite often worried that the Indians would eat them. Dickinson is consistently mistrustful of these "cannibal" Indians. At one point his captors go fishing, and despite the fact that this might have meant a full meal for the captives, he remarks, "But the sense of our Conditions stayed our hungry stomicks: for some amongst us thought they would feed us to feed themselves."[42]

Dickinson's assumption that the Indians are cannibals leads him to assume that they cannot be trusted. However, even the constant fear of being eaten by his captors, who do very little physical harm to them, especially when compared to the experiences of captives farther north, does not prevent him from mistrusting their tales of the cannibalistic practices of other groups. The Englishmen want to travel north to the Spanish, but the local cacique strongly warns against this.[43] The cacique informs them that although Spanish-controlled towns are not far, "when we came there, we should have our Throats and scalps cutt, and be shott, Burnt, and Eaten."[44] Dickinson does not trust the motives of the Indians and believes they are simply trying to steer him from his course, in a reversal of the "neighboring device" discussed in chapter 2. In this case, Dickinson believes that the Jaegas are calling out the anthropophagic practices of other groups in order to keep their captives from leaving. His lack of faith in the accusations of cannibalism in the Spanish-controlled region is curious; why does he unquestioningly, and without evidence, believe that the Indians of Jobe practice cannibalism, yet he does not trust the advice of the cacique? Perhaps Dickinson believes that anthropophagy is not likely to be practiced in regions where the European presence is strong. Despite his relatively low opinion of Spaniards (which changed slightly after the hospitality he was shown at their hands), his narrative suggests that he believes that a strong European presence of any kind might curb Indian anthropophagic desires.

Dickinson's wife, Mary, and their baby are among the captives and face their own difficult circumstances. Mary was still nursing their young child when they were taken captive, but the hardships and starvation to which they are exposed prevent her from being able to provide adequately for their child. At one point an Indian woman serves as wet-nurse, much to Mary's dismay. Both breast-feeding and cannibalism were conceived of as acts of incorporation, hearkening back to the images in chapter 2. Suckling babies were believed to do more than simply receive nutrients from their mothers; they also absorbed culture. Women's bodies were associated with food, as through their breasts they provided the most basic elements necessary for human survival.[45] In medieval European writings breast-feeding was believed to be a two-way relationship in which both mother and child received nourishment from the act. This nourishing relationship was both feared and admired. Witches were believed to have a supernumerary nipple through which they provided sustenance, usually blood, to their familiars.[46] Thus the presence of breast-feeding in captivity narratives represents another way the discourse of cannibalism permeates a variety of relationships, including between colonist and Indian, and men and women. It speaks to the pervasive fear of consumption by savagery, whether through literal consumption or the metaphoric cannibalistic link between mother and child.

For Mary Dickinson to allow a "savage, cannibalistic" Indian woman to breast-feed her child was to allow for the potential of contamination. The "savagery" of the Indian woman might literally pass into the child through the breast milk. However, as the Dickinsons continued to endure enormous hardships and periods of starvation on their journey, Mary was forced to beg Indian women to feed her child. She was intermittently able to breast-feed throughout their journey, and at one point she suckles an Indian child, risking contamination herself. Both Mary and Jonathan Dickinson express great fear that their child will become a "savage" Indian.[47] Dickinson fears incorporation by the Indians, both bodily and culturally. His presumption of the presence of cannibalism among the Florida Indians leads him to question their motives and remain constantly fearful of being consumed or corrupted by their "man-eating fury."

Dickinson's account of his captivity in Florida highlights a number of important aspects of English colonial discourse on cannibalism. First and foremost, Dickinson already presumed to know the nature of the Indians he encountered and did not need empirical evidence to back up his claims.[48] English settlers in North America were already attentive to the Indians' presumed propensity for man-eating, and thus a great number of captives, including Dickinson, expressed a fear of cannibalism without any proof of its presence. Dickinson's publisher was also well aware of the power of using the term *cannibal* in the title in order to turn a profit. It is likely that Dickinson did not originally write his account for public view but that a group of Quakers in Philadelphia urged publication. His journal became quite popular, going through fifteen reprints by 1869, including Dutch and German editions.[49] Perhaps even mentioning cannibalism in the title, with no actual occurrences within, was an attractive prospect to a seventeenth- or eighteenth-century publisher.[50] Narratives of horrific cruelties, of which cannibalism was perceived as the ultimate sign of savagery and cruelty, were incredibly popular in early English America. In fact Dickinson's work, along with those of Mary Rowlandson, John Williams, and Mary Jemison, were among the best-selling early English publications about North America.[51]

Providence plays an important role in Dickinson's narrative. After they crashed on the beach, they came face-to-face with people whom they assumed to be ferocious, cannibalistic savages. Dickinson comments on the ferocity of their captors and that they seem poised to attack the shipwrecked Europeans: "But on a sudden it pleased the Lord to Work Wonderfully for our preservation, and instantly all these savage men were struck dumb, and like men amazed the space of a Quarter of an Hour, in which time their countenances Fell, and they looked like another people." He believes that through the providence of God, the once "bloody minded *Creatures*" are rendered benign. During this transformation the plans of the Indians change as well as their outward appearance. Dickinson believes that savagery is often visible through dress, comportment, and facial expression. He remarks a number of times on his journey about the "Wild Furious Countenance[s]" of the Indians that he encountered. For Dickinson the outward manifestation of internal savagery can be changed by the grace of God.[52] Throughout his narrative he remains ambivalent as to whether or not God has actually intervened and brought the Indians closer to Christianity and thus civilization, but he nonetheless puts a great deal of stock in the power of God to protect and redeem true believers.

This theme of redemption through divine providence is quite common in captivity accounts. Unlike the Jesuit priests who sought redemption through service, sacrifice, and sometimes martyrdom, Puritan men and women believed that their redemption could come spontaneously through God's grace. God was believed to intervene actively in the lives of Puritans in New England, and in their narratives of Indian captivity writers often remark upon the ways God helped them to survive and overcome the horrors of captivity. The belief that through God's divine grace English people could triumph over the wilderness and its inhabitants helped to bolster their sense of superiority. Whereas the Jesuits desired martyrdom, the Puritans desired redemption and deliverance from captivity, which was seen as evidence of God's favor. The ability to persevere in what English colonists believed was a hostile environment peopled by savages was proof of divine providence.

A central theme of captivity narratives is the redemption of a chaste individual from the temptations of Indian "savagery." According to Richard Slotkin, "In the Indian's devilish clutches, the captive had to meet and reject the temptation of Indian marriage and/or the Indian's 'cannibal' Eucharist. To partake of the Indian's love or of his equivalent of bread and wine was to debase, to un-English the very soul."[53] The experience of captivity was akin to Satan's testing of Jesus in the desert: one had to make it through a series of hardships that were meant to test the soul and break the spirit in order to prove one's spiritual worth. If one survived intact and did not succumb to the allure of savagery, then one's soul was cleansed and God's favor was assured. In many captivity narratives cannibalism represents one of these key trials that English men and women had to face.

The prominent Puritan minister Cotton Mather wrote about redemption from captivity through God's providence. In a collection of tales of redemption entitled *Good Fetch'd out of Evil*, he discusses several different narratives. About one of these he writes, "A crue of Indians had been Three Days without any manner of sustenance. They took an English Child, and hung it before the Fire to rost it for their Supper; but that those *Cannibals* might Satiate their—I want a name for it,—as well as their hunger, they would Roast it *Alive.* The Child began to Swell. A Cannoe arrived at that Instant with a *Dog* in it. The *Lesser Devills* of the Crue, proposed their taking the *Dog* instead of the *Child*; They did so; And the Child is *yet Living!* Her name is, *Hannah Parsons.*"[54] It is clear that Mather believes God to be directly responsible for the salvation of little Hannah Parsons. Rather than allowing the death of an innocent English girl, God sent a dog to act in her stead, just as God sent a ram to Abraham to sacrifice in Isaac's stead. Mather's allusions to the famous biblical tale of redemption would likely not have been lost on his readers and would have reminded each of them that through sacrifice they could be redeemed by God's mercy. The lands and Indigenous peoples of the Americas were perceived as a test of the devotion of the faithful. By overcoming the temptations and dangers of America, Puritan settlers could triumph and receive God's blessing.

Mather acknowledged that there existed grades of savagery, as he refers to the Natives who set Parsons free as "lesser devils." However, lesser devils were still savage, especially considering that dogs were thought to be an unacceptable food source for civilized peoples. Mather admitted to being without words to express properly the vicious, cannibalistic appetites of the Indians; he believed that it was more than mere hunger that motivated their actions. By roasting the child alive, they were also satiating a cruel blood lust. The presumption of the innocence of children heightened the horror the reader was meant to experience and the outrage at the actions of the Indians.

God's intervention temporarily stayed the hands of Hannah Parsons's executioners and assured that she would survive, but interestingly Mather does not indicate that this intervention had any lasting impact on the presumed savage nature of the Indians. This pattern was repeated in several other narratives. For Elizabeth Hanson, who was taken captive near Dover Township in 1724 and redeemed six months later by her husband after spending five months with Indians and one month with the French, faith in divine providence helped her to survive a strenuous captivity and the threat of cannibalism. Hanson was captured with her child, and together they had to endure a long march through the wilderness, as did most captives. Her nameless child was quite sick at first but was soon on the mend. The child's recovery brought Hanson little comfort as her Indian master taunted her with threats, indicating that the child's recuperation portended its cannibalization. Her master even made her find a stick on which the child would be roasted. Hanson was forced to undress the child so that her master could examine it: "He began to feel its arms, legs, and thighs; and having passed this examination upon it, he informed me, that as it was not yet fat enough, I must dress it again, till it was in better case. But notwithstanding he thus acted, I could persuade myself he was in earnest, but that he did it with a view to afflict and aggravate me: neither could I think but that our lives would be preserved from his barbarous hands, by the over-ruling power of Him, in whose Providence I put my trust both night and day."[55] Hanson believed that only through faith could she endure the trials of captivity. Her acknowledgment that her master was taunting her and even that he may not have been sincere in his threats did little to bring her comfort. In her narrative, just as in Mather's account of the redemption of Hannah Parsons and in Dickinson's report, captives seem to live under constant threat of cannibalization. By representing cannibalism in such a way, Mather, Hanson, and Dickinson emphasize the power of God over their destinies but not over the souls of Indians.

Cannibalism served as a key metaphor for the threat of incorporation into savagery. The fact that in the accounts of Mather and Hanson the threats were directed at children reinforced the vulnerability of the young and the importance of constant vigilance against the possibility of descent into savagery and wildness. Whether Hanson's master actually intended to consume her child or merely threatened to do so as psychological torture is less important than the fact that by facing savage cannibals and surviving, Hanson served as a symbol of the redemptive power of English civilization and Christianity.

Captives who were not Puritans also wrote about the importance of divine providence. Briton Hammon escaped slavery only to face Indian captors who threatened him with death and consumption, "but the Providence of God order'd it otherways."[56] Henry Grace described being redeemed twice from the jaws of cannibals. The first time, he feared that his captors would consume him for want of food, but just as in the tale of Hannah Parsons, the Indians chose to kill and consume dogs instead; the second time, another tribe, the Cherokee, prevented him from being consumed.[57] The common thread in all of these tales of redemption from cannibalism, or the threat of cannibalism, is that redemption was possible only through the intervention of God and that through God's providence, English men and women could prove their superiority over the lands and peoples of North America. In these narratives cannibalism served the specific purpose of representing the fear of the descent into savagery through incorporation into the Other. The ability to overcome it reinforced English identity and ultimately enabled later English writers to assert their masculine power over the wilderness and its inhabitants.

Even in captivity narratives that did not directly describe incidents of man-eating, the influence of the discourse of cannibalism is still evident. In the popular account of his captivity, John Williams did not record any anthropophagic incidents, nor did he write much about the torture of captives. Even though he said that many were killed along their forced march to Canada (mostly women who were unable to keep up), he did not come upon the prolific scenes of torture and cruelty that many other captivity writers recorded. He was not brought to an Indian village and forced to run the gauntlet, nor did he participate in a formal adoption ceremony. Unlike most captives, he did not experience long periods of starvation. The only torture he details occurred at the hands of French Catholics who tried to force stubborn English captives to convert, and the vast majority of Williams's account is taken up by his defense of Protestantism to these Jesuits. However, despite the lack of ethnographic detail, his account is nonetheless quite telling. He writes that in 1704 in Deerfield, Massachusetts, where he was captured, they were attacked by both "Indians and Macquas."[58] *Macqua* is an English transliteration of an Algonquian word for man-eater. Although this term originally referred to the Mohawk, Williams applies it unevenly and uses it to refer to members of either the Huron or Mohawk tribes.[59] It is not particularly remarkable that Williams refers to the Mohawk as the Macquas, but it is remarkable that he divided Native Americans into two categories, Indian and Macquas, which is reminiscent of earlier divisions between good and bad, cannibals and noncannibals. He underscored a lasting assumption about cannibalism in the Americas: that there were two distinct types of people, one of whom considered man-eating a normal practice, the other who abhorred it. The reputation of the Mohawk as man-eaters most likely came about as an epithet lodged by their enemies. Calling another group cannibalistic persisted as an insult implying barbarity, viciousness, and brutishness.

In 1634 the Englishman and proto-ethnologist William Wood wrote a tidy summary of the view that many colonists held about the Mohawk in early New England:

> These [Mohawks] are a cruel bloody people which were wont to come down upon their poor neighbors with more than brutish savageness, spoiling their corn, burning their houses, slaying men, ravishing women; yea very cannibals they were, sometimes eating on a man, one part after another, before his face and while yet living, in so much that the very name of a Mohawk would strike the heart of a poor Aberginian [a member of one of the tribes living north of the colony] dead, were there not hopes at hand of relief from the English to succor them. . . . That which they most hunt after is the flesh of man; their custom is if they get a stranger near their habitations not to butcher him immediately, but keeping him in as good plight as they can, feeding him with the best victuals they have. As a near-neighboring Indian assured me . . . a rough-hewn satyr cutteth a gobbit of flesh from his brawny arm, eating it in his view.[60]

It should not be surprising that Wood did not actually witness the act of cannibalism but recorded secondhand information as truth. Nor should Wood's assertion that a member of a neighboring tribe told him of the horrific cannibalistic practices of the Mohawk come as a surprise. Indians often lodged accusations of cannibalism (and all of its implied savagery) at rival groups in order to cement a friendship with the Europeans. This dynamic took on a unique character for English settlers, as the accused cannibals were their (unwelcome) neighbors. In order to maintain an English presence in the New World it was necessary to disavow a connection to the Indians, even as the English relied on them as allies and trading partners. This complex relationship rested on a mutual lack of understanding of cultural practices. In order for the English to maintain their sense of superiority and their rightful claim to the land, it was necessary to denigrate their enemies, a common practice throughout North America.[61] The trope of cannibalism continued to function in the seventeenth and eighteenth centuries as a justification for certain actions against a perceived enemy, even if it often went unspoken.

Starvation was another common theme in early captivity narratives, as almost all captives were forced to endure long periods of extreme deprivation. While they lamented their circumstances, few captives were willing to connect their suffering with the often equivalent circumstances endured by their Indian masters. For example the captive Isaac Hollister remarked that several of the Seneca Indians with whom he was traveling died of starvation on their journey.[62] Captivity writers established a hierarchy of suffering in which the trials they endured were always worse than those suffered by the Indians. Puritan writers tended to see suffering as a necessary condition of human life. More important, however, their suffering could be relieved by divine Providence, which was not afforded to the savage Indians. For Puritan writers like Mary Rowlandson, the suffering that she endured during her captivity was part of God's divine plan, and from these sufferings she could renew her faith and revel in the power of redemption. She asserted that long periods of starvation and marching through the frigid wilderness was natural to those who led a savage existence.[63] No captivity writer acknowledged the fact that the arrival of Europeans was at least partially responsible for their difficult circumstances.[64]

Dire circumstances occasionally drove English captives to cannibalism, and several eighteenth-century narratives include passages about these desperate acts. Thirteen-year-old Isaac Hollister was taken captive on the banks of the Susquehanna River on October 15, 1763. After several months of captivity, he and a fellow captive decided to make their escape. His companion, a Dutchman, convinced him that they should leave as soon as possible, even though it was still winter. The two wandered around the woods and eventually ran out of food. At one point they survived on tree bark alone for ten days. When the unfortunate Dutchman could go no farther, Hollister sat with him and offered comfort, but there was little to be had. Shortly before his death, the Dutchman told him "that *if he died first, he would not have me afraid to eat of his flesh, for I am determin'd, says he, to eat of yours, if you should die before me.*" Rather than balking at this suggestion, Hollister took the words to heart: "And now I was left all alone, stript of every comfort of life, and knew not which way to turn myself. I thought the absolute necessity I was in, would excuse my pursuing the advice he gave me of eating his flesh as soon as dead: I went immediately about performing the disagreeable operation and cut off 5 or 6 pounds of his legs and thighs:—I left the rest, and made the best way I could down the Creek." After cutting apart his companion, Hollister resumed his wanderings and eventually arrived at an Indian town, where he was promptly returned to his master. He then spent a year living with the Seneca.[65] In his attempt to escape the "savagery" of his captors, Hollister turned to cannibalism, subverting the long-standing connection between cannibalism and savagery. His attempt to return to civilization led to his temporary descent into savagery. Hollister's survival rested on the consumption of his Dutch companion, just as English successes in the New World insisted on the sacrifice of both Indian and European competitors. By resorting to the savagery of cannibalism (at the urging of the Dutchman) Hollister symbolically enacted the triumph of English imperial claims in North America. His tale was a reminder that English people would do whatever was necessary to maintain their God-given right to the New World. Rather than representing weakness, his desperate acts proved his resourcefulness and reinforced the preeminence of masculine English power. The nature of English imperial power in eighteenth-century North America insisted upon the domination of the wilderness; while individuals like Hollister might have been faced with the possibility of succumbing to wildness, their ingenuity and masculine prowess allowed them to triumph over savagery.

Another captive, Thomas Brown, whose scouting patrol was captured by Indians near Montreal during the Seven Years War in 1759, was also driven to cannibalism. After his capture and imprisonment in Montreal, Brown and an English companion escaped and marched toward Crown Point for twenty-two days, on fifteen of which they were without food. Finally, when Brown's companion died, desperation led him to cut the flesh from his friend's bones and wrap it in a handkerchief. After burying his unfortunate companion, Brown continued on his journey. The next day he found three frogs to eat; while the frogs did not restore him fully, he was able to put off eating his friend. Brown described his trepidation at eating human flesh: "Being weak and tired, about 9 o'clock I sat down; but could not eat my Friend's Flesh. I expected to die myself; and while I was commending my Soul to God, I saw a partridge light just by me, which I tho't was sent by Providence; I was so weak, that I could not hold out my Gun; but by resting, I bro't my Piece to bear so that I kill'd the Partridge. While I was eating of it, there came two Pigeons, so near that I kill'd them both."[66] Brown claimed he did not actually consume human flesh but was merely tempted to do so. Instead he was divinely redeemed. It seems unlikely that after weeks of starvation and being driven to carve up his companion, he would suddenly find food readily available or that he would have delayed in eating his friend, but this discursive turn of events reinforced God's ability to triumph over savagery.

That Hollister and Brown were willing to include these unpleasant scenes in their published narratives speaks to an important shift in the discursive representation of cannibalism. They offered a justification of cannibalism that emphasized the importance of strength and self-reliance to survival rather than presenting accounts of horrific exploitation at the hands of tempting women. Portending the great masculine frontier heroes of the nineteenth century, Hollister and Brown represent themselves as survivalists who were driven to commit atrocious acts by their encounter with savagery, but did so only in hopes of redemption through the return to civilization. English settlers had begun to foster an understanding of themselves as part of the wilderness and to accept that the wilderness could drive an individual to commit acts that defied the very fabric of civilization. Yet the acts of cannibalism in these narratives demonstrate the inevitable triumph of the resourcefulness and endurance of civilization.

In January 1752 a group of English soldiers participated in an act of cannibalism. This incident is distinct from the anthropophagous acts of Hollister and Brown, who resorted to cannibalism only alone in the wilderness, far away from the discipline of military life. After a mutiny at Oswego, New York, a group of soldiers abandoned their posts and headed for New France. When their provisions ran out, they turned on one another and consumed four or five individuals.[67] These soldiers symbolically abandoned their Englishness as they headed toward French territory and engaged in cannibalism. Unlike Hollister and Brown, their cannibalism did not represent the ingenuity of an individual on a quest for survival. Rather the soldiers were cowards who shirked their duties and tried to escape to the enemy. In doing so they succumbed to savagery.

The Seven Years War was a time of crisis and rearticulation for Anglo-American masculinity. The years leading up to the war reflected a change from Indian to French threats against English power and dominance in the northeastern United States. The already gendered arena of war also involved virulent anti-Catholicism; the English believed both French and Indian societies were led by inadequate patriarchs who brought their people to poverty, degradation, and damnation rather than civilization, growth, and prosperity. The way English writers represented the French in the years bracketing the Seven Years War was quite similar to their descriptions of Native peoples.[68] The descriptions of cannibalism also reflected this shift, and more French people were accused of participating in this savage act.

In some cases English writers did not directly accuse the French of anthropophagous acts but instead upbraided them for sanctioning Indian cruelties. John Maylem's "Gallic Perfidy: A Poem" from 1758 contains a detailed description of "Savage Furies" and "fell *Canadian* Rage" expressed though acts of cannibalism and cruelty. The title of the poem itself is an indictment of French disloyalty and treachery. By allowing such cruelties to be performed against English citizens, the French were just as guilty as their Indian allies. Maylem also mentions that English responses to Gallic perfidy involved "the Mother's Shrieks, and the Father's manlier grief."[69] This poem not only asserts English superiority but also emphasizes the importance of gendered responses to threats to imperial power. Outpourings of manly grief helped to solidify community identity and foster hatred and distrust of outsiders.[70]

In some cases it was not just the French who were indicted for these actions but all adherents of the Catholic Faith.[71] Cotton Mather wrote, "On this side they [the English settlers] saw their Wives and Children, their Fathers, Mothers, etc. butchered daily by a Handful of Barbarous Indians; on t'other side, little or no resistance made by their armies which [were] Commanded by those of the *Romish* Religion; insomuch that it seem'd rather an intended Massacre, than a desire of putting an End to a Diabolick and Bloody War."[72] Some captives, like John Gyles, were very fearful of corruption by Catholics. When a Jesuit priest gave him a biscuit, he buried it rather than eating it because he feared that it contained a potion that would trick him into believing in Catholicism. As he was only a young child at the time, he took reports of Jesuit torture of Protestants very seriously. He was not alone in his hatred of Jesuits, for his mother remarked upon hearing that he was to be sold to them, "Oh, my dear child, if it were God's will, I had rather follow you to your grave, or never see you more in this world, that you should be sold to a Jesuit, for a Jesuit will ruin you, body and soul!"[73] Her pathological hatred of the Jesuits may be difficult for modern readers to comprehend, but the contest for imperial dominance in the Americas involved exclusionary understandings of the right to rule. Englishmen, and therefore the British Empire, solidified their power by strongly asserting communal standards and demonstrating the superiority of their moral character, for moral superiority translated into power.

John Norton, who was captured during King George's War in 1746, recorded an incident in which French and Indian soldiers consumed human flesh: "After some Time the Indians seemed to be in a Ruffle; and presently rushed up in the Watchbox, brought down the dead Corpse, carried it out of the Fort, scalped it, and cut off the Head and Arms. A young Frenchman took one of the arms and flayed it, roasted the Flesh and offered some of it to *Daniel Smeed*, one of the prisoners, to eat, but he refused it. The Frenchman dressed the Skin of the Arm (as I afterwards heard) and made a Tobacco pouch of it."[74] Norton underscores what he believes to be the important differences between the English and their enemies, whether French or Indian: the Frenchman's willingness to participate in the cannibal ritual of the Indians symbolically and tangibly connects him with savagery, while the refusal of the English prisoner to consume flesh sets him above his captors. Norton further emphasizes that this was not a desperate act of starvation by the young Frenchman, as he carried a tobacco pouch made out of his prey. English captives like Norton feared falling victim to the cannibal kettle of their Indian enemies, but they also were frightened of descending into savagery by identifying too closely with the Indians. It was necessary for Norton to see himself as completely separate from the French and Indians who took him captive in order to maintain his own sense of English superiority and to assure that his masculinity was not corrupted. In Norton's narrative God's providence delivers the English from the savages, heathens, and Catholics.

Examinations of gender must include the ways in which gender categories relate to power by legitimating various forms of oppression and domination and also the ways gender helps to shape relationships between individuals and groups. As Anne Lombard argues, for English colonists "the source of manhood . . . was not inside the individuals but without, in the attribution of virtues that signified a community's agreement that a man had fulfilled its expectations for the male role."[75] Manliness was not innate; it was earned through demonstration of culturally determined morality. How English colonists, especially Puritans, understood manhood reinforced the importance of community. While this earlier model is quite different from the rugged individual frontier version of masculinity of the nineteenth century, these early depictions of masculinity paved the way for the frontier hero to emerge. In this way savage landscapes and savage people were not impediments to success but rather were necessary for the development of masculine virtues. The act of cannibalism posed a threat to masculine imperial power in North America, and in order to deal with its threat to both the community and the individual, English writers negotiated their sense of self-identity in relation to competing groups. Thus anyone who posed a threat to English dominion in North America risked being called a cannibal. In doing so English men were able to rearticulate and reassert their masculine dominance of the American landscape and its people.

# 6 / Understanding Cannibals: Conclusions and Questions

The Seven Years War, or the French and Indian War, as it was called in the American colonies, ended in 1763. The resulting Treaty of Paris radically reshaped the political contours of eastern North America. England gained control of almost all of the lands east of the Mississippi River, with the exception of those bordering the Gulf of Mexico. France lost claim to nearly all of its possessions in North America, holding onto the small Canadian islands of Saint Pierre and Miquelon and the Caribbean island of Guadalupe, which it considered more important than all of Canada. Spain, which joined France late in the war, fared slightly better, maintaining its hold on most of its territorial claims in North America. But these three imperial powers were not the only groups fighting in the North American theater of the war. Diverse groups of Indians fought alongside and against continental and creole soldiers, yet the Treaty of Paris did not substantively address Indian land claims or losses. At war's end Indian groups that had allied with the French found themselves residing in enemy territory. Other groups, like the Iroquois, who had skillfully carved out a place for themselves as middlemen, mediators, and suzerains, were no longer able to manipulate the interests of European empires for their own benefit. The war signaled a change in the way Indians and Europeans interacted, even for those groups like the Iroquois who fought on the winning side. While it is a bit of an oversimplification, the end of the Seven Years War was also the end of the conquest of and contest by European powers over the mainland of Atlantic North America.[1]

Things changed in Mexico and other parts of the Spanish Empire in the second half of the eighteenth century as well. There were no major exchanges of land in these regions, and Spain was still actively conquering the Indians living on the fringes of its empire. But even if the conquest continued in the borderlands of Spanish America, the Enlightenment brought with it a change in the way many educated Spaniards thought about Indians and Spain's relationship to them. Enlightenment thinkers did not consider Indians civilized, or even other than savage, but they did begin to explain the differences they perceived between themselves and Native Americans in new ways.[2]

Thus by the dawn of the eighteenth century European empires in North America had changed dramatically, and the place of Indians and the dichotomous construction of civilization and savagery within those empires also underwent important changes. Even though power structures throughout the Americas were dynamic and shifting, there was a generalized trend away from constructing the New World as a place in which civilized Europeans encountered and conquered savage Americans. As American colonies gained their independence from their European masters, the leaders of these newly independent nations would no longer be able to maintain the same narrative of conquest as the triumph of European civility over American savagery. The residents in the infant United States were no longer outsiders or colonists; they were Americans.[3] Yet other regions of the world were still subject to Europe's power; thus as European empires departed the Americas, the paradigm of the savage cannibal Indian was replaced by the paradigm of the cannibal African or Pacific Islander.[4] The changing of the imperial guard in the Americas did not end the tale of the cannibal Other, but it did relocate it.

In each of the specific imperial and geographic contexts I have explored in this book, the discourse of cannibalism played an important part in the establishment and maintenance of imperial power, and in each case this discourse was gendered. Imperial power is always gendered and cannot be adequately understood without an acknowledgment of this component. Following this line of thought, although the nature of imperial power changed according to temporal, geographic, imperial, and cultural circumstances, what remained consistent was the way Europeans connected cannibalism with savagery. Furthermore the power of the binary construction of civilization and savagery insisted upon a gendered hierarchy that privileged specific notions of masculinity over femininity.

European settlers, conquerors, missionaries, and explorers in the Americas constructed their encounters with Native peoples in terms that cast Natives as savage and feminine and Europeans as civilized and masculine. The construction of the idea of civilization rested on the assumption of superiority. In order to establish and maintain their notion of their own superiority, Europeans consistently accused Indians of practices at odds with civilization. Chief among these was cannibalism. However, these accusations of cannibalism should not be separated from the assumptions about gender and sexuality that always accompanied them. The descriptions of the earliest encounters in the Caribbean indicate that the participation of women in presumed acts of cannibalism elicited a specific fear from the male explorers. The fear of women whose appetites, both sexual and gastronomic, seemed out of order demonstrated the fragile nature of European masculine power.

In the context of the conquest of Mexico, however, Cortés was much more confident in his power than his predecessors in the Caribbean. The establishment of the Spanish Empire in the Caribbean allowed him to draw from an existing base of power and use the dictates of the empire and Spanish cultural norms to construct himself as a virile masculine hero who had come to liberate the Mayas from the tyranny of the savage, cannibalistic Aztecs. The formation of power in the Yucatán and the justification for his entire enterprise rested upon the assumption that the disordered practices of Indians needed to be corrected, through violence if necessary. Cortés thus fought on two fronts: the battlefield and the body. Rather than fearing the appetites of anthropophagous savage women, he used his power to dominate and incorporate them into his entourage, thereby undermining Native understandings of gender and sexuality and replacing them with a version of imperialist patriarchy.

The work of French Jesuit missionaries in what is now Canada supported an affirmation of their own masculinity against the challenges of Protestantism. Just as in the Caribbean and Mexico, the threat of cannibalism drew men from Europe to the Americas. The Jesuits' encounters with Iroquois man-eaters allowed them to demonstrate their commitment to missionary work and to prove their status as masculine soldiers for God.

For English settlers in eastern North America, the presence of cannibals was a hindrance to, not a catalyst for, expansion. Despite this, they still constructed their identities as civilized Englishmen in opposition to cannibalistic Indians. In a fashion similar to that of the French Jesuits, the English colonists' triumph over savagery allowed them to prove their commitment to and justify their presence in lands that did not belong to them. The captivity narrative in particular demonstrated how writers positioned cannibalism as a continued threat to the empire and used anthropophagous accusations against both the French and the Indians to establish their dominion and their superior masculinity.

## Cannibals in the Nineteenth Century and Beyond

The shift from cannibal women as a significant threat to the European civilizing agenda to the use of accusations of cannibalism to establish and maintain masculine power is an important one. By the start of the nineteenth century, the association between cannibalism and disordered female sexuality was no longer as prominent as the fear of bloodthirsty male warriors who threatened to devour innocent settlers. Thus as western European patriarchal power became more firmly entrenched in the Americas, anthropophagous men became the chief threat. Certainly the fear of women's power and appetites had not wholly disappeared, but from the perspective of imperial discourse, the control and maintenance of power in the Americas, which was supported by the assumption of the hierarchical relationship between civilization and savagery, necessitated the construction of an imperial masculinity that had to prove itself superior to Indigenous men. European imperial power in the Americas was maintained by the remaking of Indigenous ideas about gender and sexuality.[5] Women's power was largely eliminated through the civilizing process, and as such, the fear of consumption at their hands lessened.

While this book stops in the late eighteenth century, the story of the discourse of cannibalism and its relationship to imperial power certainly does not end there. In fact if my analysis were to continue into the nineteenth, twentieth, and even twenty-first century, it would reveal that many of the established patterns remain active. One important thing that has changed is the significance of race in this discourse. As the concept of race became more well-defined and entrenched in culture, it also became more important in the discourse of cannibalism. People accused of cannibalism in the nineteenth century were almost always described in terms of their perceived race. As a whole, the writers I have examined did not understand the differences that they observed between themselves and Indians in terms of race in the modern sense. Rather they believed that there existed hierarchical divisions within humanity, which were sometimes tied to skin color but were more closely tied to religion, geography, and cultural practices. Race, as it is predominantly understood in North America today, did not come into being until the nineteenth century, and thus the racialized dynamics at play in this book should not be confused with the systematic, phenotypical racism of later colonialism.[6]

Racialization was a slow process in which early imperial beliefs about civilization and savagery became linked with biological inferiority. The factors that once differentiated between the civilized and the savage in hegemonic European discourse, such as food choices, sexual practices, gendered norms, and agricultural practices, became disassociated from culture and reasserted as biological by the nineteenth century. However, from 1492 to 1763 European discourse about alterity was more mutable, and savagery was most often understood not as something innate but as a step in the process toward proper civilization. At the intersections of the discourses of cannibalism, gender, sexuality, and empire, it becomes evident that European writers held complex views about Native Americans that changed based on geographic, cultural, and temporal contexts. This book focused on how the discourses of gender and cannibalism together played an important role in the establishment and maintenance of imperial power, which is key to understanding later processes of racialization. Within the period to which this study is limited, the relationship between gender and cannibalism was more important than it would be later, when the discourse of race predominated.

By the nineteenth century European empires were rapidly expanding to new parts of the world. They brought the intellectual legacies of the discourse of cannibalism with them to these new regions, just as Columbus inherited the discourses of Herodotus and Marco Polo. In fact while the prototypical cannibal in the context of this project was Native American, as empires grew and changed, new groups were accused of heinous acts of anthropophagy. For example, by the close of the nineteenth century the Dahomey of West Africa were renowned for their man-eating, and by the start of the twentieth century cannibals were said to inhabit remote islands of the South Pacific.[7]

There are numerous more recent examples that demonstrate the continued relevance of the discourse of cannibalism in later centuries. For example, the 1893 World's Columbian Exposition in Chicago drew nearly 27 million visitors and offered a gathering of amazing inventions, curiosities, artifacts, art, and scholarship never before seen. The fair was intended to be a celebration of the discoveries made by Columbus and their legacy. In its title alone the fair reinforced America as a conquered land with no relevant history before its discovery by western Europeans. The exhibits were a glorification of colonialism and of the subjugation of the land and its inhabitants. Chicago itself had recently been a "hostile" land occupied by Native Americans. Placing the World's Fair far from the eastern seaboard, in the middle of the nation, acknowledged the successful expansion of the United States and emphasized the accessibility of the frontier. The beauty and grandeur of the fair emphasized the resiliency of American lands and people. In many ways the fair also inaugurated a reinvigorated sense of "Americanness," a celebration of the American spirit and culture.

The exhibition's Midway Plaisance, a collection of curiosities and exhibits from around the globe, was designed to entertain and titillate; accuracy and education were not primary goals. The arrangement of these ethnological exhibits allowed the visitor to travel from displays of civilization to those of savagery. Walking from west to east through the Midway was a journey through the categories of humanity.[8] At the east end were displays of the technological innovations of mankind—the tools of civilization.[9] The western end focused more on ethnological displays and war entertainment shows. At the terminus of the cultural displays was a model of a Dahomey village.[10] The exhibit emphasized the Dahomeys' reputation for cannibalism, sacrifice, and other acts of savagery. Even Frederick Douglass remarked that the achievement of the African American who had come "from Dahomey" should not be measured by the standards of Anglo-American culture but "from the depths out of which he has risen."[11]

In the late nineteenth century the Dahomey, who lived in what is now the Republic of Benin, engaged in a series of armed conflicts with the French, and tales of their reported savagery circulated throughout the Western World.[12] What set them apart was not only their reputation for ferocity but also the presence of female soldiers. These armed "Amazons" were "crueller and fiercer than most men."[13] According to explorers like Sir Richard Burton, the Dahomey practiced sacrifice and cannibalism.[14] Thus the nadir of the Midway Plaisance was occupied by a group of people notorious for their cannibalism and for violating Western gendered norms. These Dahomey men and women

were the inheritors of the discourse of cannibalism. The French justified their conquest of West Africa by employing the same methods
that were used in the sixteenth and seventeenth centuries. They called
into question the right of the Dahomey people to possess land and to
wield power by emphasizing their most savage characteristics, including their immodesty, their ferocity, their gendered practices, and their
reported man-eating.

The figure of the cannibal followed the paths of imperialism and
colonialism, moving from the Americas to Africa and finally to the
Pacific Rim, which became famous for housing cannibals after the
death of Captain James Cook in 1779. Even in the twentieth century
lurid tales of cannibalism among the people of New Guinea were
widespread.[15]

## Cannibalism and the Other

The discourse of cannibalism remains central to the ways difference
is constructed and experienced in the West. Christopher Columbus
and Amerigo Vespucci based their relationships with Indians in the
Caribbean on preexisting notions of alterity. Columbus structured his
interactions with the Arawaks on his knowledge of medieval travel
literature. Vespucci, on the other hand, emphasized the exoticness of
the people he encountered, their lasciviousness, and their refusal to
abide by the tenets of civilization. As exploration and conquest in the
Caribbean continued, the differences between Europeans and Indians
became an important foundation on which atrocities were justified
and Native peoples were subjugated. In descriptions of the Caribbean
in the late fifteenth and early sixteenth centuries, the two most significant and overlapping "crimes" of which the Natives were accused
were cannibalism and violations of norms of gender and sexuality. In
explicit descriptions of aberrant sexuality and man-eating, European
writers developed an imperialist worldview that defined civilization
as powerful, masculine, and European. Conversely Indian men and
women were largely described as savages, who, even if they were brave,
strong, and sometimes successful in repelling Europeans through acts
of violence, did not do so for proper reasons and therefore were unable
to access the power of civilization.

In each imperial context that I have discussed, the discourse of
cannibalism functioned in a slightly different way. However, there
are several unifying characteristics that enable conclusions to be

drawn about the relationship between accusations of cannibalism and imperial power. The most prominent of these is the clear association between acts of cannibalism and savagery. In each imperial context a range of subjects saw cannibalism as a significant, defining characteristic of savagery. Another important connecting feature is that the link between cannibalism and savagery was further strengthened by the association between cannibalism and discourses of the body. While different writers and empires gendered the discourse of cannibalism in slightly different ways, they all demonstrated a sustained connection between emerging European ideas about masculinity and patriarchy and descriptions of cannibalism. Finally, and perhaps most important, the discourse of cannibalism is inextricable from discussions of imperial power. Empires justified their conquest of the Americas with accusations of Indian savagery and cannibalism. Through their actions in the Americas the Spanish, the French, and the English developed a sense of their own identities and right to rule. The discourse of cannibalism was fundamental in helping to establish European imperial power in the Americas and was an important force in establishing early modern ideas about civilization, savagery, masculinity, femininity, and European superiority.

# NOTES

Notes to the Introduction

1. Michel de Montaigne, "Of Cannibals," in *The Complete Essays of Michel de Montaigne*, 159. The scholarship on Montaigne's essay and its interpretation is vast, but for a few examples of work that is relevant to the context of this book, see Celestin, "Montaigne and the Cannibals"; de Certeau, *Heterologies*; Duval, "Lessons of the New World"; Greenblatt, *Marvelous Possessions*; Hoffman, "Anatomy of the Mass"; Lestringant, *Cannibals*; Lutri, "Montaigne on the Noble Savage"; Marchi, "Montaigne and the New World"; Moore-Gilbert, "'New Worlds, New Selves'"; David Quint, "A Reconsideration of Montaigne's *Des Cannibales*," in Kupperman, *America in European Consciousness*, 166–91; Rawson, "'Indians' and Irish"; Todorov, "L'etre and l'Autre."

2. Montaigne, "Of Cannibals," 156. "I may call these people barbarians, in respect to the rules of reason, but not in respect to ourselves, who surpass them in every kind of barbarity."

3. Ibid., 159.

4. Quint, "A Reconsideration of Montaigne's *Des Cannibales*," 166–67.

5. Montaigne, "Of Cannibals," 150.

6. See Foucault, *History of Sexuality* vol. 1 and Foucault, *Power/Knowledge*. I refer here to discourse in the Foucauldian sense, although I recognize that the specificities of Foucault's nineteenth-century model cannot be simply transferred to the sixteenth, seventeenth, or eighteenth century. In *History of Sexuality*, Foucault writes, "Discourses are not once and for all subservient to power or raised up against it, any more than silences are. I must make allowance for the concept's complex and unstable process whereby discourse can be both an instrument and an effect of power, but also a hindrance, a stumbling block, a point of resistance and a starting point for an opposing strategy. Discourse transmits and produces power; it reinforces it, but also undermines and exposes it, renders it fragile and makes it possible to thwart it" (101).

7. Gordon-Grube, "Anthropophagy in Post-Renaissance Europe," 407. See also Gordon-Grube, "Evidence of Medicinal Cannibalism in Puritan New England"; Himmelman, "The Medicinal Body"; Noble, *Medicinal Cannibalism in Early Modern English Literature and Culture*; Sugg, "'Good Physic but Bad Food'"; Sugg, *Mummies, Cannibals, and Vampires*.

8. Sugg, "'Good Physic but Bad Food,'" 226.

9. See Conklin, *Consuming Grief*; Vilaça, "Relations between Funerary Cannibalism and Warfare Cannibalism"; Goldman, *The Anthropology of Cannibalism*.

10. Sicoli and Tartabini, "Amerindian Cannibalism," 254.

11. For more on this see Arens, *The Man-Eating Myth*.

12. McClintock et al., *Dangerous Liaisons*, 89.

13. Stoler, *Carnal Knowledge and Imperial Power*, 10.

14. Foucault, *The History of Sexuality* vol. 1. Foucault defines biopower as the disciplining force that is enacted upon the body from the state as a technology of control over the bodies of its citizens.

15. Although it focuses primarily on the twentieth century, Omi and Winant's book *Racial Formation in the United States* is quite useful for understanding the processes of racialization.

16. The belief that climate was instrumental in the development of human characteristics, often called environmental or climatic determinism, was common from the early modern world well into the twentieth century. Climate was believed to affect appearance, temperament, intelligence, and level of civilization. For example, tropical climates were believed to create especially lazy, savage peoples. John Smith, referring to the African continent, remarked that "in regard of the heat of the Country, and their extremities of Nature, make strange copulations, and so ingender those extraordinary monsters" (quoted in Kupperman, "Fear of Hot Climates in the Anglo-American Colonial Experience," 231). See also Isaac, *The Invention of Racism in Classical Antiquity*; Manley, "The Revival of Climatic Determinism."

17. Dickason, *The Myth of the Savage*, 66–67; Hart, *Representing the New World*, 182–85.

18. McClintock, *Imperial Leather*, 89. McClintock writes, "Women are represented as the atavistic and authentic body of national tradition (inert, backward-looking, and natural). . . . Men, by contrast, represent the progressive agent of national modernity (forward-thrusting, potent, and historic)" (92).

19. While the evidence for a Viking presence in the Americas is indisputable, there are a number of other proposed "discoveries." Regardless of the veracity of the presence of African explorers in the Americas, for example, giving sole credit to western Europe for the "discovery" of the Americas reinforces the notion that the continents were a blank slate before Columbus arrived. While much of the evidence that he uses is unconvincing and questionable, Jan Carew's essays on the connection between the origins of racism and the Columbian encounter are a useful reminder to challenge Western and Eurocentric frameworks. Carew, "Columbus and the Origins of Racism in the Americas: Part One"; Carew, "Columbus and the Origins of Racism in the Americas: Part Two."

20. See Zerubavel, *Terra Cognita*.

21. Klein, *The Selected Melanie Klein*.

22. Kilgour, *From Communion to Cannibalism*.

23. Barker et al., *Cannibalism and the Colonial World*.

24. See Hulme and Sherman, *"The Tempest" and Its Travels*; Hulme, *Remnants of Conquest*; Hulme, *Colonial Encounters*; Hulme and Whitehead, *Wild Majesty*; Whitehead, *Hans Staden's True History*; Whitehead, "Hans Staden and the Cultural Politics of Cannibalism"; Whitehead, "Carib Cannibalism"; Whitehead, *Lords of the Tiger Spirit*.

25. Harris, *Good to Eat*; Harris, *Cannibals and Kings*.

26. Shankman, "Le Rôti et la Bouilli," 54; Lévi-Strauss, *The Raw and the Cooked*.

27. "One could infer that cannibalism (which by definition is an endo-cuisine in respect to the human race) ordinarily employs boiling rather than roasting, and that where bodies are roasted—cases vouched for by ethnographic literature—must be more frequent in exo-cannibalism (eating the body of an enemy) than in endo-cannibalism (eating a relative)" (quoted in Shankman, "Le Rôti et le Bouilli," 58).

28. Abler, "Iroquois Cannibalism," 309.

29. In his essay "Rethinking Anthropophagy" Arens writes, "Firstly, even for the skeptics, cannibalism, does exist: it exists as a term within colonial discourse to describe the ferocious devouring of human flesh supposedly practiced by some savages. That existence, within discourse, is no less historical whether or not the term cannibalism describes an attested or extant social custom." In Barker et al., *Cannibalism and the Colonial World*, 4.

30. Abler, "Iroquois Cannibalism," 309. In a separate piece, Abler also confronts Peggy Reeves Sanday's discussion of Iroquois cannibalism in her well-known book, *Divine Hunger: Cannibalism as a Cultural System*. See Abler, "A Mythical Myth," in *Cannibalism and the Colonial World*.

31. Abler, "Iroquois Cannibalism," 312.

32. Meinig, *The Shaping of America*, vol. 1. As with any general and comprehensive theory, there are certainly limitations to Meinig's model. I use Meinig's categorizations simply as a heuristic model, recognizing that it is perhaps an oversimplification.

33. Seed, *American Pentimento*, 60, 62–65.

34. Ibid., 62–63; Elliott, *Imperial Spain*, 56–76.

35. Ibid., 70.

36. Ibid., 12.

37. Bhabha, *The Location of Culture*, 95.

38. Barker et al., *Cannibalism and the Colonial World*, 6.

39. Jahoda, *Images of Savages*, 109. This phenomenon was even more common among African victims of the slave trade. See Pierson, *Black Legacy*, 3–34; Thornton, "Cannibals, Witches, and Slave Traders in the Atlantic World."

40. Jahoda, *Images of Savages*, 97.

41. William F. Keegan, "Columbus Was a Cannibal: Myths and the First Encounters," in Paquette and Engerman, *The Lesser Antilles in the Age of European Expansion*, 29.

42. See Hulme, *Colonial Encounters*, chapter 1, "Columbus and the Cannibals," 13–43; Louise Allaire, "Visions of Cannibals: Distant Islands and Distant Lands in the Taino World Image," in Paquette and Engerman, *The Lesser Antilles in the Age of European Expansion*, 33–49; Davis and Goodwin, "Island Carib Origins."

Interestingly, ancient Greeks used two different forms of the word for "man-eater"; one, *androphagoi*, is roughly equivalent to the modern term *cannibal* as it was used as an ethnic designation, while the second, *anthropophagoi*, was used to refer to all creatures who consumed human flesh. Pliny uses the term *anthropophagoi* in his writings as Latin did not have this subtle distinction. See McGowan, "Eating People," 416n10.

43. Barker et al., *Cannibalism and the Colonial World*, 4.

44. Smith, "The Generall Historie of Virginia, New England, and the Summer Isles," 205; Núñez Cabeza de Vaca, *Chronicle of the Narváez Expedition*.

45. Savigny, *Narrative of a Voyage to Senegal*; Simpson, *Cannibalism and the Common Law*; Hanson, *The Custom of the Sea*.

46. Lestringant, *Cannibals*, 75.

## Notes to Chapter 1

1. There are numerous versions of this myth. One example can be found in (Pseudo) Apollodurus, *The Library*, 1.1–11—2.2.

2. Herodotus, *The Histories*, 33.

3. Ibid., 49, 50–54, 55, 179, 180.

4. Ibid., 235–38, 241.

5. Ibid., 243.

6. Ibid., 242, 243, 185.

7. Murphy and Mallory, "Herodotus and the Cannibals."

8. Strabo, *Geography*, 260–61.

9. Pliny the Elder, *Natural History*, book VII, sections 2, I. I have chosen to list references in this work by book and section number rather than by page number as it is in the public domain and available in a wide variety of formats for which pagination is not always provided.

10. Ibid., book VI, section 35. These imaginary regions are inhabited by "the Nigroi, whose King is said to have only one eye, in his forehead; the Wild-beast-eaters, who live chiefly on the flesh of panthers and lions; the Eatalls, who devour everything; the Man-Eaters, whose die is human flesh; the Dog-milkers, who have dogs' heads; the Artibatitae who have four legs and rove about like wild animals."

11. Ibid., book IV, section 12; book V, section 8.

12. Ibid., book V, section 8.

13. Ibid., book VI, section 20.

14. Ibid., book VII, section 2.

15. Ibid., book VII, sections 3, 4, 6.

16. Ibid., book VII, sections 15, 17.

17. McGowan, "Eating People," 413–14.

18. Bettenson, *Documents of the Christian Church*, 3, 4.

19. Athenagoras, "A Plea for the Christians," in Schaff, *Ante-Nicene Fathers*, 285.

20. Wagemakers, "Incest, Infanticide, and Cannibalism," 4.

21. Athenagoras, "A Plea for the Christians," 327, 330.

22. Minucius Felix wrote, "On a Solemn day they [the Christians] assemble at the feast, with all their children, sisters, mothers, people of every sex and of every age. There, after much feasting, when the fellowship has grown warm, and

the fervor of incestuous lust has grown hot with drunkenness, a dog that has been tied to the chandelier is provoked, by throwing a small piece of offal beyond the length of a line [to] which he is bound, to rush and spring; and thus the conscious light being overturned and extinguished in the shameless darkness, the connections of abominable lust in the uncertainty of fate. Although not all in fact, yet in consciousness all are alike incestuous, since by the desire of all of them everything is sought for which can happen in the act of each individual" (quoted in Wagemakers, "Incest, Infanticide, and Cannibalism," 2–3).

23. Ibid., 3.

24. Bettenson, *Documents of the Christian Church*, 4.

25. Other groups were certainly well known for their reported cannibalism throughout the ancient and medieval world, including groups in India, Gaul, and Briton, but discursively at least, the Scythians dominated.

26. Bohak, "Ethnic Portraits in Greco-Roman Literature," 218–20.

27. Quoted in ibid., 219.

28. Pliny the Elder, *Natural History*, book VII, section 2.

29. Quoted in Wagemakers, "Incest, Infanticide, and Cannibalism," 9.

30. For clarity I will refer to this version as *The Acts of Andrew and Matthias*. Sharp, "The Acts of Matthew and Andrew in the City of Cannibals"; Root, *Acts of Andrew*.

31. Sharp, "Acts of Matthew and Andrew in the City of Cannibals," verses 3–4, 12–17, 105–6, 164–76, 190–203.

32. For general discussions of cannibalism in medieval Europe see Price, *Consuming Passions*; Charnock, "Cannibalism in Europe"; Blurton, *Cannibalism in High Medieval English Literature*; Doueihi, *A Perverse History of the Human Heart*; Heng, *Empire of Magic*; Kilgour, *From Communion to Cannibalism*; Cohen, *Of Giants, Monsters, and the Middle Ages*; McAvoy and Walters, *Consuming Narratives*.

33. Barney et al., *The Etymologies of Isidore of Seville*, 24, 7–14, 196. 199.

34. Ibid., 243, 244–45, 288.

35. Ibid., 198.

36. Rubenstein, "Cannibals and Crusaders," 526, 528–29, 530.

37. See Price, *Consuming Passions*.

38. Morison, *Admiral of the Ocean Sea*, 64.

39. Polo, *The Travels of Marco Polo*, 197, 88, 92.

40. Ibid., 110, 231, 248, 253.

41. Ibid., 253–54, 256.

42. The Andaman Islands (along with the Nicobar Islands) are part of the modern state of India but are geographically closer to Myanmar and Thailand.

43. Polo, *The Travels of Marco Polo*, 258.

44. Mandeville, *The Travels of Sir John Mandeville: The Fantastic 14th-Century Account*, vi–vii, viii–ix, xiii, 17, 19, 103–4, 105, 145.

45. Ibid., 161–64, 187, 182.

46. Mandeville, *The Travels of Sir John Mandeville: The Version from the Cotton Manuscript*, 119, 120, 187, 203.

47. Odoric of Pordenone, "The Journal of Friar Odoric" (1876), 151. "In Tibet when a man dies they bring the body to the priest who cuts off the head and gives

it the son and then they cut up the rest and parade it through the city allowing carrion birds to take the body. Once the body has been taken by the carrion, which they rejoice at. And so he [the son] takes his father's head, and straightway cooks it and eats it; and of the skull he maketh a goblet from which he and all of the family always drink devoutly to the memory of the deceased father. And they say that by acting in this way they show great respect for their father. And many other preposterous and abominable customs have they."

48. Ibid., 97.

49. Mandeville, *The Travels of Sir John Mandeville: The Version from the Cotton Manuscript*, 90.

## Notes to Chapter 2

1. Morison, *Admiral of the Ocean Sea*, 236. I find Morison's language in this excerpt troubling and discomforting. To describe an encounter desired by and orchestrated by only one participant as a willing sexual act replicates a whole host of assumptions about women's sexuality and desire.

2. In the first chapter of *Imperial Leather*, Anne McClintock nicely encapsulates the feminization of colonial lands in the context of both Africa and the Americas.

3. These islands are sometimes called the Caribbees and include the Leeward and Windward Islands of the western Antilles and the Netherlands Antilles off the coast of Venezuela. The major islands of this group are (in modern terms) Barbuda, Dominica, Guadeloupe, Montserrat, Martinique, St. Lucia, Grenada, Barbados, Aruba, Curaçao, and Trinidad and Tobago, as well as smaller islands. Carib-speaking groups also inhabited parts of the South American mainland.

4. Vespucci makes no real distinction between the groups other than location, and given the complexity and inaccuracies of his geographic and ethnological data, separating the Caribs in his writings is somewhat counterproductive. There are significant debates over the relationships between the Island Caribs, the Arawaks, and the Mainland Caribs, which, in some ways, renders moot the distinctions drawn by the authors in this chapter. In other words, while men like Vespucci separated Indians in the Caribbean into distinct tribal groups, it is not clear whether this reflected empirical data or merely a flawed system of categorization based on observed levels of "civilization." In "Island Carib Origins" Davis and Goodwin argue that the delineation between Island Caribs and other Caribbean groups is itself flawed; not only is the terminology used in early documents to refer to Caribbean Indians confusing and unclear, but the association between the Island Caribs and the Mainland Carib groups is also a problem as the so-called Island Caribs did not speak a Cariban language. Traditionally the Island Caribs are said to be the descendants of a migration of Carib-speaking groups from the mainland in the centuries preceding Columbus's arrival, and while there is little doubt that there were significant migrations of Carib-speaking people to the Caribbean, the story is much more complex than that, as is evidenced by the linguistic record. On the island of Dominica, which has historically been labeled a Carib island and indeed maintains a Carib Reserve to this day, three languages were reported by seventeenth-century observers: one spoken by women, one by men, and one used primarily for war and special occasions. The men's and women's languages contain significant elements of both Cariban and Arawakan tongues. As Davis

and Goodwin argue, the possibility exists that the Island Caribs were actually Arawakan peoples who were influenced by Cariban peoples, instead of the other way around, as is traditionally argued. Much of the difficulty in elucidating the origins of the Island Caribs comes from attempting to square the historic record with the archaeological and linguistic records. Thus, as I am examining primarily historic records, my discussion here will have no impact on the debate over exactly who these people were and where they lived. In fact in this chapter I examine the development of the precedents in the historic literature that have created the separation between the Island Caribs and the Arawakan peoples of the Caribbean that makes the determination of tribal origins so difficult.

5. See Zerubavel, *Terra Cognita*. Although this "discovery" has been undeniably important for Western history, it was not readily received as such at the time.

6. In the decades and centuries that would follow, the Caribs would be somewhat replaced by various Tupí-speaking peoples in Brazil. Tales of Tupí cannibalism gained popular attention at least in part through the captivity narrative of Hans Staden as well as the writings of missionaries in the region. See Forsyth, "The Beginnings of Brazilian Anthropology"; Whitehead, "Hans Staden and the Cultural Politics of Cannibalism"; Whitehead, *Hans Staden's True History*; Léry, *History of a Voyage to the Land of Brazil*; McGinness, "Christianity and Cannibalism."

7. There is significant controversy and debate over the names of Caribbean tribes. Historians and anthropologists have vacillated between Taíno and Arawak. Arawak is also a designation for a group of related languages that were spoken by peoples throughout Central and South America. Carib can refer to groups inhabiting the northern coast of South America or to groups in the Caribbean, although some scholars prefer to differentiate by referring to the latter as Island Caribs. To complicate matters further, Caribs can also be referred to as Kalinago. There is considerable debate over whether or not the distinction between the various groups in the Caribbean even makes sense, as discussed in note 4 of this chapter. For consistency with the sources that I am using, I have chosen to use Carib and Arawak, although I do so with some reservation as both names are external rather than self-designations. For more on the questions of naming, see Rouse, *The Tainos*; Hulme and Whitehead, *Wild Majesty*; Boucher, *Cannibal Encounters*; Davis and Goodwin, "Island Carib Origins."

8. See the introduction in Boucher, *Cannibal Encounters*. Scholars continue to debate whether the long-standing dispute between the Caribs and the Arawaks was real or imagined, or perhaps exaggerated by Europeans.

9. Chanca, "Letter of Dr. Chanca on the Second Voyage of Columbus," 286–87; Allesandro Zorzi, in Symcox, *Italian Reports on the Americas*, 107.

10. Dickason, *The Myth of the Savage*, 63. Europeans had certainly come into contact before with peoples they considered strange and savage. For example, while Marco Polo's travel writings brought much new information about the places and peoples in the East and their savagery, these lands were already known to exist. The peoples of the Americas were (almost) completely unknown to Europe, and the discovery of such a vast amount of undiscovered land and people challenged much conventional wisdom.

11. Ibid.

12. Jahoda, *Images of Savages*, 15.

13. Todorov, *The Conquest of America*, 15.

14. Morison, *Admiral of the Ocean Sea*, 64, 243, 315, 377, 454, 458.

15. The only surviving pieces of Columbus's journal are found in the writings of Bartolomé de las Casas and Columbus's son Ferdinand, with the greater portion presented by Las Casas. It is clear that both Ferdinand and Las Casas had copies of the original journal as they both quote it at length as well as provide summaries of some parts. For the sake of clarity, I will refer to Columbus as the author of this journal, despite the fact that its authorship is far more complex. See Keegan, "Columbus Was a Cannibal," 18–19.

16. Columbus, *The* Diario, 133.

17. Mandeville, *The Travels of Sir John Mandeville: The Version from the Cotton Manuscript*, 130.

18. Columbus, *The* Diario, 321.

19. Todorov refers to this as a "finalist strategy" (*The Conquest of America*, 15); Morison, *Admiral of the Ocean Sea*, 243.

20. Christopher Columbus, "Letter of Columbus to Luis de Santángel," 271.

21. Columbus, "Journal of the First Voyage of Columbus," 87.

22. Santángel financed most of Columbus's Columbus's second voyage.

23. Christopher Columbus, "Letter to Santángel," in Columbus, *The* Diario, 269.

24. Ibid., 270, 269–70; Morison, *Admiral of the Ocean Sea*, 315.

25. Morison, *Admiral of the Ocean Sea*, 154.

26. For more on the important debates about the historical differences and similarities between the Arawaks and the Caribs see Paquette and Engerman, *The Lesser Antilles in the Age of Imperial Expansion*; Whitehead, *Lords of the Tiger Spirit*.

27. See Columbus, "Letter to Santángel"; Ferdinand Columbus, *The Life of the Admiral*.

28. Ferdinand Columbus, *The Life of the Admiral*, 61.

29. Columbus, *The* Diario, 67.

30. According to Rouse, *bohío* is actually a Taíno term for a kind of dwelling (*The Tainos*, 9).

31. Columbus, *The* Diario, 167, 329.

32. Ibid., 339–43.

33. Herodotus, *The Histories*, 271–73.

34. Columbus, "Letter of Columbus to Sántangel," 265; Columbus,, *The* Diario, 65, 233, 235, 255, 281.

35. Columbus, *The* Diario, 225, 255.

36. Columbus, "Letter of Columbus to Sántangel," 269.

37. Allegretto Allegretti, in Symcox, *Italian Reports on the Americas*, 27.

38. Columbus, "Letter of Columbus to Sántangel," 270.

39. Domenico Malipiero, in Symcox, *Italian Reports on the Americas*, 28.

40. Giacomo Filippo Forest da Bergamo, in Symcox, *Italian Reports on the Americas*, 30.

41. Martyr, *De Orbe Novo*, 1: 63.

42. Chanca, "Letter of Dr. Chanca on the Second Voyage of Columbus," 286–87.

43. Zorzi, in Symcox, *Italian Reports on the Americas*, 107.

44. Chanca, "Letter of Dr. Chanca on the Second Voyage of Columbus," 281; Gerbi, *Nature in the New World*, 27.

45. Ferdinand Columbus, *The Life of the Admiral*, 113.

46. Ibid., 114, 170.

47. For more on Chanca's training and education as well as his motivations for joining the crew, see Chanca and Bernáldez, *Christopher Columbus's Discoveries*, 213–16, 225–29.

48. The portion of Bernáldez's text about of the voyages of Columbus relied heavily on Chanca's writings. He claims to have consulted a number of other testimonies from the second voyage of Columbus but does not name them specifically. He may have had access to reports that are no longer extant. Chanca and Bernáldez, *Christopher Columbus's Discoveries*, 7, 269.

49. Chanca, "Letter of Dr. Chanca on the Second Voyage of Columbus," 286–87.

50. Ibid., 288.

51. Quoted in ibid., 289n1.

52. Boucher, *Cannibal Encounters*, 15.

53. Chanca, "Letter of Dr. Chanca on the Second Voyage of Columbus," 288.

54. Chanca and Bernáldez, *Christopher Columbus's Discoveries*, 89.

55. Michele da Cuneo, in Symcox, *Italian Reports on the Americas*, 51.

56. Chanca, "Letter of Dr. Chanca on the Second Voyage of Columbus," 290–91.

57. Bernáldez refers to a third cultural group residing on the modern-day island of Puerto Rico: "The natives here do not own any canoes nor are they able to travel by sea; however, they use bows and arrows like the Caribs against whom they fight and defend themselves, and, when by chance they happen to overcome the attackers, they eat them like the Caribs do with them" (Chanca and Bernáldez, *Christopher Columbus's Discoveries*, 101).

58. Chanca and Bernáldez, *Christopher Columbus's Discoveries*, 93.

59. Cuneo, in Symcox, *Italian Reports on the Americas*, 51.

60. Even prominent scholars of Columbus treat the incident with little regard. Morison says only this: "The Spaniards were much impressed by the stout courage of the Caribs, whom Columbus ever after held to be the implacable enemies of his Sovereigns and of their Arawak subjects. Even more surprising was the conduct of a 'very beautiful Carib girl,' whom Michele de Cuneo captured personally in the fight and whom Columbus let him keep as a slave." He then quotes the relevant portion of Cuneo's text and moves on. How exactly the young Carib woman's behavior is "surprising" is left unremarked (*Admiral of the Ocean Sea*, 417).

61. Cuneo, in Symcox, *Italian Reports on the Americas*, 56–58, 57, 56, 57–58, 52.

62. Simone dal Verde, in Symcox, *Italian Reports on the Americas*, 32.

63. Ibid.

64. Nicolò Scillacio, in Symcox, *Italian Reports on the Americas*, 39.

65. Ibid., 40; Marcantonio Coccio, in Symcox, *Italian Reports on the Americas*, 69; Angelo Trevisan, in Symcox, *Italian Reports on the Americas*, 83.

66. Trevisan, in Symcox, *Italian Reports on the Americas*, 86.

67. Coccio, in Symcox, *Italian Reports on the Americas*, 69. "The Spaniards found visible proof of these reports [that they ate men, kept the women as slaves, and ate their children] when they broke into the houses which the Cannibals had abandoned: the tables were set, and on them were bowls like ours, filled with parrots, other birds the size of pheasants, and human flesh. Nearby hung a human head, still dripping blood."

68. Zorzi, in Symcox, *Italian Reports on the Americas*, 112.

69. Whitehead, "Carib Cannibalism," 71.

70. "Let it be known that my Lord the King and I, intending that all people who live and are on the islands and Terra Firma of the Ocean Sea become Christians and be converted to our Holy Catholic Faith, have ordered by means of a letter of ours that no person or persons who by our command went to those islands and Terra Firma should dare to apprehend or capture any person or persons of the Indians . . . in order to take them to any other place, and that no injury either to their persons or their property be done unto them, under certain penalties spelled out in our letter, even if the motive be to help the Indians" (quoted in Michael Palencia Roth, "The Cannibal Law of 1503," in Williams and Lewis, *Early Images of the Americas*, 23).

71. Ibid., 24.

72. Whitehead, "Carib Cannibalism," 71.

73. Ibid., 71. Deriving from the Spanish verb meaning "to entrust," *encomenderos* were individuals who were granted allotments of Indian labor. They were not officially the owners of the lands that Indians worked, which theoretically remained in Indian hands. Rather they were given the fruits of Indian labor as tribute.

74. Whitehead, "Carib Cannibalism," 71; Thomas, *Rivers of Gold*, 427–28.

75. See Las Casas, *History of the Indies*; Schwartz, "The Greatest Misnomer on Planet Earth."

76. Formisano, *Letters from a New World*, xx–xxi.

77. Ibid., xxii–xxv.

78. Vespucci, "Mundus Novus," in Formisano, *Letters from a New World*, 48, 49.

79. Vespucci, "Letter to Soderini," in Formisano, *Letters from a New World*, 63.

80. Vespucci, "Mundus Novus," in Formisano, *Letters from a New World*, 50.

81. Vespucci, "Letter to Soderini," in Formisano, *Letters from a New World*, 63.

82. Vespucci, "Mundus Novus," in Formisano, *Letters from a New World*, 50–51.

83. Vespucci, "Letter to Soderini," in Formisano, *Letters from a New World*, 63. "They [Indian women] showed themselves to be very desirous to copulate with us Christians."

84. Ibid., 65.

85. Vespucci, "Mundus Novus," in Formisano, *Letters from a New World*, 50.

86. Trexler, *Sex and Conquest*, 56, 174.

87. Vespucci, "Letter to Soderini," in Formisano, *Letters from a New World*, 66.

88. Ibid., 80, 81.

89. Ibid., 88.

90. For more on the medieval traditions see Bynum, *Holy Feast and Holy Fast*; Price, *Consuming Passions*.

91. Groesen, "The De Bry Collection of Voyages"; Jones, "Ethnographer's Sketch, Sensational Engraving, Full-Length Portrait," 140.

92. McClintock, *Imperial Leather*, 21, 22.

93. Bynum, *Holy Feast and Holy Fast*, 269–70.

94. Schreffler, "Vespucci Rediscovers America," 295–96.

95. Todorov argues that the narrative style of Vespucci lends itself to more spectacular and enthralling images (*The Morals of History*, 109).

96. Montrose, "The Work of Gender in the Discourse of Discovery," 3, 4.

97. Schreffler, "Vespucci Rediscovers America," 297, 299, 301.

98. Montrose, "The Work of Gender in the Discourse of Discovery," 5.

99. Schreffler, "Vespucci Rediscovers America," 304.

100. Ibid.

101. Montrose, "The Work of Gender in the Discourse of Discovery," 4, 5.

102. McClintock, *Imperial Leather*, 26.

103. Ibid. "Here, women mark, quite literally, the margins of the new world but they do so in such way as to suggest a profound ambivalence in the European male. In the foreground, the explorer is of a piece—fully armored, erect and magisterial, the incarnation of male imperial power. Caught in his gaze, the woman is naked, subservient and vulnerable to his advance. In the background, however, the male body is quite literally in pieces, while the women are actively and powerfully engaged. The dismembered leg roasting on the spit evokes a disordering of the body so catastrophic as to be fatal."

104. Ibid., 27.

## Notes to Chapter 3

1. Juan Ginés de Sepúlveda, "The Controversy between the Bishop of Chiapas and Doctor Sepúlveda in the Year 1552, in which the Bishop Condemned the Right of Western Conquests and the Doctor Defended it with Elegance," in Lane, *Defending the Conquest*, 52.

2. The term *gendered genesis* comes from Powers, *Women in the Crucible of Conquest*.

3. Seed, *American Pentimento*, 107.

4. For example see Durán, *The History of the Indies of New Spain*; Schwartz, *Victors and Vanquished*; Chimalpahin Cuauhtlehuanitzin, *Annals of His Time*.

5. Townsend, "Burying the White Gods," 665.

6. Sigal, "The *Cuiloni*, the *Patlache*, and the Abominable Sin," 561.

7. The *encomienda* system revolved around the ownership of labor, not people.

8. Adorno, "Discourses on Colonialism," 252.

9. Elliott, *Empires of the Atlantic World*, 3–4, 21.

10. *Chontal Maya* derives from a Nahua term for "foreigner" and denotes the Maya peoples of the Yucatan generally, and more specifically those of the modern state of Tabasco, but has been used to refer to a variety of different Maya ethnic groups throughout Mexico. *Nahuas* (or Nahua peoples) were Uto-Aztecan peoples who spoke variations of the Nahuatl language. This group includes the Toltecs, Aztecs, Tlaxcaltec, Xochimilica, and others. The term *Mexica* is also used occasionally; it refers specifically to the ruling ethnic group of the Aztec Empire, who were a Nahuatl-speaking group. *Aztec* refers to the Mexica of Tenochtitlan but can also be extended to the Nahuatl-speaking people of the allied cities of Texcoco and Tlacopan, and even more generally it can refer to all those living within the Aztec Empire who spoke Nahuatl and shared related cultural patterns.

11. Wagner, *Discovery of Yucatan by Francisco Hernández de Córdoba*, 41, 48, 49, 54; Elliott, *Empires of the Atlantic World*, 88–89; Martyr, *De Orbe Novo*, 2: 78.

12. The encounters between Spaniards and the Indians of Florida arguably followed a pattern somewhere between that of the island tribes of the Caribbean and the "civilizations" of Mexico.

13. Seed, *Ceremonies of Possession in Europe's Conquest of the New World*, 85; Elliott, *Empires of the Atlantic World*, 20; Durán, *The History of the Indies of New Spain*, 434; Gómara, *Cortés*, 114; Anonymous Conqueror, in Fuentes, *The Conquistadors*, 75.

14. Meinig, *The Shaping of America*, 1: 72.

15. Trexler, *Sex and Conquest*, 63, 73, 121. The extent to which the precontact Mayas and Nahuas actually sanctioned homosexuality is still the subject of enormous debate. See Sigal, "The *Cuiloni*, the *Patlache*, and the Abominable Sin."

16. Trexler, *Sex and Conquest*, 147, 167.

17. Although she is discussing gender parallelism and gender complementarity in the context of the Andean societies, Powers's definitions of these terms are quite useful for our purposes: "In gender-parallel societies women and men operate in two separate, but equivalent spheres, each gender enjoying autonomy in its own sphere." Gender complementarity refers to "societies in which women and men performed distinct social, political, and economic roles, but roles that were perceived as equally important to the successful operation of the society, whether performed by women or by men. Women's roles were not seen as subordinate to or less significant than those of men; instead women's and men's contributions were equally valued, considered essential one to the other and to the whole of society; that is, they were complementary. Women's roles were not auxiliary; rather women and men were partners in the business of life" ("Andeans and Spaniards in the Contact Zone," 511–12).

18. Dyer, "Seduction by Promise of Marriage," 440–41.

19. Vollendorf, "Good Sex, Bad Sex," 3.

20. Behrend-Martínez, "Manhood and the Neutered Body in Early Modern Spain," 1073. In the mid-seventeenth century the redefinition of masculinity meant that there was an increasing emphasis on biological sex rather than gender. In other words, being a man was more than just a set of gendered performances that demonstrated masculinity; it also meant possessing physiological indicators of male sex.

21. Price, *Consuming Passions*, 84, 98.

22. Malintzin was also sometimes referred to as Doña Marina or La Malinche. It is possible that none of these names are accurate, but I have chosen to use Malintzin as it was neither given to her by the Spanish, as was Doña Marina, nor used as a derogatory term, like La Malinche. For example see Durán, *The History of the Indies of New Spain*, 511, 523; Martyr, *De Orbe Novo*, 2: 35.

23. Powers, *Women in the Crucible of Conquest*, 53.

24. Sigal, *From Moon Goddesses to Virgins*, 40.

25. Trexler, *Sex and Conquest*, 59, 45.

26. My translation. "Estas gentes tienan la *tria peccatela* que decia el Italiano: no creen en Dios; son casi todos sodomitas: comen carne humana." Alonso Zuazo, "Carta Del Licenciado Alonso Zuazo," in Icazbalceta, *Colección de Documentos para la Historia de México*, 565.

27. Sigal, "The *Cuiloni*, the *Patlache*, and the Abominable Sin," 560–61.

28. Wagner, *The Rise of Fernando Cortés*, 104–5.

29. Pagden, *The Fall of Natural Man*, 82; Hay, "The Windigo Psychosis"; Podruchny, "Werewolves and Windigos."

30. Díaz, *The Discovery and Conquest of Mexico*, 48–50.

31. Adorno, "Discourses on Colonialism," 241, 212, 213.

32. Zuazo was one of the three men left in charge of Cortés's government when the he left for Honduras, in addition to having other important positions in the Spanish government in the Americas. See Zuazo, "Carta del Licenciado Alonso Zuazo," in Icazbalceta, *Coleccion de Documentos para la Historia de México*, 558–67.

33. For a discussion of some of the differences between the textual sources of the conquest see Greene, "The Conquest of Mexico."

34. Schwartz, *Victors and Vanquished*, 115.

35. The accounts of Tapia, Aguilar, and the Anonymous Conqueror are in Fuentes, *The Conquistadors*.

36. Stabler and Kieza, "Ruy González's 1553 Letter to Emperor Charles V."

37. Greene, "The Conquest of Mexico," 164.

38. Myers, *Fernández de Oviedo's Chronicle of America*, 121–22.

39. Cortés, *Letters from Mexico*, 146.

40. Myers, *Fernández de Oviedo's Chronicle of America*, 123. Oviedo says there is classical evidence for the existence of savage customs like cannibalism and sodomy. Martyr is more explicit about considering cultures on their own terms. He expresses his disgust at the Indian practice of wearing lip plates, yet he writes, "This example proves the blindness and the foolishness of the human race: it likewise proves how we deceive ourselves. The Ethiopian thinks that black is a more beautiful colour than white, while the white man thinks the opposite.... We are influenced by passion rather than guided by reason, and the human race accepts these foolish notions, each country following its own fancy. In deference to another's opinion, we prefer foolish things while we reject solid and certain ones" (Martyr, *De Orbe Novo*, 2: 39).

41. Gómara, *Cortés*, 114.

42. Wagner, *The Rise of Fernando Cortés*, 369.

43. Díaz, *The Discovery and Conquest of Mexico*, 170.

44. Anonymous Conqueror, in Fuentes, *The Conquistadors*, 75.

45. Vollendorf, "Good Sex, Bad Sex," 4.

46. Anonymous Conqueror, in Fuentes, *The Conquistadors*, 79–80.

47. Zuazo, "Carta Del Licenciado Alonso Zuazo," in Icazbalceta, *Colección de Documentos para la Historia de México*, 565.

48. Sigal, "The *Cuiloni*, the *Patlache*, and the Abominable Sin," 557, 562.

49. Sigal, *From Moon Goddesses to Virgins*, 44.

50. Groups that were conquered by the Aztecs retained some autonomy but were expected to provide tribute in the form of goods or labor to the empire. These tribute burdens were often excessive and led many of the outlying cities and towns to greatly resent their Aztec lords.

51. Townsend, *Malintzin's Choices*, 72.

52. Gómara, *Cortés*, 116.

53. Ibid., 118; Townsend, *Malintzin's Choices*, 72.

54. Díaz, *The Discovery and Conquest of Mexico*, 102, 62–63, 122, 136, 153–54.

55. Kellogg, *Weaving the Past*, 60.

56. Díaz, *The Discovery and Conquest of Mexico*, 106, 140. At one point Cortés was also given five slaves and asked to prove that he was a god by consuming their

flesh (Gómara, *Cortés*, 105). It is likely that Cortés and his men were not actually perceived as gods, and that this is a fabrication. See Townsend, "Burying the White Gods."

57. Díaz, *The Discovery and Conquest of Mexico*, 236.

58. Ibid., 153–54.

59. The genealogy of Malintzin's name is quite complicated. Townsend suggests that *Malintzin* was a corruption of the name Marina, which was given to her by the Spaniards. The suffix -tzin was added as an honorific, and based on prevailing linguistic forms of address, she was called Malintze. In turn, this was corrupted by the Spaniards into Malinche (*Malintzin's Choices*, 55).

60. Ibid.

61. Díaz, *The Discovery and Conquest of Mexico*, 135.

62. Kellogg, *Weaving the Past*, 7, 25, 30, 32.

63. Díaz, *The Discovery and Conquest of Mexico*, 66–67.

64. Ibid., 208–9.

65. Price, *Consuming Passions*, 95.

66. Trexler, *Sex and Conquest*, 10.

67. Price, *Consuming Passions*, 102.

68. Sigal, "The *Cuiloni*, the *Patlache*, and the Abominable Sin," 564.

69. Trexler, *Sex and Conquest*, 147–48.

70. Pagden, *The Fall of the Natural Man*, 81.

71. Such debates certainly continued for decades, but they tended to focus more on the status of Indians as lesser humans or natural slaves, not as nonhumans. For example the famous Valladolid debate between Las Casas and Sepúlveda in 1550 hinged on the place of Native Americans in the natural order.

72. Pagden, *The Fall of the Natural Man*, 82–83.

73. Myers, *Fernández de Oviedo's Chronicle of America*, 121; Wagner, *The Rise of Fernando Cortés*, 369.

74. Adorno, "The Discursive Encounter of Spain and America," 220.

75. Pagden, *The Fall of the Natural Man*, 85, 95.

76. Adorno, "The Discursive Encounter of Spain and America," 211.

77. Las Casas, *In Defense of the Indians*, 28, 30, 32.

78. Ibid., 42–43, 51, 191.

79. In the vast majority of accounts, cannibalism and sacrifice are linked. It is often assumed, sometimes without any corroborating evidence, that acts of cannibalism followed temple sacrifices. The two were often talked about as equivalently barbaric crimes. However, particularly in the context of the battlefield, cannibalism was much more of a threat. Aztecs and Mayas often sacrificed a portion of the population of the losing army, and some of them may have been cannibalized as well. However, the desecration of the fallen soldiers and the consumption of their bodies was recognized as singularly abhorrent. Deaths in battle were not seen as sacrifices; those were reserved for the temple. But acts of cannibalism were said to occur on the battlefield and in the town center.

80. Trexler, *Sex and Conquest*, 84.

81. Lane, *Defending the Conquest*, 60, 96–97, 61, 63–64.

82. Ibid., 66–67.

83. Ibid., 70, 71.

## Notes to Chapter 4

1. Lev. 26:27–33; Duet. 28:53–57; 2 Kings 6:28–29; Isa. 9:19–20, 49:26; Jer. 19:1–9; Lam. 4:10, 2:20; Ezek. 5:7–12, 24:10–12; Mic. 3:2–4; Zec. 11:9; 1 Cor. 10:28; Gal. 5:15; 1 Pet. 5:8, New Revised Standard Version (NRSV).

2. Jer. 19:1–9 NRSV.

3. Mic. 3:2–4 NRSV.

4. While French missionary efforts were not limited to what is now Canada and parts of the northern United States, it is on these regions that this chapter focuses. There were also a number of other missionary sects, including the Récollets (a branch of the Franciscans) and the Sulpicians, who were active in New France at various times.

5. Thwaites, *The Jesuit Relations*. The Thwaites edition includes the original languages (French, Italian, and Latin) alongside the English translation. I reference the English translations both in the text and in citations; the original language can be found on the facing pages.

6. The fund-raising aspect of the *Relations*, along with the biases and motivations of the priests themselves, rightly leads Daniel Richter to call for care and caution when using Jesuit accounts to draw conclusions about Indigenous practices ("Iroquois versus Iroquois," 1). But as my focus here is on the power of discourse, the fact that the Jesuits might have been willing to embellish or misrepresent their experiences in New France speaks to the power of descriptions of savagery and cannibalism.

7. Ulrike Strasser, "'The First Form and Grace': Ignatius of Loyola and the Reformation of Masculinity," in Hendrix and Karant-Nunn, *Masculinity in the Reformation Era*, 45, 46.

8. Ibid., 47, 48–49, 51.

9. Ignatius, *A Pilgrim's Journey*.

10. Strasser, "'The First Form and Grace,'" 53. For more on the history and significance of religious celibacy see Abbot, *The History of Celibacy*; Olsen, *Celibacy and Religious Tradition*; Pagels, *Adam, Eve, and the Serpent*.

11. Ibid., 55, 58.

12. Ibid., 60, 61.

13. Ibid., 62, 64–65, 67.

14. While homosociality was important to the Jesuits, it was equally important that they actively police any hints of homosexual behavior (Marín, "Heterosexual Melancholia and Mysticism in the Early Society of Jesus," 126).

15. Abé, *The Jesuit Mission to New France*, 48–49.

16. Forsyth, "The Beginnings of Brazilian Anthropology."

17. Indeed the Jesuits has a complicated relationship with various empires throughout the colonial period, culminating most famously in their expulsion from the New World by Spain in 1767. See Roehner, "Jesuits and the State."

18. In fact the eight missionaries who died in New France were canonized in 1930 and are collectively known as the Canadian Martyrs. They are Saint Jean de Brébeuf, Saint Noël Chabanel, Saint Antoine Daniel, Saint Charles Garnier, Saint René Goupil, Saint Isaac Jogues, Saint Jean de Lalande, and Saint Gabriel Lalemant (Moore, *Indian and Jesuit*, 11; Greer, *The Jesuit Relations*).

19. Moore, *Indian and Jesuit*, 44, 138.

20. Kennedy, *Jesuit and Savage in New France*, 63.

21. Blackburn, *Harvest of Souls*, 21–22, 27, 29–31.

22. Kennedy, *Jesuit and Savage in New France*, 65–67. Meinig characterized the particular nature of French expansion in the Americas as a strategy of articulation (*The Shaping of America*, 1: 72).

23. Healy, "The French Jesuits and the Idea of the Noble Savage," 145.

24. Moore, *Indian and Jesuit*, 129.

25. Ibid., 82–83, 105, 130; Healy, "The French Jesuits and the Idea of the Noble Savage." 151.

26. See Brandão, *Your Fyre Shall Burn No More*, 48, appendix A. The tribal designation, Montagnais in French documents refers to one of two groups of Innu people (the other being the Naskapi). The modern-day people self-designate as Innu, not Montagnais.

27. Healy, "The French Jesuits and the Idea of the Noble Savage," 145, 149.

28. In fact the Jesuits strongly discouraged contact between French habitants and Indians out of fear of the corrupting influence of the rabble (ibid., 153).

29. Ibid., 155.

30. Jaenen, "'Les Sauvages Ameriquains,'" 43, 45. Jaenen writes, "There was a continuing preoccupation with Europe, so that the new World and its native cultures were employed to evaluate Old World society, and sometimes simply criticize in indirect fashion both church and state, European man and European institutions."

31. Abler, "Iroquois Cannibalism"; Abler, "A Mythical Myth"; Jamieson, "An Examination of Prisoner-Sacrifice and Cannibalism at the St. Lawrence Iroquoian Roebuck Site," 174.

32. The archaeological evidence for Iroquois cannibalism prior to European conquest is fairly convincing, but combining this evidence with the ethnohistorical record, it seems reasonable to assert that as competition of land, power, and resources increased in Iroquoia, the torture and sometimes cannibalization of captives increased as well (Jamieson, "An Examination of Prisoner-Sacrifice and Cannibalism at the St. Lawrence Iroquoian Roebuck Site," 174).

33. Trigger, *Children of Aataentsic*, 74–5, 143–58.

34. Thwaites, *Jesuit Relations*. Out of 134 references to cannibalism, seventy-two are about the Iroquois. The group with the next largest number of references is the Huron, with nineteen. For more on Huron cannibalistic practices see Trigger, *Children of Aataentsic*, 74–75.

35. As the English translation of *The Jesuit Relations* uses the term *Huron* rather than the more modern and precise term *Wyandotte* (or even *Wendat*), for the sake of consistency and clarity I will maintain this usage. The Huron/Wyandotte were not one tribe but a confederacy of tribes sharing an Iroquoian language. Similarly the term *Iroquois* refers to a confederacy of tribes that are more correctly called the Haudenosaunee.

36. Richter, "Iroquois versus Iroquois," 3; Moore, *Indian and Jesuit*, 33.

37. Thwaites, *Jesuit Relations*, 34: 231–33, 38: 181.

38. Ibid., 35: 21.

39. Ibid., 35: 89.

40. For examples of Huron cannibalism in Thwaites, *Jesuit Relations* see 10: 227–29, 12: 255, 13: 61, 79, 171, 187, 15: 173, 17: 75, 99, 18: 33, 19: 201, 20: 39, 23: 173, 26: 57, 27: 275, 295, 33: 45, 40: 49.

41. Ibid., 35: 23, 97, 189.

42. Ibid., 34: 197, 35: 79.

43. A few examples of this should suffice. See Thwaites, *Jesuit Relations*, 21: 65–67, 121, 22: 249, 255–57, 265, 272, 31: 85, 38: 47, 46: 61, 57: 95.

44. Richter, *Ordeal of the Longhouse*, 21–22.

45. Knowles, "The Torture of Captives by the Indians of Eastern North America."

46. Thwaites, *Jesuit Relations*, 31: 175, 32: 19, 43: 85, 44: 81, 173, 49: 231, 34: 197.

47. Richter, *The Ordeal of the Longhouse*, 50ff.

48. Richter, "War and Culture," 529. For more on the relationship between cannibalism, sacrifice, torture, and warfare see Trigger, *Children of Aataentsic*, 143–46.

49. Shoemaker, "An Alliance between Men"; Tyler Boulware, "'We are Men': Native American and Euroamerican Projections of Masculinity During the Seven Years' War," in Foster *New Men*, 51–70.

50. Richter, *Ordeal of the Longhouse*, 33.

51. Thwaites, *Jesuit Relations*, 21: 119.

52. Ibid., 21: 67, 22: 265, 25: 265–67, 27: 213, 41: 53, 55: 275, 21: 119.

53. For example see ibid., 22: 257, 265, 271.

54. Ibid., 22: 253–55.

55. For an in-depth discussion of Jesuit ideas about the role of the devil in New France see Goddard, "The Devil in New France."

56. Jahoda, *Images of Savages*, 97–99.

57. Thwaites, *Jesuit Relations*, 21: 67.

58. Ibid., 22: 271, 38: 45.

59. The last reference to Iroquois cannibalism in Thwaites, *Jesuit Relations* comes from volume 62. Father Thierry Beschefer remarks, "It is not only the Iroquois who benefit by the labors of the fathers who dwell among them. As they never return from war without bringing some Captives with them, a portion of who are destined to the fire. There are but a few of them who have not The Happiness of being baptized before death. God's providence seeks Them out in Their country, and makes Them come hither to find eternal blessedness amid the fires of these Man-eaters" (62: 241).

60. Ibid., 34: 215–17.

61. Archaeological evidence also seems to support that women were less commonly tortured, sacrificed, or cannibalized (Jamieson, "An Examination of Prisoner-Sacrifice and Cannibalism at the St. Lawrence Iroquoian Roebuck Site," 174; Trigger *Children of Aataentsic*, 145–46).

62. Thwaites, *Jesuit Relations*, 22: 263, Ibid., 22: 265. As Nancy Shoemaker argues, it was common for Indians to lodge insults that employed metaphors of gender and generation ("An Alliance Between Men," 245).

63. Thwaites, *Jesuit Relations*, 22: 265.

64. Ibid., 22: 265, 27: 275.

65. Ibid., 34: 31.

66. Ibid., 34: 27.

67. Ibid., 34: 29.

68. Huron people living among the Iroquois likely took the lead in this action (Trigger, *Children of Aataentsic*, 389–90, 764).

69. Richter argues convincingly that individuals who were adopted by the Iroquois often brought their knowledge of Christianity and Christian rituals with them to their new community. Their experiences, along with the more limited contact between the Iroquois themselves and the Jesuits, meant that Christianity and the presence of missionaries in Iroquois communities was divisive for the Iroquois in the mid-seventeenth century. He also argues that both sides believed they understood the other, or as he puts it, "Just as the Jesuits thought they knew the Iroquois, Iroquois thought they knew the Jesuits." Thus incidents like this one demonstrate Iroquois knowledge of Christian traditions as well as the way that knowledge could make the job of missionaries more challenging ("Iroquois versus Iroquois," 2).

70. Thwaites, *Jesuit Relations*, 34: 27–29.

71. Richter, *Ordeal of the Longhouse*, 56.

72. Thwaites, *Jesuit Relations*, 26: 33.

73. Ibid., 46: 41.

74. Ibid., 46: 43.

75. Ibid., 46: 47.

76. Ibid., 31: 35.

77. Jogues initially earned a reputation for bravery for his ability to withstand the torture inflicted on him in 1642. He was then adopted into the Mohawk, where he stayed for two years before escaping. He returned to the village in 1646 as part of a diplomatic mission and left again on good terms with a promise to return. However, in his absence conditions in the village deteriorated, and when he came back later that year it would be for the last time; he was tortured and killed by the Iroquois in spite of the protests of his adoptive clan relatives (Richter, "Iroquois versus Iroquois," 5).

78. Anderson, *Chain Her by One Foot*, 18.

79. For a useful discussion of the prophetic dreams and gender see Anne Marie Plane, "Indian and English Dreams: Colonial Hierarchy and Manly Restraint in Seventeenth-Century New England," in Foster, *New Men*, 31–47.

80. Thwaites, *Jesuit Relations*, 42: 153.

81. Ibid., 52: 173.

82. Ibid., 30: 259.

83. Ibid., 62: 59, 71.

84. Richter, *Ordeal of the Longhouse*, 144.

85. Thwaites, *Jesuit Relations*, 23: 157, 159.

## Notes to Chapter 5

1. Swift, *A Modest Proposal*, 10.

2. Jean Lowry, "A Journal of the Captivity of Jean Lowry," 1760, in Washburn, *The Garland Library of Narratives of North American Indian Captivities*, 8: 27.

3. Elliott, *Empires of the Atlantic World*, xvii, 6. Obviously there were English explorers and soldiers dispatched to the New World in the sixteenth century, but that English colonization did not see a great deal of development until well into the seventeenth century, especially in North America.

4. Ibid., 65.

5. Ibid., 59–60.

6. Peter Cook, "Kings, Captains, and Kin: French Views of Native American Political Culture in Sixteenth and Early Seventeenth Centuries," in Mancall, *The Atlantic World and Virginia*, 346–47; Elliot, *Empires of the Atlantic World*, xvii.

7. "I have read in Relations of the *Indians* amongst the *Spaniards* that they would not eat a *Spaniard* till they had kept him two or three days to wax tender, because their flesh was hard. At *Matins* vineyard, and Island that lyes South to *Plimout* in the way to *Virginia*, certain *Indians* (whilst I was in the Countrey) seised upon a Boat that put into a By-*Cove*, kill'd the men and eat them up in a short time before they were discovered" (Josselyn, *An Account of Two Voyages to New England*, 98).

8. Josselyn identified Native Americans with Tartars. Additionally he says the Mohawks spoke a Turkish tongue (ibid., 96, 97). Using earlier European models for understanding difference, which often employed eastern Europe as a point of reference, was common in English descriptions of Indians.

9. Ibid., 98.

10. Elliott, *Empires of the Atlantic World*, 17, 24.

11. Slotkin, *Regeneration through Violence*, 38.

12. Obviously there were many sincere efforts at Indian conversion throughout the English colonies, and many English men and women engaged in the exchange of goods and cultural practices with the Indians. Generally, however, these efforts were less widespread and were more individually based, as opposed to the imperial support for conversion in New France and New Spain. England did not export vast numbers of missionaries and priests. The unique Protestant Christianity of England (and its many divisions), rather than the Catholicism of France and Spain, set forth a different path toward colonization and conversion. Among colonists (not necessarily the planters), who often were religious dissenters themselves, religion tended to be a more individual process in which one's relation to God and God's community was preeminent. Thus the Puritans emphasized self-examination and the personal experience of conversion. They eschewed the hierarchies and bureaucracies that allowed the Franciscans and Jesuits to have such an enormous impact in the Americas. However, I do not want to assert that the English were unconcerned with the souls of Indians. The importance of conversion and proselytization was evident from the outset in early Virginia. The writings of Richard Hakluyt make this quite evident. See David Harris Sack, "Discourse on Western Planting: Richard Hakluyt and the Making of the Atlantic World," in Mancall, *The Atlantic World and Virginia*. Additionally, as Elliott points out, England's mission was to give savages what they needed: "1. civility for their bodies, 2. Christianity for their souls" (*Empires of the Atlantic World*, 11–12).

13. See Gallay, *The Indian Slave Trade*.

14. Elliott, *Empires of the Atlantic World*, 8–9. For example, the Jamestown settlers included a jeweler, two refiners, and two goldsmiths (John Smith, "The Proceedings of the English Colonie in Virginia," in Horn, *Captain John Smith*, 59).

15. John Smith, "A Description of New-England, by Captaine John Smith," in Horn, *Captain John Smith*, 133, 145. At other times Smith made promises of great wealth to be obtained by the sale of other agricultural and natural materials (139).

16. Elliott, *Empires of the Atlantic World*, 13–14, 16.

17. De Bry, *Thomas Hariot's Virginia*, 5.

18. Elliott, *Empires of the Atlantic World*, 25–27.

19. Hariot and White, *A Briefe and True Report*.

20. Other colonies, such as Massachusetts Bay, reflected a general lack of imperial interest in the early stages of American colonization (Elliott, *Empires of the Atlantic World*, 27).

21. Meinig, *The Shaping of America*, 1: 70.

22. Josselyn details the punishments meted out for certain offenses in the Massachusetts Bay Colony. For example, "an *English* woman suffering an *Indian* to have carnal knowledge of her, had an *Indian* cut out exactly in red cloth sewed upon her right Arm, and injoyned to wear it twelve months" (*An Account of Two Voyages to New England*, 137).

23. Elliott, *Empires of the Atlantic World*, 182–83. *Métis* and *mestizo* are the French and Spanish terms, respectively, for individuals with both Indian and European parentage.

24. Ibid., 78. For more on English views about race and skin color see Kupperman, *Indians and English*, chapter 2, "Reading Indian Bodies" 41–76.

25. Josselyn, *An Account of Two Voyages to New England*, 143.

26. Elliott, *Empires of the Atlantic World*, 79.

27. For more on the Great Chain of Being see Lovejoy, *The Great Chain of Being*; duBois, *Centaurs and Amazons*; Kuntz and Kuntz, *Jacob's Ladder and the Tree of Life*.

28. Seed, *American Pentimento*, 46–49, 53, 113.

29. Ibid., 113.

30. Smith, "Generall Historie of Virginia," 204. Smith often referred to himself in the third person.

31. The population estimates for Virginia are a matter of debate. Most sources assert that there were nearly five hundred colonists in Jamestown just before the Starving Time, ignoring the fact that this figure includes the population of two other settlements that did not suffer the same deprivation. There were likely closer to 300 or 350 people in Jamestown itself, including a disproportionate number of women, children, the elderly, and the sick (Bernhard, "'Men, Women, and Children' at Jamestown," 609). Herrmann, "The 'Tragicall Historie,'" 49–52. The preceding growing season had been abnormally dry, causing agricultural production that was far lower than expected; given that there were not enough farmers among the settlers, they were ill-equipped to feed themselves without help from the Indians and supplies from England. The resupply ship they expected was delayed by a hurricane in the Caribbean and arrived months late, bearing more colonists but few supplies. To make matters worse, their relationship with the local Powhatan Indians was at a low point, and the colonists were forced to hide behind their fortifications out of fear of Indian attacks. They also lacked access to consistent fresh water.

32. Neely, "Jamestown Colonists Resorted to Cannibalism."

33. Smith, "The Generall Historie of Virginia, New England, and the Summer Isles," 205. Smith's account is not the only reference to acts of cannibalism between Europeans. In the well-known story of Alvar Nuñez Cabeza de Vaca, *Chronicle of the Narváez Expedition*, there is an episode of cannibalism among stranded Spaniards.

34. Smith, "The Generall Historie of Virginia, New England, and the Summer Isles," 205.

35. Percy, "A Trewe Relacyon," 261. "The Spanyards plantacyon in the River of plate and the streightes of MAGELANE Suffered also in soe mutche thatt haveinge eaten upp all their horses to susteine themselves wthall, mutenies did Aryse and growe Amongste them for the wch the general DIEGO MENDOSA cawsed some of them to be executed Extremity of hunger in forceinge other secrettly in the night to cutt downe Their deade fellowes from of the gallowes and bury them in their hungry Bowelles."

36. Ibid., 266–67.

37. Herrmann, "The 'Tragicall Historie,'" 52, 56, 57.

38. Council for Virginia, "A True Declaration"; William Strachey, "A True Reportory," in Horn, *Captain John Smith*, 979–1037.

39. Mary Rowlandson's account of her captivity, "A True History of the Captivity and Restoration of Mrs. Mary Rowlandson," best illustrates the struggle against the environment and the importance of divine providence.

40. Wilcomb Washburn, introduction to Vaughan, *Narratives of North American Captivity*, xii–xxxvii.

41. Dickinson, "God's Protecting Providence," 2, 5, 9.

42. Ibid., 14, 60.

43. *Cacique*, while technically a Taíno term, was commonly used by European writers to refer to a wide array of Indian leaders and chiefs.

44. Dickinson, "God's Protecting Providence," 10. Dickinson reports that one member of their group spoke limited Spanish and could communicate with the Natives, who also knew some Spanish. Obviously the issue of translation is an important factor here (Dickinson, "God's Protecting Providence," 6).

45. Bynum, *Holy Feast and Holy Fast*, 269–70.

46. Price, *Consuming Passions*, 26ff, 60ff. For a discussion of the continuation of this trope in colonial New England see Karlsen, *The Devil in the Shape of a Woman*.

47. "To be devoured or swallowed up is to be incorporated within an Other, transformed into an Other. This possibility, horrifying as it was, did not constitute Jonathan and Mary Dickinson's ultimate nightmare. They were most fearful for their six-month-old son—not so much that he would be physically devoured by their captors but that he would live to become one of them" (Strong, *Captive Selves, Captivating Others*, 156).

48. Todorov, *The Conquest of America*, 17.

49. Andrews, "God's Protecting Providence," 8, 10. Andrews's essay contains a helpful publication history of Dickinson's work.

50. Similar to the way the publishing family the De Brys knew that salacious images of savage cannibals would sell books, Dickinson's publisher likely suspected that putting the word *cannibal* in the title would encourage sales.

51. Vaughan, *Narratives of North American Captivity*, xi.

52. Dickinson, 7, 5.

53. Slotkin, *Regeneration through Violence*, 94.

54. Cotton Mather, "Good Fetch'd out of Evil," 1706, in Washburn, *The Garland Library of Narratives of North American Indian Captivities*, 4: 34.

55. Elizabeth Hanson, "An Account of the Captivity of Elizabeth Hanson, Now or Late of Kachecky, in New England: Who, with Four of her Children and Servant-Maid, was taken captive by the Indians, and carried into Canada. Setting forth The various remarkable Occurrences, sore Trials, and wonderful Deliverances which befell them after their Departure, to the Time of their Redemption. Taken in Substance from her own Mouth, by Samuel Bownas," in VanDerBeets, *Held Captive by Indians*, 143.

56. Briton Hammon, "A Narrative of the Sufferings and Deliverance of Briton Hammon," 1760, in Washburn, *The Garland Library of Narratives of North American Indian Captivities*, 8: 7. The substitution of dogs for human victims has an interesting trajectory in anthropological interpretations of Iroquois rituals. See Blau, "The Iroquois White Dog Sacrifice."

57. Henry Grace, "History of the Life and Sufferings of Henry Grace," 1764, in Washburn, *The Garland Library of Narratives of North American Indian Captivities*, 8: 40, 43.

58. Williams, *The Redeemed Captive Returning to Zion*, 12, 20, 23.

59. Evan Haefeli and Kevin Sweeney, "Revisiting *The Redeemed Captive*: New Perspectives on the 1704 Attack on Deerfield," in Calloway, *After King Philip's War*, 56.

60. Wood, *New England's Prospect*, 75–76.

61. Abler, "Scalping, Torture, Cannibalism, and Rape," 4. Abler wrote, "One hears cries of atrocity and 'barbaric' activity because societies justify their wars by citing the deviant behaviour of the enemy. One is justified in killing and maiming someone who is less human than oneself, so typically enemy violations of a common code will receive wide publicity while the violation made by one's own forces will be denied or excused and justified as 'retaliation.'"

62. Isaac Hollister, "A Brief Narration of the Captivity of Isaac Hollister," 1767, in Washburn, *The Garland Library of Narratives of North American Indian Captivities*, 8: 7.

63. See Rowlandson, "A True History of the Captivity and Restoration of Mrs. Mary Rowlandson."

64. Archaeological evidence suggests that the Iroquois increased their fortifications with a corresponding uptick in violence from around the thirteenth century onward. The evidence is also fairly conclusive that the Iroquois did practice cannibalism before the arrival of Europeans. However, the archaeological and textual evidence suggests that after 1525 they began consolidating and fortifying villages in response to new threats. While it cannot at this time be conclusively proved, it seems fairly clear that as violence and instability increased in Iroquoia after the arrival of Europeans, so did man-eating. See Trigger, *Children of Aataentsic*, 144, 158; Bradley, *The Evolution of the Onondaga Iroquois*, 34–37, 54; Snow, *The Iroquois*, 53.

65. Hollister, "A Brief Narration of the Captivity of Isaac Hollister," in Washburn, *The Garland Library of Narratives of North American Indian Captivities*, 8: 2–5, 5–7.

66. Thomas Brown, "A Plain Narrative," 1760, in Washburn, *The Garland Library of Narratives of North American Indian Captivities*, 8: 20–21.

67. Peter Way, "The Cutting Edge of Culture: British Soldiers Encounter Native Americans in the French and Indian War," in Daunton and Halpern, *Empire and Others*, 135.

68. Little, *Abraham at Arms.*

69. John Maylem, "Gallic Perfidy: A Poem," 1758, in Washburn, *The Garland Library of Narratives of North American Captivities*, 8: 9, 12, 15, 10.

70. For a discussion of the connection between emotions and Anglo-American masculinity see Eustace, *Passion Is the Gale.*

71. For an interesting example of accusations of French Eucharistic cannibalism see Lowry, "A Journal of the Captivity of Jean Lowry," in Washburn, *The Garland Library of Narratives of North American Indian Captivities*, 8: 27.

72. Cotton Mather, "A Memorial of the Deplorable State of New England," 1707, in Washburn, *The Garland Library of Narratives of North American Captivities*, vol. 8.

73. John Gyles, "Memoirs of Odd Adventures, Strange Deliverances etc. in the Captivity of John Gyles esq., Commander of the Garrison on St. George River, in the District of Maine. Written by Himself," in VanDerBeets, *Held Captive by Indians*, 97–98.

74. John Norton, "The Redeemed Captive," 1758, in Washburn, *The Garland Library of Narratives of North American Captivities*, 6: 10.

75. Lombard, *Making Manhood*, 16, 9.

## Notes to Chapter 6

1. See Anderson, *Crucible of War*; Hofstra, *Cultures in Conflict.*

2. Weber, *Bárbaros*, 12, 34–51, 39.

3. Obviously many Indian groups considered the Americans interlopers, but I am referring to their self-identification.

4. Certainly all discussion of Indian cannibalism did not simply end, but the frequency of accusations of cannibalism and the power of these accusations to influence policy declined markedly.

5. In addition to myriad other sources discussed thus far, Anderson's *Chain Her by One Foot* is a wonderful example of how the process of imperialism reshaped Indian gender roles.

6. Almaguer, *Racial Faultlines*, 19–21.

7. I do not want to downplay the importance of the Tupínamba of Brazil as absolutely central to understanding cannibalism in the Americas, but as my focus has been on North America, I have chosen to place my emphasis elsewhere. For another fascinating example of the discourse of cannibalism in West Africa, the trials of the so-called Human Leopards highlight the continued Western fascination with the presumed cannibalism of the Other. See Beatty, *Human Leopards.*

8. Rydell, *All the World's a Fair*, 60, 46–47. One visitor remarked about the Midway Plaisance, "The best way of looking at the races is to behold them on an ascending scale, in the progressive movement; thus, we can march forward with them starting with the lowest specimens of humanity, and reaching continually upward to the highest stage" (quoted on 65).

9. I use the word *mankind* rather than *humankind* purposefully here. Although the fair displayed the innovations of both men and women, women's works were placed in their own building, reinforcing the naturalness and neutrality of men as inventors and innovators.

10. Rydell, *All the World's a Fair*, 56; Kruger, "'White Cities,' 'Diamond Zulus,' and the 'African Contribution to Human Advancement.'" For more on the representation of Native Americans see Rinehart, "To Hell with Wigs!"

11. Quoted in Rydell, *All the World's a Fair*, 53.

12. Bay, *Wives of the Leopard*, 278.

13. Isabel Burton, quoted in ibid., 278.

14. Bay, *Wives of the Leopard*, 66, 278; Wright, *The Life of Sir Richard Burton*, 67; Burton, *A mission to Gelele, King of Dahome*, 303–4.

15. See Banivanua-Mar, "Cannibalism and Colonialism"; Brantlinger, "Missionaries and Cannibals in Nineteenth-century Fiji"; Lindenbaum, *Kuru Sorcery*; Obeyesekere, *Cannibal Talk*; Salmond, *The Trial of the Cannibal Dog*.

# BIBLIOGRAPHY

Abé, Takao. *The Jesuit Mission to New France: A New Interpretation in the Light of the Earlier Jesuit Experiences in Japan.* Boston: Brill, 2011.

Abler, Thomas. "Iroquois Cannibalism: Fact Not Fiction." Special Iroquois issue, *Ethnohistory* 27, no. 4 (1980).

———. "A Mythical Myth: Comments on Sanday's Explanation of Iroquoian Cannibalism." *American Anthropologist* 90, no. 4 (1988): 967–69.

———. "Scalping Torture, Cannibalism, and Rape: An Ethnohistorical Analysis of Conflicting Cultural Values in War." *Anthropologica* 34 (1992): 3–20.

Abbott, Elizabeth. *A History of Celibacy.* Cambridge, MA: Da Capo Press, 2001.

Acosta, José de. *Natural and Moral History of the Indies.* Edited by Jane Mangan. Translated by Frances López-Morillas. Chronicles of the New World Encounter Series. Durham, NC: Duke University Press, 2002.

Adorno, Rolena. "Discourses on Colonialism: Bernal Díaz, Las Casas, and the Twentieth-Century Reader." Hispanic issue, *MLN* 103, no 2 (1988): 239–58.

———. "The Discursive Encounter of Spain and America: The Authority of Eyewitness Testimony in the Writing of History." *William and Mary Quarterly*, 3rd series, 49, no. 2 (1992): 210–28.

Almaguer, Tomás. *Racial Faultlines: The Historical Origins of White Supremacy in California.* Berkeley: University of California Press, 1994.

Anderson, Fred. *Crucible of War: The Seven Years' War and the Fate of Empire in British North America, 1754–1766.* Reprint edition. New York: Viking, 2001.

Anderson, Karen. *Chain Her by One Foot: The Subjugation of Women in Seventeenth Century New France*. New York: Routledge, 1991.

Andrews, Charles M. "God's Protecting Providence: A Journal by Jonathan Dickinson." *Florida Historical Quarterly* 21, no. 2 (1942): 107–26.

(Pseudo) Apollodorus. *The Library*, vol. 1. Translated by James George Frazer. New York: G. P. Putnam's Sons, 1921.

Arens, William. *The Man-Eating Myth: Anthropology and Anthropophagy*. New York: Oxford University Press, 1980.

Avramescu, Cătălin. *An Intellectual History of Cannibalism*. Translated by Alistair Ian Blyth. Princeton, NJ: Princeton University Press, 2011.

Axtell, James, ed. *After Columbus: Essays in the Ethnohistory of Colonial North America*. New York: Oxford University Press, 1988.

———. *Natives and Newcomers: The Cultural Origins of North America*. New York: Oxford University Press, 2001.

Banivanua-Mar, Tracey. "Cannibalism and Colonialism: Charting Colonies and Frontiers in Nineteenth Century Fiji." *Comparative Studies in Society and History* 52, no. 2 (2010): 255–81.

Barker, Francis, Peter Hulme, and Margaret Iversen, eds. *Cannibalism and the Colonial World*. Cultural Margins. New York: Cambridge University Press, 1998.

Barney, Stephen A., W. J. Lewis, J. A. Beach, and Oliver Berghof, eds. *The Etymologies of Isidore of Seville*. Cambridge, UK: Cambridge University Press, 2006.

Bay, Edna. *Wives of the Leopard: Gender, Politics, and Culture in the Kingdom of Dahomey*. Charlottesville: University of Virginia Press, 1998.

Beatty, Sir Kenneth James. *Human Leopards: An Account of the Trials of Human Leopards before the Special Commission Court. With a Note on Sierra Leone, Past and Present*. New York: AMS Press, 1978.

Beau, B. *A Defense of Cannibalism*. International Conciliation. New York: American Association for International Conciliation, 1914.

Behrend-Martínez, Edward. "Manhood and the Neutered Body in Early Modern Spain." *Journal of Social History* 38, no. 4 (2005): 1073–93.

Berglund, Jeff. *Cannibal Fictions: American Explorations of Colonialism, Race, Gender and Sexuality*. Madison: University of Wisconsin Press, 2006.

Bernhard, Virginia. "'Men, Women, and Children' at Jamestown: Population and Gender in Early Virginia, 1607-1610. *Journal of Southern History* vol. 58, no. 4 (Nov. 1992): 599-618.

Bettenson, Henry, ed. *Documents of the Christian Church*. 2nd edition. New York: Oxford University Press, 1967.

Bhabha, Homi K. *The Location of Culture*. New York: Routledge, 2004.

Blackburn, Carole. *Harvest of Souls: The Jesuit Missions and Colonialism in North America, 1632–1650*. Montréal: McGill-Queen's University Press, 2000.

Blau, Harold. "The Iroquois White Dog Sacrifice: Its Evolution and Symbolism." *Ethnohistory* 11, no. 2 (1964): 97–119.

Blurton, Heather. *Cannibalism in High Medieval English Literature.* New Middle Ages Series. New York: Palgrave Macmillan, 2007.

Bohak, Gideon. "Ethnic Portraits in Greco-Roman Literature." In *Cultural Borrowings and Ethnic Appropriation in Antiquity.* Edited by Erich S. Gruen Stuttgart: Franz Steiner Verlag, 2005.

Bonvillain, Nancy. "Gender Relations in Native North America." *American Indian Culture and Research Journal* 13, no. 2 (1969): 1–28.

———. *Women and Men: Cultural Constructs of Gender.* Upper Saddle River, NJ: Prentice Hall, 1998.

Boucher, Philip P. *Cannibal Encounters: Europeans and Island Caribs, 1492–1763.* Baltimore: Johns Hopkins University Press, 1992.

Bradley, James W. *The Evolution of the Onondaga Iroquois: Accommodating Change, 1500–1655.* Syracuse, NY: Syracuse University Press, 1987.

Bragdon, Kathleen. "Gender as a Social Category in Native Southern New England." *Ethnohistory* 43, no. 4 (1996): 573–92.

Brandão, José António, ed. and trans. *Nation Iroquoise: A Seventeenth-Century Ethnography of the Iroquois.* Lincoln: University of Nebraska Press, 2003.

———. *Your Fyre Shall Burn No More: Iroquois Policy toward New France and Its Native Allies to 1701.* Lincoln: University of Nebraska Press, 1997.

Brantlinger, Patrick. "Missionaries and Cannibals in Nineteenth-century Fiji." *History and Anthropology* 17, no. 1 (2006): 21–38.

Brightman, Robert A. "The Windigo in the Material World." *Ethnohistory* 33, no. 4 (1988): 337–79.

Brown, Kathleen M. "Brave New Worlds: Women's and Gender History." *William and Mary Quarterly* 50, no. 2 (1993): 311–28.

Brown, Paula, and Donald F. Tuzin. *The Ethnography of Cannibalism.* Washington, DC: Society for Psychological Anthropology, 1983.

Burton, Sir Richard Francis. *A mission to Gelele, King of Dahome: With notices of the so called "Amazons," the grand customs, the yearly customs, the human sacrifices, the present state of the slave trade, and the Negro's place in nature.* London: Tylston and Edwards, 1893.

Butler, Joseph T., Jr. "The Atakapa Indians: Cannibals of Louisiana." *Louisiana History: The Journal of the Louisiana Historical Association* 11, no. 2 (1970): 167–76.

Bynum, Caroline Walker. *Holy Feast and Holy Fast: The Religious Significance of Food to Medieval Women.* New York: Zone Books, 1991.

Cabeza de Vaca, Alvar Núñez. *Chronicle of the Narváez Expedition.* Translated by Fanny Bandelier. New York: Penguin Books, 2002.

Calloway, Colin G., ed. *After King Philip's War: Presence and Persistence in Indian New England.* Hanover, NH: University Press of New England, 1997.

———. "An Uncertain Destiny: Indian Captivities on the Upper Connecticut River." *Journal of American Studies* 17, no. 2 (1983): 189–210.

Campbell, Mary. *The Witness and the Other World: Exotic European Travel Writing, 400–1600.* Ithaca, NY: Cornell University Press, 1988.

Cañizares-Esguerra, Jorge. *Puritan Conquistadors: Iberianizing the Atlantic, 1550–1700.* Stanford: Stanford University Press, 2006.

Carew, Jan. "Columbus and the Origins of Racism in the Americas: Part One." *Race and Class* 29, no. 4 (1988): 1–19.

———. "Columbus and the Origins of Racism in the Americas: Part Two." *Race and Class* 30, no. 1 (1988): 33–57.

Carrasco, David. *City of Sacrifice: The Aztec Empire and the Role of Violence in Civilization.* Boston: Beacon Press, 1999.

Celestin, Roger. "Montaigne and the Cannibals: Toward a Redefinition of Exoticism." *Cultural Anthropology* 5, no. 3 (1990): 292–313.

Chanca, Diego Alvarez. "Letter of Dr. Chanca on the Second Voyage of Columbus." American Journeys Collection, document AJ-065. Wisconsin Historical Digital Library and Archives. http://content.wisconsinhistory.org/cdm/ref/collection/aj/id/4408.

Chanca, Diego Alvarez, and Andrés Bernáldez. *Christopher Columbus's Discoveries in the Testimonies of Diego Alvarez Chanca and Andrés Bernáldez.* Translated by Gioacchino Tiolo and Luciana F. Farina. Nuova Raccolta Colombiana. Rome: Istituto Poligrafico E. Zecca Dello Stato— Libreria Dello Stato, 1992.

Charnock, Richard Stephen. "Cannibalism in Europe." *Journal of the Anthropological Society of London* 4 (1866): xxii–xxxi.

Chesley Baity, Elizabeth. *Americans before Columbus.* New York: Viking Press, 1961.

Chimalpahin Cuauhtlehuanitzin, Domingo Francisco de San Antón Muñón. *Annals of His Time: Don Domingo de San Antón Muñón Chimalpahin Quauhtlehuanitzin.* Edited and translated by James Lockhart, Susan Schroeder, and Doris Namala. Stanford: Stanford University Press, 2006.

Clendinnen, Inga. *Ambivalent Conquests: Maya and Spaniard in Yucatan, 1517–1570.* New York: Cambridge University Press, 2003.

———. *Aztecs: An Interpretation.* New York: Cambridge University Press, 1991.

Cobley, Alan, ed. *Crossroads of Empire: The European-Caribbean Connection 1492–1992.* Cave Hill, Barbados: Department of History, University of the West Indies, 1994.

Cohen, Jeffrey Jerome. *Of Giants, Monsters, and the Middle Ages.* Medieval Cultures Book 17. Minneapolis: University of Minnesota Press, 1999.

Columbus, Christopher. *The Columbus Letter of 1493: A Facsimile of the Copy in the Willia R. Clements Library.* Translated by Frank Robbins. Ann Arbor: Clements Library Associates, 1952.

——. *The* Diario *of Christopher Columbus's First Voyage to America, 1492–1493.* Abstracted by Fray Bartolomé de las Casas. Translated by Oliver Dunn and James E. Kelley Jr. Norman: University of Oklahoma Press, 1989.

——. *The Four Voyages: Being His Own Log-Book, Letters, and Dispatches with Connecting Narrative Drawn from the Life of the Admiral by his son Hernando Colon and other Contemporary Historians.* Edited and translated by J. M. Cohen. London: Penguin Books, 1969.

——. *His Own Book of Privileges.* 1502. Translated by George R. Barwick. London: B. F. Stevens, 1894.

——. "Journal of the First Voyage of Columbus." American Journeys Collection, document AJ-062. Wisconsin Historical Digital Library and Archives. http://www.americanjourneys.org/aj-062/index.asp.

——. "Letter of Columbus to Luis de Santángel." American Journeys Collection, document AJ-063. Wisconsin Historical Digital Library and Archives. http://www.americanjourneys.org/aj-063/index.asp.

Columbus, Ferdinand. *Historie Concerning the Life and Deeds of the Admiral Don Christopher Columbus.* Edited by Paolo Emilio Taviani and Ilaria Luzzana Caraci. Translated by Luciano F. Farina. Nuova Raccolta Colombiana. Rome: Istituto Poligrafico E Zecca Dello Stato—Libreria Dello Stato, 1998.

——. *The Life of the Admiral Christopher Columbus by his Son Ferdinand.* Translated by Benjamin Keen. New Brunswick, NJ: Rutgers University Press, 1992.

Conklin, Beth A. *Consuming Grief: Compassionate Cannibalism in an Amazonian Society.* Austin: University of Texas Press, 2001.

Constable, Olivia Remie, ed. *Medieval Iberia: Readings from Christian, Muslim, and Jewish Sources.* Philadelphia: University of Pennsylvania Press, 1997.

Corfis, Ivy, and Ray Harris-Northall, eds. *Medieval Iberia: Changing Societies and Cultures in Contact and Transition.* Rochester, NY: Tamesis, 2007.

Council for Virginia. "A True Declaration of the estate of the Colonie in Virginia, With a confutation of such scandalous reports as have tended to the disgrace of so worthy an enterprise." London, 1610. Virtual Jamestown Project. http://etext.lib.virginia.edu/etcbin/jamestown-browse?id=J1059.

Curry, Dennis. *Feast of the Dead: Aboriginal Ossuaries in Maryland.* For the Archaeological Society of Maryland, Inc. Crownsville, MD: Maryland Historical Trust Press, 1999.

Cortés, Hernán. *Letters from Mexico.* Translated by Anthony Pagden. Revised edition. New Haven, CT: Yale University Press, 1986.

Danvers, Gail. "Gendered Encounters: Warriors, Women, and William Johnson." *Journal of American Studies* 35, no. 2 (2001): 187–202.

Daunton, M. J., and Rick Halpern, eds. *Empire and Others: British Encounters with Indigenous Peoples, 1600–1850.* Philadelphia: University of Pennsylvania Press, 1999.

Davis, Dave D., and R. Christopher Goodwin. "Island Carib Origins: Evidence and Nonevidence." *American Antiquity* 55, no. 1 (1990): 37–48.

de Bry, Theodore. *Thomas Hariot's Virginia.* Ann Arbor, MI: University Microfilms, 1966.

de Certeau, Michel. *Heterologies: Discourse on the Other.* Translated by Brian Massumi. Vol. 17, *Theory and History of Literature.* Minneapolis: University of Minnesota Press, 1986.

Derounian-Stodala, Kathryn Zabelle, and James Arthur Levernier. *The Indian Captivity Narrative, 1550–1900.* New York: Twayne, 1993.

Díaz del Castillo, Bernal. *The Discovery and Conquest of Mexico, 1517–1521.* Translated by A. P. Maudsley. New York: Farrar, Strauss, and Cudahy, 1956.

Dickason, Olive Patricia. *The Myth of the Savage and the Beginnings of French Colonialism in the Americas.* Edmonton: University of Alberta Press, 1984.

Dickinson, Jonathan. "God's Protecting Providence." 1707. In *The Garland Library of North American Indian Captivities*, vol. 4, edited by Wilcomb Washburn. New York: Garland Publishers, 1977.

Doueihi, Milad. *A Perverse History of the Human Heart.* Cambridge, MA: Harvard University Press, 1997.

Downs, Laura Lee. *Writing Gender History.* New York: Oxford University Press, 2004.

Drake, Sir Francis. *The World Encompassed.* 1628. March of American Facsimile Series, no. 11. Ann Arbor, MI: University Microfilms, 1966.

duBois, Page. *Centaurs and Amazons: Women and the Pre-history of the Great Chain of Being.* Ann Arbor: University of Michigan Press, 1982.

Durán, Diego. *The History of the Indies of New Spain.* Translated by Doris Heyden and Fernando Horcasitias. New York: Orion Press, 1964.

Duval, Edwin M. "Lessons of the New World: Design and Meaning in Montaigne's 'Des Cannibales' and 'Des Coches.'" Montaigne: Essays in Reading, *Yale French Studies*, no. 64 (1983): 95–112.

Dyer, Abigail. "Seduction by Promise of Marriage: Law, Sex, and Culture in Seventeenth-Century Spain." *Sixteenth Century Journal* 34, no. 2 (2003): 439–55.

Eccles, W. C. *Essays on New France.* Toronto: Oxford University Press, 1987.

Eden, Richard, ed. *The First Three English Books on America.* Edited by Edward Arber. Translated by Richard Eden. Westminster, UK: Archibald, Constable, 1895.

Elberg, Nathan. "Aztec Cannibalism and the Caloric Obsession." *American Anthropologist*, new series 83, no. 3 (1981): 622.

Elias, Norbert. *The Civilizing Process: The History of Manners.* New York: Urizen Books, 1978.

Elliott, J. H. *Empires of the Atlantic World: Britain and Spain in America, 1492–1830.* New Haven, CT: Yale University Press, 2006.

———. *Imperial Spain, 1469–1716.* 1963. London: Penguin Books, 2002.

Endicott, Kirk M., and Robert Louis Welsch. *Taking Sides: Clashing Views on Controversial Issues in Anthropology.* Dubuque, IA: McGraw-Hill/Dushkin, 2005.

Eustace, Nicole. *Passion Is the Gale: Emotion, Power, and the Coming of the American Revolution.* Omohundro Institute of Early American History and Culture. Chapel Hill: University of North Carolina Press, 2008.

Fanon, Frantz. *Black Skin, White Masks.* New York: Grove Press, 1991.

Feldman, George Franklin. *Cannibalism, Headhunting, and Human Sacrifice in North America: A History Forgotten.* Chambersburg, PA: Alan C. Hood, 2008.

Fenster, Thelma S., and Clare A. Lees. *Gender in Debate from the Early Middle Ages to the Renaissance.* The New Middle Ages. New York: Palgrave, 2002.

Fernández-Armesto, Felipe. *Amerigo: The Man Who Gave His Name to America.* London: Weidenfeld & Nicolson, 2006.

Fernández de Oviedo y Valdés, Gonzalo. *Natural History of the West Indies.* Chapel Hill: University of North Carolina Press, 1969.

Fitzmaurice, Andrew. *Humanism and America: An Intellectual History of English Colonization.* Cambridge, UK: Cambridge University Press, 2003.

Floyd, Troy S. *The Columbus Dynasty in the Caribbean: 1492–1526.* Albuquerque: University of New Mexico Press, 1973.

Formisano, Luciano, ed. *Letters from a New World: Amerigo Vespucci's Discovery of America.* Translated by David Jacobson. New York: Marsilio, 1992.

Forsyth, Donald W. "The Beginnings of Brazilian Anthropology: Jesuits and Tupinamba Cannibalism." *Journal of Anthropological Research* 38, no. 2 (1983), 147–78.

Foster, Thomas A., ed. *New Men: Manliness in Early America.* New York: New York University Press, 2011.

Foucault, Michel. *The History of Sexuality. Volume 1: An Introduction.* Translated by Robert Hurley. New York: Vintage Books, 1990.

———. *The Order of Things: An Archaeology of the Human Sciences.* New York: Pantheon Books, 1971.

———. *Power/Knowledge: Selected Interviews and Other Writings, 1972–1977.* Translated by C. Gordon. New York: Pantheon Books, 1980.

Franklin, Wayne. *Discoverers, Explorers, Settlers: The Diligent Writers of Early America.* Chicago: University of Chicago Press, 1979.

Fuentes, Patricia de. *The Conquistadors: First-Person Accounts of the Conquest of Mexico.* Norman: University of Oklahoma Press, 1993.

Gallay, Alan. *The Indian Slave Trade: The Rise of the English Empire in the American South, 1670–1717.* New Haven, CT: Yale University Press, 2002.

Galvano, Antonie. *The Discoveries of the World from their first orginall unto the yeere of our Lord 1555.* Edited by Richard Hakluyt. London: Impensis G. Bishop, 1601.

Gardyner, George. *A Description of the New World. Or, America Islands and Continent: and what people those regions are now inhabited. And what places there desolate and without Inhabitants.* London: Robert Leybourn, 1651.

Gaudio, Michael. *Engraving the Savage: The New World and Techniques of Civilization.* Minneapolis: University of Minnesota Press, 2008.

Gerbi, Antonello. *Nature in the New World: From Christopher Columbus to Gonzalo Fernandez de Oviedo.* Translated by Jeremy Moyle. Reissue edition. Pittsburgh: University of Pittsburgh Press, 2010.

Gibson, Charles. *Spain in America.* New York: Harper and Row, 1966.

Godbeer, Richard. *Sexual Revolution in Early America.* Gender Relations in the American Experience. Baltimore: Johns Hopkins University Press, 2002.

Goddard, Peter A. "The Devil in New France: Jesuit Demonology, 1611–1650." *Canadian Historical Review* 78, no. 1 (1997): 40–62.

Goetzmann, William H., and Glyndwr Williams. *The Atlas of North American Exploration: From the Norse Voyages to the Race to the Pole.* New York: Prentice Hall, 1992.

Goldman, Laurence R., ed. *The Anthropology of Cannibalism.* Westport, CT: Bergin and Garvey, 1999.

Gómara, Francisco López de. *The Conquest of the West India.* Translated by Thomas Nicholas. March of the Americas Facsimile Series, no. 6. Ann Arbor, MI: University Microfilms, 1966.

———. *Cortés: The Life of the Conqueror by His Secretary.* Translated by Leslie Byrd Simpson. Berkeley: University of California Press, 1964.

Goody, Jack. *The Domestication of the Savage Mind.* Cambridge, UK: Cambridge University Press, 1977.

Gordon-Grube, Karen. "Anthropophagy in Post-Renaissance Europe: The Tradition of Medicinal Cannibalism." *American Anthropologist,* new series 90, no. 2 (1988): 405–9.

———. "Evidence of Medicinal Cannibalism in Puritan New England: 'Mummy' and Related Remedies in Edward Taylor's 'Dispensatory.'" *Early American Literature* 28, no. 3 (1993): 185–221.

Greenblatt, Stephen. *Marvelous Possessions: The Wonder of the New World.* New York: Clarendon Press, 1991.

———, ed. *New World Encounters.* Berkeley: University of California Press, 1993.

Greene, Paul E. "The Conquest of Mexico: The View of the Chroniclers." *Americas* 31, no. 2 (1974): 164–71.

Greer, Allan, ed. *The Jesuit Relations: Natives and Missionaries in Seventeenth-Century North America*. Bedford Series in History and Culture. Boston: Bedford/St. Martin's Press, 2000.

———. *The People of New France*. Themes in Canadian Social History. Toronto: University of Toronto Press, 1997.

Grimshaw, Ivan Gerould, and Edward F. Colerick. *Cannibals of Indiana*. Ft. Wayne, IN: Public Library of Fort Wayne and Allen County, 1955.

Groesen, Michiel van. "The De Bry Collection of Voyages (1590–1634): Early America Reconsidered." *Journal of Early Modern History* 12 (2008): 1–24.

Guest, Kristen, ed. *Eating Their Words: Cannibalism and the Boundaries of Cultural Identity*. Albany: State University of New York Press, 2001.

Gustafson, Lowell S., and Amelia M. Trevelyan, eds. *Ancient Maya Gender Identity and Relations*. Westport, CT: Bergin & Garvey, 2002.

Gutiérrez, Ramón A. *When Jesus Came, the Corn Mothers Went Away: Marriage, Sexuality, and Power in New Mexico, 1500–1846*. Stanford: Stanford University Press, 1991.

Hakluyt, Richard, ed. *Divers Voyages Touching the Discoverie of America*. Ann Arbor, MI: University Microfilms, 1966.

Hakluyt, Richard, and Edmund Goldsmid, eds. *The Principal Navigations, Voyages, Traffiques, and Discoveries of the English Nation*. Vol. 12, America Part I. Edinburgh: E. & G. Goldsmid, 1889.

———. *The Principal Navigations, Voyages, Traffiques, and Discoveries of the English Nation*. Vol. 13, America Part II. Edinburgh: E. & G. Goldsmid, 1889.

———. *The Principal Navigations, Voyages, Traffiques, and Discoveries of the English Nation..* Vol. 14, America Part III. Edinburgh: E. & G. Goldsmid, 1890.

———. *The Principal Navigations, Voyages, Traffiques, and Discoveries of the English Nation*. Vol. 15, America Part IV. Edinburgh: E. & G. Goldsmid, 1890.

Hamlin, William H. "Imagined Apotheoses: Drake, Harriot, and Ralegh in the Americas." *Journal of the History of Ideas* 57, no. 3 (1996): 405–28.

Hanson, Neil. *The Custom of the Sea: A Shocking True Tale of Shipwreck, Murder, and the Last Taboo*. New York: John Wiley and Sons, 1999.

Harner, Michael. *The Ecological Basis for Aztec Sacrifice*. Washington, DC: American Anthropological Association, 1977.

Hariot, Thomas, and John White. *A Briefe and True Report of the New Found Land of Virginia of the Commodities and of the Nature and Manners of the Naturall Inhabitants Discoupered by the English Colony There Seated by Sir Richard Greinuile Knight in the Yeere 1585*. Francoforti ad Moenvm [Frankfurt am Main]: Typis Ioannis Wecheli, svmtbis vero Theodori de Bry, 1590.

Harris, Marvin. *Cannibals and Kings: The Origin of Cultures*. Vintage Books edition. New York: Random House, 1991.

———. *Good to Eat: Riddles of Food and Culture*. Reissue edition. Long Grove, IL: Waveland Press, 1998.

Hart, Jonathan Locke. *Representing the New World: The English and French Uses of the Example of Spain*. New York: Palgrave, 2001.

Hay, Thomas H. "The Windigo Psychosis: Psychodynamic, Cultural, and Social Factors in Aberrant Behavior." *American Anthropologists* 73, no. 1 (1971): 1–19.

Healy, George R. "The French Jesuits and the Idea of the Noble Savage." *William and Mary Quarterly*, 3rd series 15, no. 2 (1958): 144–67.

Hendrix, Scott H., and Susan C. Karant-Nunn, eds. *Masculinity in the Reformation Era*. Kirksville, MO: Truman State University Press, 2008.

Heng, Geraldine. "Cannibalism, the First Crusade, and the Genesis of Medieval Romance." *Differences: A Journal of Feminist Cultural Studies* 10, no. 1 (2001): 98–174.

———. *Empire of Magic: Medieval Romance and the Politics of Cultural Fantasy*. New York: Columbia University Press, 2004.

Hennepin, Louis. *A New Discovery of a Vast Country in America by Father Louis Hennipin*. Reprinted from the second London issue of 1698. 2 vols. Edited by Rueben Gold Thwaites. Chicago: A. C. McClurg, 1903.

Herdt, Gilbert H. *Third Sex, Third Gender: Beyond Sexual Dimorphism in Culture and History*. New York: Zone Books, 1994.

Herodotus. *The Histories*. Translated by Robin Waterfield. London: Oxford University Press, 2008.

Herrmann, Rachel B. "The 'Tragicall Historie': Cannibalism and Abundance in Colonial Jamestown." *William and Mary Quarterly*, 3rd series 68, no. 1 (2011): 47–74.

Himmelman, P. Kenneth. "The Medicinal Body: An Analysis of Medicinal Cannibalism in Europe, 1300–1700." *Dialectical Anthropology* 22, no. 2 (1997): 183–203.

Hoffman, George. "Anatomy of the Mass: Montaigne's 'Cannibals.'" *PMLA* 117, no. 2 (2002): 207–21.

Hofstra, Warren R., ed. *Cultures in Conflict: The Seven Years' War in North America*. Lanham, MD: Rowman and Littlefield, 2007.

Hogg, Gary. *Cannibalism and Human Sacrifice*. London: Hale, 1958.

Hook, Brian S. "Oedipus and Thyestes among the Philosophers: Incest and Cannibalism in Plato, Diogenes, and Zeno." *Classical Philology* 100, no. 1 (2005): 17–40.

Horn, James, ed. *Captain John Smith: Writings and Other Narratives of Roanoke, Jamestown, and the First English Settlement of America*. New York: Library of America, 2007.

Horowitz, Maryanne Cline. *Race, Gender, and Rank: Early Modern Ideas of Humanity*. Library of the History of Ideas, vol. 8. Rochester, NY: University of Rochester Press, 1992.

Householder, Michael. *Inventing Americans in the Age of Discovery: Narratives of Encounter*. Farnham, UK: Ashgate, 2011.

Hulme, Peter. *Colonial Encounters: Europe and Native Caribbean, 1492–1797.* New York: Methuen, 1986.

———. *Remnants of Conquest: The Island Caribs and Their Visitors, 1877–1998*. New York: Oxford University Press, 2000.

Hulme, Peter, and William H. Sherman, eds. *"The Tempest" and Its* Travels. Philadelphia: University of Pennsylvania Press, 2000.

Hulme, Peter, and Neil L. Whitehead, eds. *Wild Majesty: Encounters with the Caribs from Columbus to the Present Day*. New York: Oxford University Press, 1992.

Hurtado, Albert L., and Peter Iverson. *Major Problems in American Indian History: Documents and Essays*. Boston: Houghton Mifflin, 2001.

Icazbalceta, Joaquin García. *Coleccion de Documentos para la Historia de México*. Mexico City: Libreria de J. M. Andrade, 1858.

Ignatius of Loyola. *A Pilgrim's Journey: The Autobiography of Ignatius of Loyola*. Translated by Joseph Tylenda. Revised edition. San Francisco: Ignatius Press, 2001.

Isaac, Barry L. "Nahua versus Spanish and Mestizo Accounts in the Valley of Mexico." *Ancient Mesoamerica* 16 (2005): 1–10.

Isaac, Benjamin H. *The Invention of Racism in Classical Antiquity*. Princeton, NJ: Princeton University Press, 2004.

Jaenen, Cornelius J. "'Les Sauvages Ameriquains': Persistence into the 18th Century of Traditional French Concepts and Constructs for Comprehending Amerindians." *Ethnohistory* 29, no. 1 (1982): 43–56.

Jaffary, Nora E. *Gender, Race and Religion in the Colonization of the Americas*. Women and Gender in the Early Modern World. Burlington, VT: Ashgate, 2007.

Jahoda, Gustav. *Images of Savages: Ancient Roots of Modern Prejudice in Western Culture*. New York: Routledge, 1999.

Jamieson, James B. "An Examination of Prisoner-Sacrifice and Cannibalism at the St. Lawrence Iroquoian Roebuck Site." *Canadian Journal of Archaeology* 7, no. 2 (1983): 159–75.

Jara, René, and Nicholas Spadaccini, eds. *Amerindian Images and the Legacy of Columbus*. Minneapolis: University of Minnesota Press, 1992.

Jennings, Francis. *The Invasion of America: Indians, Colonialism, and the Cant of Conquest*. Chapel Hill: University of North Carolina Press for the Institute of Early American History and Culture, 1975.

Jones, Ann Rosalind. "Ethnographer's Sketch, Sensational Engraving, Full-Length Portrait: Print Genres for Spanish America in Girolamo Benzoni, the De Brys, and Cesare Vecellio." *Journal of Medieval and Early Modern Studies* 41, no. 1 (2011): 137–71.

Josephy, Alvin M., Jr., ed. *American in 1492: The World of the Indian Peoples before the Arrival of Columbus*. New York: Knopf, 1992.

Josselyn, John. *An Account of Two Voyages to New England made during the years 1638, 1663*. Boston: William Veazie, 1865.

Juall, Scott D. "'Beaucoup plus barbares que les Sauvages mesmes': Cannibalism, Savagery, and Religious Alterity in Jean de Léry's *Histoire d'un voyage faict en la terre du Brésil* (1599–1600)." *L'Esprit Créateur* 48, no. 1 (2008): 58–71.

Karlsen, Carol. *The Devil in the Shape of a Woman: Witchcraft in Colonial New England*. New York: Norton, 1998.

Kellogg, Susan, *Weaving the Past: A History of Latin America's Indigenous Women from the Prehispanic Period to the Present*. New York: Oxford University Press, 2005.

Kennedy, J. H. *Jesuit and Savage in New France*. New Haven, CT: Yale University Press, 1950.

Kenseth, Joy, ed. *The Age of the Marvelous*. Chicago: University of Chicago Press, 1991.

Kilgour, Maggie. *From Communion to Cannibalism: An Anatomy of Metaphors of Incorporation*. Princeton, NJ: Princeton University Press, 1990.

King, C. Richard. "The (Mis)uses of Cannibalism in Contemporary Cultural Critique." *Diacritics* 30, no. 1 (2000): 106–23.

Klein, Melanie. *The Selected Melanie Klein*. Edited by Juliet Mitchell. New York: Free Press, 1987.

Knight, Franklin W. *The Caribbean: The Genesis of a Fragmented Nationalism*. 2nd edition. New York: Oxford University Press, 1990.

Knowles, Nathaniel. "The Torture of Captives by the Indians of Eastern North America." *Proceedings of the American Philosophical Society* 82, no. 2 (1940): 151–225.

Kristeva, Julia. *The Powers of Horror: An Essay on Abjection*. Translated by Leon Roudiez. New York: Columbia University Press, 1982.

Kruger, Loren. "'White Cities,' 'Diamond Zulus,' and the 'African Contribution to Human Advancement': African Modernities and the World's Fairs." *TDR: The Drama Review* 51, no. 3 (2007): 19–45.

Kuntz, Marion, and Paul Kuntz, eds. *Jacob's Ladder and the Tree of Life: Concepts of Hierarchy and the Great Chain of Being*. American University Studies, series 5, Philosophy vol. 14. New York: P. Lang, 1987.

Kupperman, Karen Ordahl, ed. *America in European Consciousness, 1493–1750*. Chapel Hill: University of North Carolina Press for the Institute of Early American History and Culture, 1995.

———. "Apathy and Death in Early Jamestown." *Journal of American History* 66, no. 1 (1979): 24–40.

———. *The Atlantic in World History*. New York: Oxford University Press, 2012.

———. *Captain John Smith: A Select Edition of His Writings*. Chapel Hill:

University of North Carolina Press for the Institute of Early American History and Culture, 1988.

——. "Fear of Hot Climates in the Anglo-American Colonial Experience." *William and Mary Quarterly*, 3rd series 41, no. 2 (1984): 213–40.

——. *Indians and English: Facing Off in Early America*. Ithaca, NY: Cornell University Press, 2000.

——. *The Jamestown Project*. Cambridge, MA: Harvard University Press, 2007.

——. *North America and the Beginnings of European Colonization*. Essays on the Columbian Encounter. Washington, DC: American Historical Association, 1992.

Landa, Friar Diego de. *The Maya: Diego de Landa's Account of the Affairs of Yucatan*. Edited and translated by A. R. Pagden. Chicago: J. P. O'Hara, 1975.

——. *Yucatan before and after the Conquest with Other Related Document, Maps, and Illustrations*. 1566. Translated by William Gates. New York: Dover, 1978.

Lane, Kris, ed. *Defending the Conquest: Bernardo de Machuca's Defense and Discourse of the Western Conquests*. Translated by Timothy F. Johnson. Latin American Originals. University Park: Penn State University Press, 2010.

Las Casas, Bartolomé de. *History of the Indies*. Translated by Andree Collard. New York: Harper and Row, 1971.

——. *In Defense of the Indians: A Defense of the Most Reverend Lord, Don Fray Bartolomé de las Casas, order of the Preachers, late Bishop of Chiapa, against the Persecutors and slanderers of the Peoples of the New World discovered across the seas*. Translated by Stafford Poole. DeKalb: Northern Illinois University Press, 1992.

Lavrin, Ascunsión, ed. *Sexuality and Marriage in Colonial Latin America*. Lincoln: University of Nebraska Press, 1989.

Lefebvre, Martin. "Conspicuous Cannibals: The Figure of the Serial Killer as Cannibal in the Age of Capitalism." *Theory, Culture, and Society* 22, no. 3 (2005): 43–62.

Lepore, Jill. *The Name of War: King Phillip's War and the Origins of American Identity*. New York: Knopf, 1998.

Léry, Jean de. *History of a Voyage to the Land of Brazil, Otherwise Called America*. Berkeley: University of California Press, 1990.

Lestringant, Frank. *Cannibals: The Discovery and Representation of the Cannibal from Columbus to Jules Verne*. Berkeley: University of California Press, 1997.

Levenson, Jay A., ed. *Circa 1492: Art in the Age of Exploration*. Washington, DC: National Gallery of Art, Yale University Press, 1991.

Lévi-Strauss, Claude. *Myth and Meaning*. New York: Schocken Books, 1979.

——. *The Raw and the Cooked*. Translated by John Weightman and Doreen

Weightman. Introduction to the Science of Mythology. New York: Harper and Row, 1969.

———. *The Savage Mind*. Nature of Human Societies Series. Chicago: University of Chicago Press, 1966.

———. *Tristes Tropiques*. New York: Atheneum, 1974.

Lindenbaum, Shirley. *Kuru Sorcery: Disease and Danger in the New Guinea Highlands*. 2nd edition. Boulder, CO: Paradigm, 2013.

———. "Thinking about Cannibalism." *Annual Review of Anthropology* 33 (2004): 475–98.

Little, Ann. *Abraham at Arms: War and Gender in Colonial New England*. Philadelphia: University of Pennsylvania Press, 2007.

Lockhart, James. *The Nahuas after Conquest: A Social and Cultural History of the Indians of Central Mexico, Sixteenth through Eighteenth Centuries*. Stanford: Stanford University Press, 1992.

Loeb, Edwin Meyer. *The Blood Sacrifice Complex*. Vol. 30, *American Anthropological Society Memoirs*. New York: Kraus, 1964.

Lombard, Anne S. *Making Manhood: Growing Up Male in Colonial New England*. Cambridge, MA: Harvard University Press, 2003.

López de Mariscal, Blanca. "A Thousands Words: The Interface of Text and Image in Accounts of New World Travels." *Arcadia: International Journal of Literary Culture* 46 (2011): 293–317.

Lorant, Stefan, John White, and Jacques Le Moyne de Morgues, eds. *The New World: The First Pictures of America*. New York: Duell, Sloan, and Pearce, 1946.

Lovejoy, Arthur. *The Great Chain of Being: A Study of the History of an Idea*. Cambridge, MA: Harvard University Press, 1936.

Lugones, Maria. "Heterosexualism and the Colonial/Modern Gender System." *Hypatia* 22, no. 1 (2007): 186–209.

Lutri, Joseph R. de. "Montaigne on the Noble Savage: A Shift in Perspective." *French Review* 49, no. 2 (1975): 206–11.

MacCormick, Alex. *The Mammoth Book of Maneaters*. London: Robinson, 2003.

Mackenthun, Gesa. *Metaphors of Dispossession: American Beginnings and the Translation of Empire, 1492–1637*. Norman: University of Oklahoma Press, 1997.

Madureira, Luís. "A Cannibal Recipe to Turn a Dessert Country into the Main Course: Brazilian *Antropofagia* and the Dilemma of Development." *Luso-Brazilian Review* 41, no. 2 (2005): 96–125.

Mancall, Peter, ed. *The Atlantic World and Virginia: 1550–1624*. Chapel Hill: University of North Carolina Press, 2007.

———. *Travel Narratives from the Age of Discovery: An Anthology*. New York: Oxford University Press, 2006.

Mancall, Peter C., and James Hart Merrell, eds. *American Encounters:*

*Natives and Newcomers from European Contact to Indian Removal, 1500–1850.* 2nd edition. New York: Routledge, 2007.

Mandeville, John. *The Travels of Sir John Mandeville: The Fantastic 14th-Century Account of a Journey to the East.* Mineola, NY: Dover, 2006.

———. *The Travels of Sir John Mandeville: The Version from the Cotton Manuscript in modern spelling with three narratives, in illustration of it from Hakluyt's* Navigations, Voyages, and Discoveries. London: Macmillan, 1915.

Manley, Gordon. "The Revival of Climatic Determinism." *Geographical Review* 48, no. 1 (1958): 98–105.

Marchi, Dudley M. "Montaigne and the New World: The Cannibalism of Cultural Production." *Modern Language Studies* 23, no. 4 (1993): 35–54.

Marín, Juan Miguel. "Heterosexual Melancholia and Mysticism in the Early Society of Jesus." *Theology and Sexuality* 13, no. 2 (2007): 121–35.

Martyr D'Anghera, Peter. *De Orbe Novo: The Eight Decades of Peter Martyr D'Anghera.* 2 vols. Translated by Francis Augustus MacNutt. New York: G. P. Putnam's Sons, Knickerbock Press, 1912.

McAvoy, Liz Herbert, and Teresa Walters, eds. *Consuming Narratives: Gender and Monstrous Appetite in the Middle Ages and the Renaissance.* Cardiff: University of Wales Press, 2002.

McClintock, Anne. *Imperial Leather: Race, Gender, and Sexuality in the Colonial Contest.* New York: Routledge, 1995.

McClintock, Anne, Aamir Mufti, and Ella Shohat, eds. *Dangerous Liaisons: Gender, Nation, and Postcolonial Perspectives* Minneapolis: University of Minnesota Press, 1997.

McDowell, Jim. *Hamatsa: The Enigma of Cannibalism on the Pacific Northwest Coast.* Vancouver: Ronsdale Press, 1997.

McGinness, Anne B. "Christianity and Cannibalism: Three European Views of the Tupi in the Spiritual Conquest of Brazil, 1557–1563." *World History Connected,* October 2010, http://worldhistoryconnected.press.illinois.edu/7.3/mcginness.html (accessed Sept. 2013).

McGowan, Andrew. "Eating People: Accusations of Cannibalism against Christians in the Second Century." *Journal of Early Christian Studies* 2, no. 3 (1994): 413–42.

Meinig, D. W. *The Shaping of America: A Geographical Perspective on 500 Years of History.* Vols. 1–4. New Haven, CT: Yale University Press, 1986.

Minucius Felix, Marcus. *The Octavius of Minicius Felix.* Translated by J. H. Freese. London: Society for the Promotion of Christian Knowledge, 1919.

Molho, Anthony, and Gordon S. Wood, eds. *Imagined Histories: American Historians Interpret the Past.* Princeton, NJ: Princeton University Press, 1998.

Montaigne, Michel de. *The Complete Essays of Michel de Montaigne.* Translated by Donald M. Frame. Stanford: Stanford University Press, 1976.

Montrose, Louis. "The Work of Gender in the Discourse of Discovery." The New World. Special issue, *Representations*, Winter 1991: 1–41.

Moore, James T. *Indian and Jesuit: A Seventeenth Century Encounter.* Chicago: Loyola University Press, 1982.

Moore-Gilbert, Bart. "'New Worlds, New Selves,' Montaigne, 'the Atlantic' and the Emergence of Modern Biography." *Atlantic Studies* 2, no.1 (2005): 1–14.

Morgan, Jennifer. *Laboring Women: Reproduction and Gender in New World Slavery.* Philadelphia: University of Pennsylvania Press, 2004.

Morison, Samuel E. *Admiral of the Ocean Sea: A Life of Christopher Columbus.* Boston: Northeastern University Press, 1983.

———, ed. and trans. *Journals and Other Documents on the Life and Voyages of Christopher Columbus.* New York: Heritage Press, 1963.

Morrison, Kenneth M. *The Solidarity of Kin: Ethnohistory, Religious Studies, and the Algonkian-French Religious Encounter.* Albany: State University of New York Press, 2002.

Münster, Sebastian. *Cosmographie.* Amsterdam: Theatrum Orbis Terrarum, 1968.

———. *A Treatyse of the Newe India.* Edited by Richard Eden. Ann Arbor, MI: University Microfilms, 1966.

Murphy, E. M., and J. P. Mallory. "Herodotus and the Cannibals." *Antiquity* 74, no. 284 (2000): 388–94.

Myers, Kathleen Ann. *Fernández de Oviedo's Chronicle of America: A New History for a New World.* Austin: University of Texas Press, 2007.

Myscofski, Carole A. "Imagining Cannibalism: European Encounters with Native Brazilian Women." *History of Religions* 47, nos. 2–3 (2007–2008): 142–55.

Navarrete, Martín Fernández de. *Coleccion de los viages y descubrimientos que hicieron por mar los españoles desde fines del siglo XV: Con varios documentos ineditos concernientes a la historia de la marina castellana y de los establecimientos españoles en Indias.* 5 vols. Buenos Aires: Editorial Guarania, 1945–46.

Neely, Paula. "Jamestown Colonists Resorted to Cannibalism: A Gruesome Discovery in a Trash Deposit at Jamestown Points to Cannibalism." *National Geographic News*, May 1, 2013. http://news.nationalgeographic.com/news/2013/13/130501-jamestown-cannibalism-archeology-science/.

Noble, Louise. *Medicinal Cannibalism in Early English Literature and Culture.* Early Modern Cultural Studies. New York: Palgrave Macmillan, 2011.

Núñez Cabeza de Vaca, Alvar. *Chronicle of the Narváez Expedition.* Translated by Fanny Bandelier. New York: Penguin Books, 2002.

Obeyesekere, Gananath. *The Apotheosis of Captain Cook: European Mythmaking in the Pacific.* Princeton, NJ: Princeton University Press, 1992.

———. *Cannibal Talk: The Man-Eating Myth and Human Sacrifice in the South Seas*. Berkeley: University of California Press, 2005.

Odoric of Pordenone. "The Journal of Friar Odoric." In *Cathay and the Way Thither; being a collection of medieval notices of China*. Vol. 1. Edited and translated by Henry Yule. London: Hakluyt Society, 1876.

Olson, Carl, ed. *Celibacy and Religious Tradition*. New York: Oxford University Press, 2008.

Omi, Michael, and Howard Winant. *Racial Formation in the United States: From the 1960s to the 1990s*. New York: Routledge, 1994.

Ortiz de Montellano, Bernard. "Aztec Cannibalism: An Ecological Necessity?" *Science*, new series 200, no. 4342 (1978): 611–17.

———. "Counting Skulls: Comment on the Aztec Cannibalism Theory of Harner-Harris." *American Anthropologist*, new series 85, no. 2 (1983): 403–6.

Ortner, Sherry B., and Harriet Whitehead, eds. *Sexual Meanings: The Cultural Construction of Gender and Sexuality*. New York: Cambridge University Press, 1981.

Pagden, Anthony. *The Fall of Natural Man: The American Indian and the Origins of Comparative Ethnology*. New York: Cambridge University Press, 1982.

Pagels, Elaine. *Adam, Eve, and the Serpent*. New York: Vintage Books, 1989.

Paquette, Robert L., and Stanley L. Engerman. *The Lesser Antilles in the Age of European Expansion*. Gainesville: University Press of Florida, 1996.

Percy, George. "A Trewe Relacyon." First Hand Accounts of Virginia, 1575–1705. Virtual Jamestown Project. http://etext.lib.virginia.edu/etcbin/jamestown-browse?id=J1063.

Pierson, William Dillon. *Black Legacy: America's Hidden Heritage*. Amherst: University of Massachusetts Press, 1993.

Pliny the Elder. *Natural History*. Vols. 1–10. Trans. W. H. S. Jones. Cambridge, MA: Harvard University Press, 1949–54.

Podruchny, Carolyn. "Werewolves and Windigos: Narratives of Cannibal Monsters in Canadian Voyageur Tradition." *Ethnohistory* 51, no. 4 (2004): 677–700.

Polo, Marco. *The Travels of Marco Polo*. Translated by R. E. Latham. London: Penguin Books, 1974.

Potter, Tiffany. "Writing Indigenous Femininity: Mary Rowlandson's Narrative of Captivity." *Eighteenth-Century Studies* 36, no. 2 (2003): 153–67.

Powers, Karen Vieira. "Andeans and Spaniards in the Contact Zone: A Gendered Collision." *American Indian Quarterly* 24, no. 4 (2000): 511–36.

———. *Women in the Crucible of Conquest: The Gendered Genesis of Spanish American Society, 1500–1600*. Albuquerque: University of New Mexico Press, 2005.

Prebisch, Teresa Piossek. "La Antropofagia en América en tiempos de la Conquista." *Revisita de Historia de América*, no. 123 (1998): 7–24.

Price, Merrall Llewellyn. *Consuming Passions: The Uses of Cannibalism in Late Medieval and Early Modern Europe*. New York: Routledge, 2003.

Purchas, Samuel. *Hakluytus Posthumus or Purchas His Pimgrimes*. 1625. 20 vols. Glasgow, 1906.

Quinn, David B. *Explorers and Colonies: America 1500–1625*. London: Hambledon Press, 1990.

———, ed. *New American World: A Documentary History of North America to 1612*. New York: Arno Press and Hector Bye, 1979.

Ramsay, Colin. "Cannibalism and Infant Killing: A System of 'Demonizing' Motifs in Indian Captivity Narratives." *CLIO* 24 (1994): 55–68.

Ramusio, Giovanni Battista. *Navigationi et Viaggi*. Vol. 3. Venetia: Nella Stamperia de' Givnti, 1556.

Rawson, Claude. "'Indians' and Irish: Montaigne, Swift and the Cannibal Question." *Modern Language Quarterly* 53, no. 3 (1992): 299–363.

Riches, David. *The Anthropology of Violence*. Oxford: Blackwell, 1986.

Richter, Daniel K. *Facing East from Indian Country: A Native History of Early America*. Cambridge, MA: Harvard University Press, 2001.

———. "Iroquois versus Iroquois: Jesuit Missions and Christianity in Village Politics, 1642–1686." *Ethnohistory* 32, no. 1 (1985): 1–16.

———. *The Ordeal of the Longhouse: The Peoples of the Iroquois League in the Era of European Colonization*. Chapel Hill: University of North Carolina Press, 1992.

———. "War and Culture: The Iroquois Experience." *William and Mary Quarterly*, 3rd series 40, no. 4 (1983): 528–59.

Richter, Daniel K., James Hart Merrell, and Wilcomb Washburn. *Beyond the Covenant Chain: The Iroquois and Their Neighbors in Indian North America, 1600–1800*. Syracuse, NY: Syracuse University Press, 1987.

Rinehart, Melissa. "To Hell with Wigs! Native American Representation and Resistance at the World's Columbian Exposition." *American Indian Quarterly* 36, no. 4 (2012): 403–42.

Roehner, Bertrand M. "Jesuits and the State: A Comparative Study of Their Expulsions." *Religion* 27, no. 2 (1997): 165–81.

Rogozinski, Jan. *A Brief History of the Caribbean: From the Arawak and the Carib to the Present*. New York: Facts on File, 1992.

Romm, James S. *The Edges of the Earth in Ancient Thought: Geography, Exploration, and Fiction*. Princeton, NJ: Princeton University Press, 1992.

Root, Robert Kilburn, trans. *Acts of Andrew*. New York: Henry Holt, 1899.

Rosenberg, Emily S. "Gender." *Journal of American History* 77, no. 1 (1990): 116–24.

Rouse, Irving. *The Tainos: Rise and Decline of the People who Greeted Columbus*. New Haven, CT: Yale University Press, 1992.

Rowlandson, Mary. "A True History of the Captivity and Restoration of Mrs. Mary Rowlandson." In *The Garland Library of Narratives of North*

*American Captivities*, vol. 1, edited by Wilcomb Washburn. New York: Garland, 1977.

Rubenstein, Jay. "Cannibals and Crusaders." *French Historical Studies* 31, no. 4 (2008): 525–52.

Rubies, Joan-Pau. "New Worlds and Renaissance Ethnology." *History and Anthropology* 6 nos. 2–3 (1993): 157–97.

Rushforth, Brett. "'A Little Flesh We Offer You': The Origins of Indian Slavery in New France." *William and Mary Quarterly*, 3rd series 60, no. 4 (2003), 777–808.

Rydell, Robert. *All the World's a Fair: Visions of Empire at American International Expositions, 1876–1916*. Chicago: University of Chicago Press, 1984.

Sagan, Eli. *Cannibalism: Human Aggression and Cultural Form*. New York: Harper and Row, 1974.

Sahagún, Bernardino de. *Conquest of New Spain (1585 Revision)*. Translated by Howard F. Cline. Salt Lake City: University of Utah Press, 1989.

——. *General History of the Things of New Spain*. 2nd revision. Vols. 1–12. Translated by Arthur J. O. Anderson and Charles E. Dibble. Santa Fe, NM: School of American Research, 1981.

Sale, Kirkpatrick. *The Conquest of Paradise: Christopher Columbus and the Columbian Legacy*. New York: Plume Books, 1990.

Salmond, Anne. *The Trial of the Cannibal Dog: The Remarkable Story of Captain Cook's Encounters in the South Seas*. New Haven, CT: Yale University Press, 2003.

Sanday, Peggy Reeves. *Divine Hunger: Cannibalism as a Cultural System*. New York: Cambridge University Press, 1986.

——. "Response to Abler." *American Anthropologist* 90, no. 4 (1988): 969–70.

Sartore, Richard L. *Humans Eating Humans: The Dark Shadow of Cannibalism*. Notre Dame, IN: Cross Cultural Publications, 1994.

Savigny, Jean Baptiste Henri. *Narrative of a Voyage to Senegal in 1816 Undertaken by Order of the French Government: Compromising an Account of the Shipwreck of the Medusa, Observations Respecting the Agriculture of the Western Coast of Africa*. Marlboro, VT: Marlboro Press, 1986.

Schaff, Philip, ed. *Ante-Nicene Fathers*. Vol. 2. Grand Rapids, MI: Christian Classics Ethereal Library, 1885.

Schreffler, Michael J. "Vespucci Rediscovers America: The Pictorial Rhetoric of Cannibalism in Early Modern Culture." *Art History* 28, no. 3 (2005): 295–310.

Schuller, Rudolph. "The Oldest Known Illustration of South American Indians." *Journal de la Société des Américanistes* 16, no. 1 (1924): 111–18.

Schwartz, Seymour. "The Greatest Misnomer on Planet Earth." *Proceedings of the American Philosophical Society* 146, no. 3 (2002): 264–81.

Schwartz, Stuart B. *Implicit Understandings: Observing, Reporting, and*

*Reflecting on the Encounters Between Europeans and Other Peoples in the Early Modern Era.* New York: Cambridge University Press, 1994.

————, ed. *Victors and Vanquished: Spanish and Nahua Views of the Conquest of Mexico.* Boston: Bedford/St. Martin's Press, 2000.

Scott, Joan Wallach. "Gender: A Useful Category of Historical Analysis." *American Historical Review* 91, no. 5 (1986): 1053–75.

————. *Gender and the Politics of History.* Gender and Culture. New York: Columbia University Press, 1988.

Seed, Patricia. *American Pentimento: The Invention of Indians and the Pursuit of Riches.* Minneapolis: University of Minnesota Press, 2001.

————. *Ceremonies of Possession in Europe's Conquest of the New World: 1492–1640.* New York: Cambridge University Press, 1995.

————. "'Failing to Marvel': Atahualpa's Encounter with the Word." *Latin American Research Review* 26, no. 1 (1991): 7–32.

Seeman, Erik R. *The Huron-Wendat Feast of the Dead: Indian-European Encounters in Early North America.* Baltimore: Johns Hopkins University Press, 2011.

Sepúlveda, Juan Ginés de. *Obres Completas.* 1995. Pozoblanco, Spain: Excmo. Ayuntamiento de Pozoblanco, 2003.

Shankman, Paul. "Le Rôti et le Bouilli: Lévi-Strauss' Theory of Cannibalism." *American Anthropologist,* new series 71, no. 1 (1969): 54–69.

Sharp, Tom. "The Acts of Matthew and Andrew in the City of Cannibals." *Medieval Forum* 2 (2003). http://www.sfsu.edu/~medieval/volume2.html.

Shoemaker, Nancy. "An Alliance between Men: Gender Metaphors in Eighteenth Century American Indian Diplomacy East of the Mississippi." *Ethnohistory* 46, no. 2 (1999): 239–63.

————. "How Indians Got to Be Red." *American Historical Review* 102, no. 3 (1997): 625–44.

Sicoli, F. M., and A. Tartabini. "Amerindian Cannibalism: Practice and Discursive Strategy." *Human Evolution* 9, no. 3 (1994): 249–55.

Sigal, Peter. "The *Cuiloni,* the *Patlache,* and the Abominable Sin: Homosexualities in Early Colonial Nahua Society." *Hispanic American Historical Review* 85, no. 4 (2005): 555–93.

————. *From Moon Goddesses to Virgins: The Colonization of Yucatecan Maya Sexual Desire.* Austin: University of Texas Press, 2000.

Silverblatt, Irene. "Lessons of Gender and Ethnohistory in Mesoamerica." *Ethnohistory* 42, no. 4 (1995): 639–50.

Simpson, A. W. Brian. *Cannibalism and the Common Law: The Story of the Tragic Last Voyage of the Mignonette and the Strange Legal Proceedings to Which It Gave Rise.* Chicago: University of Chicago Press, 1984.

Sloan, Kim. *A New World: England's First View of America.* Chapel Hill: University of North Carolina Press, 2007.

Slotkin, Richard. *Regeneration through Violence: The Mythology of the*

*American Frontier, 1600–1800.* Middletown, CT: Wesleyan University Press, 1973.

Smith, John. "The Generall Historie of Virginia, New England, and the Summer Isles. Together with the True Travels, Adventures and Observations, and A Sea Grammar." In *The Travels of Captaine John Smith, Volume I.* Glasgow: Glasgow University Press, 1907.

Smith, Merrill D., ed. *Sex and Sexuality in Early America.* New York: New York University Press, 1998.

Snow, Dean. *The Iroquois.* Cambridge, MA: Blackwell, 1994.

Spivak, Gayatri Chakravorty. "Can the Subaltern Speak?" In *Colonial Discourse and Post-Colonial Theory: A Reader.* Edited by Patrick Williams and Laura Chrisman. New York: Columbia University Press, 1994.

Spivak, Gayatri Chakravorty, and Ranajit Guha, eds. *Selected Subaltern Studies.* New York: Oxford University Press, 1998.

Stabler, Arthur P., and John E. Kieza. "Ruy González's 1553 Letter to Emperor Charles V: An Annotated Translation." *Americas* 42, no. 4 (1986): 473–87.

Staden, Hans. *Hans Staden's True History: An Account of Cannibal Captivity in Brazil.* Durham, NC: Duke University Press, 2008.

Stallybrass, Peter, and Allon White. *The Politics and Poetics of Transgression.* Ithaca, NY: Cornell University Press, 1986.

Stearns, Peter. *Gender in World History.* New York: Routledge, 2006.

Sterns, Steve J. "Paradigms of Conquest: History, Historiography, and Politics." Quincentenary supplement, The Colonial and Post Colonial Experiences: Five Centuries of Spanish and Portuguese America, *Journal of Latin American Studies* 24 (1992): 1–34.

Stevens, Llan. *The Oxford Book of Latin American Essays.* New York: Oxford University Press, 1997.

Stoler, Ann Laura. *Carnal Knowledge and Imperial Power: Race and the Intimate in Colonial Rule.* Berkeley: University of California Press, 2002.

Strabo. *Geography.* Vol. 2, books 3–5. Translated by H. L. Jones. Cambridge, MA: Harvard University Press, 1923.

Strong, Pauline Turner. *Captive Selves, Captivating Others: The Politics and Poetics of Colonial American Captivity Narratives.* Boulder, CO: Westview Press, 1999.

Stross, Brian. *Love in the Armpit: Tzeltal Tales of Love, Murder, and Cannibalism.* Museum brief. Columbia: Museum of Anthropology, University of Missouri–Columbia, 1977.

Sugg, Richard. "'Good Physic but Bad Food': Early Modern Attitudes to Medicinal Cannibalism and Its Suppliers." *Social History of Medicine* 19, no. 2 (2006): 225–40.

———. *Mummies, Cannibals, and Vampires: The History of Corpse Medicine from the Renaissance to the Victorians.* New York: Routledge, 2011.

Swift, Jonathan. *A Modest Proposal for Preventing the Children of Poor People from Being a Burthen to their Parents or the Country, And for Making them Beneficial to the Publick.* 3rd edition. London: Weaver, Bickerton, 1730.

Symcox, Geoffrey, ed. *Italian Reports on the Americas, 1493–1552: Accounts by Contemporary Observers.* Turnhout, Belgium: Brepols, 2002.

Takaki, Ronald. "The Tempest in the Wilderness: The Racialization of Savagery." Discovering America, special issue, *Journal of American History* 79, no. 3 (1992): 892–912.

Tannahill, Reay. *Flesh and Blood: A History of the Cannibal Complex.* New York: Stein and Day, 1975.

Taylor, Diana. *The Archive and the Repertoire: Performing Cultural Memory in the Americas.* Durham, NC: Duke University Press, 2003.

Thevet, André. *André Thevet's North America: A Sixteenth Century View.* Translated by Roger Schlesinger and Arthur P. Stabler. Kingston: McGill-Queens University Press, 1986.

———. *The New Found Worlde or Antarctike.* Amsterdam: Theatrum Orbis Terrarum, Da Capo Press, 1971.

Thomas, Hugh. *Conquest: Montezuma, Cortés, and the Fall of Old Mexico.* New York: Touchstone/Simon and Schuster, 1993.

———. *Rivers of Gold: The Rise of the Spanish Empire, from Columbus to Magellan.* New York: Random House, 2003.

Thornton, John. "Cannibals, Witches, and Slave Traders in the Atlantic World." *William and Mary Quarterly,* 3rd series 60, no. 2 (2003): 273–94.

Thwaites, Rueben Gold, ed. *Early Western Travels, 1748–1846: A Series of Annotated Reprints of some of the best and rarest contemporary volumes of travel: Descriptive of Aborigines and social and economic conditions in the middle and far west, during the period of early American settlement.* 32 vols. Cleveland, OH: A. H. Clark, 1904–7.

———. *The Jesuit Relations and Allied Documents: Travels and Explorations of the Jesuit Missionaries in North America (1610–1791).* New York: Pageant, 1959.

Todorov, Tzvetan. *The Conquest of America: The Question of the Other.* Translated by Richard Howard. New York: Harper and Row, 1984.

———. "L'etre and l'Autre: Montaigne." *Yale French Studies,* no. 64 (1983): 113–44.

———. *The Morals of History.* Translated by Alyson Waters. Minneapolis: University of Minnesota Press, 1995.

Townsend, Camilla. "Burying the White Gods: New Perspectives on the Conquest of Mexico." *American Historical Review* 103, no. 3 (2003): 659–87.

———. *Malintzin's Choices: An Indian Woman in the Conquest of Mexico.* Albuquerque: University of New Mexico Press, 2006.

Trexler, Richard C. *Sex and Conquest: Gendered Violence, Political Order, and European Conquest of the Americas*. Ithaca, NY: Cornell University Press, 1995.

Trigger, Bruce G. *Children of Aataentsic: A History of the Huron People to 1660*. Revised edition. Montréal: McGill-Queen's University Press, 1987.

VanDerBeets, Richard, ed. *Held Captive by Indians: Selected Narratives, 1642–1836*. Revised edition. Knoxville: University of Tennessee Press, 1994.

Vaughan, Alden T. *Narratives of North American Captivity: A Selective Bibliography*. New York: Garland, 1983.

Vecsey, Christopher. "The Story and Structure of the Iroquois Confederacy." *Journal of the American Academy of Religion* 54, no. 1 (1986): 79–106.

Vespucci, Amerigo. *The Letters of Amerigo Vespucci and Other Documents Illustrative of His Career*. Translated by Clements R. Markham. London: Hakluyt Society, 1964.

Vickers, Daniel. *A Companion to Colonial America*. Blackwell Companions to American History. Malden, MA: Blackwell, 2003.

Vilaça, Aparecida. "Relations between Funerary Cannibalism and Warfare Cannibalism: The Question of Predation." *Ethnos* 65, no. 1 (2000): 83–106.

Vincent, Philip. *A True Relation of the Late Battell fought in New England between the English, and the Salvages*. London: M.P. for Nathanial Butters, 1637.

Vollendorf, Lisa. "Good Sex, Bad Sex: Women and Intimacy in Early Modern Spain." *Hispania* 87, no. 1 (2004): 1–12.

Wagemakers, Bart. "Incest, Infanticide, and Cannibalism: Anti-Christian Imputations in the Roman Empire." *Greece & Rome* 57, no. 2 (2010): 337–54.

Wagner, Henry, ed. *Discovery of Yucatan by Francisco Hernández de Córdoba*. Translated by Henry Wagner. Whittier, CA: Cortes Society, 1942.

———. *The Rise of Fernando Córtes*. New York: Kraus Reprint for the Cortés Society, 1969.

Waldseemüller, Martin. *The Cosmographie Introduction of Martin Waldseemüller*. Translated by Edward Burke. Freeport, NY: Books for Libraries Press, 1969.

Walton, Priscilla L. *Our Cannibals, Ourselves*. Urbana: University of Illinois Press, 2004.

Washburn, Wilcomb, ed. *The Garland Library of North American Indian Captivities*. Vols. 1, 4, 6, 8. New York: Garland, 1977–78.

Weaver-Hightower, Rebecca. *Empire Islands: Castaways, Cannibals, and Fantasies of Conquest*. Minneapolis: University of Minnesota Press, 2007.

Weber, David J. *Bárbaros: Spaniards and Their Savages in the Age of Enlightenment*. New Haven, CT: Yale University Press, 2005.

———. "The Spanish Borderlands, Historiography Redux." *History Teacher* 39, no. 1 (2005): 43–56.

White, Hayden. *Tropics of Discourse: Essays in Cultural Criticism*. Baltimore: Johns Hopkins University Press, 1985.

White, Richard. *The Middle Ground: Indians, Empires, and Republics in the Great Lakes Region, 1650–1815*. Cambridge, UK: Cambridge University Press, 1991.

Whitehead, Neil L. "Carib Cannibalism: The Historical Evidence." *Journal de la Société des Américanistes* 70, no.1 (1984): 69–87.

———. "Hans Staden and the Cultural Politics of Cannibalism." *Hispanic American Historical Review* 80, no. 4. (2000): 721–51.

———, ed. *Hans Staden's True History: an Account of Cannibal Captivity in Brazil*. Durham, NC: Duke University Press, 2008.

———. *Lords of the Tiger Spirit: A History of the Caribs in Colonial Venezuela and Guyana, 1498–1820*. Dordrecht, Holland: Foris, 1988.

Williams, Jerry M., and Robert E. Lewis, eds. *Early Images of the Americas: Transfer and Invention*. Tucson: University of Arizona Press, 1993.

Williams, John. *The Redeemed Captive Returning to Zion*. Reprint of the 1853 Northampton edition. Bedford, MA: Applewood Books, 1987.

Wood, Peter H., Gregory A. Waselkov, and M. Thomas Hatley. *Powhatan's Mantle: Indians in the Colonial Southeast*. Indians of the Southeast. Lincoln: University of Nebraska Press, 1989.

Wood, William. *New England's Prospect*. Edited by Alden T. Vaughn. Amherst: University of Massachusetts Press, 1994.

Wright, Thomas. *The Life of Sir Richard Burton*. New York: G. P. Putnam's Sons, 1906.

Zerubavel, Eviatar. *Terra Cognita: The Mental Discovery of America*. New Brunswick, NJ: Rutgers University Press, 1992.

Zika, Charles. "Cannibalism and Witchcraft in Early Modern Europe: Reading the Visual Images." *History Workshop Journal*, no. 44 (Autumn 1997): 77–105.

# Index

# About the Author

Kelly L. Watson is an assistant professor of history and a member of the faculty in women's and gender studies at Avila University in Kansas City.

# EARLY AMERICAN PLACES